A Place to Stand

Recently Published in the Series:

Queerly Phrased: Language, Gender, and Sexuality
Edited by Anna Livia and Kira Hall

Kids Talk: Strategic Language Use in Later Childhood
Edited by Susan Hoyle and Carolyn Adger

*Talking About Treatment: Recommendations for Breast Cancer
    Adjuvant Treatment*
Felicia D. Roberts

Language In Time: The Rhythm and Tempo of Spoken Interaction
Peter Auer, Elizabeth Couper-Kuhlen, Frank Müller

*Whales, Candlelight, and Stuff Like That: General Extenders
    in English Discourse*
Maryann Overstreet

A Place to Stand

*Politics and Persuasion
in a Working-Class Bar*

Julie Lindquist

UNIVERSITY PRESS

2002

OXFORD
UNIVERSITY PRESS

Oxford   New York
Athens   Auckland   Bangkok   Bogotá   Buenos Aires   Cape Town
Chennai   Dar es Salaam   Delhi   Florence   Hong Kong   Istanbul   Karachi
Kolkata   Kuala Lumpur   Madrid   Melbourne   Mexico City   Mumbai   Nairobi
Paris   São Paulo   Shanghai   Singapore   Taipei   Tokyo   Toronto   Warsaw

and associated companies in
Berlin   Ibadan

Library of Congress Cataloging-in-Publication Data
Lindquist, Julie.
A place to stand : politics and persuasion in a working-class bar / Julie Lindquist.
p. cm.—(Oxford studies in sociolinguistics)
Includes bibliographical references.
ISBN 0-19-514037-0; ISBN 0-19-514038-9 (pbk.)
1. English language—Social aspects—Illinois—Chicago. 2. Bars (Drinking
establishments)—Social aspects—Illinois—Chicago. 3. English language—
Spoken English—Illinois—Chicago. 4. Rhetoric—Political aspects—
Illinois—Chicago. 5. Oral communication—Illinois—Chicago.
6. Chicago (Ill)—Social life and customs. 7. Chicago (Ill)—
Politics and government. 8. Working class—Illinois—
Chicago. 9. Persuasion (Rhetoric) I. Title. II. Series.
PE3101.I4 L56 2002
306.44'09773'11—dc21
2001036855

1 3 5 7 9 8 6 4 2

Printed in the United States of America
on acid-free paper

Preface

"You don't know shit from Shinola!" concludes Walter about me, setting his JB-and-soda down hard on the bar. He has made this observation before, and it is beginning to acquire the status of a ritual. We are arguing, as usual, about the presidential campaign. I'd never admit it to him, but it occurs to me that maybe he's right—maybe I do have something to learn from him, something about politics even.

This work, an attempt to learn Walter's (and others') ways of separating the shit from the Shinola, is the product of that revelation. In the years I have spent acquiring this education, the bar at the Smokehouse Inn has been my classroom.

The first time I saw the inside of a bar, I was fifteen. Like many working-class teens, I was eager for the heady possibilities for sociability that came with adulthood; to wait until I was of legal drinking age to go to the bar would have been to give in to the indignities of childhood. Even then, I knew that the way to adult pleasures, and adult wisdoms, was through the dark heavy door of a tavern. The name of that first bar was, provocatively, Hazy Daze; it, like so many of its kind, was a repository of neighborhood lore. I immediately took my place as engaged spectator. The smoke cleared to reveal a world of garrulous animation, of longing for an imagined past and hope for the future. I thought, though I could not then articulate it, that here was a place where people drop out of life for a while in order to live a little, where they defy the authority of social codes in order to enforce the rules with a vengeance. Here was a pocket of life-out-of-life where moments ticked by with suspended anxieties and fatalistic optimisms, where leisure was pursued with aggressive abandon. It was obvious to me even then that there was much to be learned about "life" in a place like this, even if what I most wanted to learn at the time was how to find a place in this scene where idle learning is imagined as a luxury to be indulged at the expense of those who have *real* jobs.

There are two places in time, two moments when this ethnography of the Smokehouse, this story of a very particular place-in-time, can be said to begin: one stretches the length of my childhood in a working-class community; the other is that moment when I first walked into a bar and discovered the scripted spontaneity of adult leisure. My own history has invented a memory of that first bar as a parallel universe that enacted and commented on the terms of the domestic and work routines of everyday life yet remained apart from them. I remember seeing a local barroom celebrity—a man who, in the twilight of the tavern, had been young and vigorous, boasting and flirting at the head of the bar—shopping for supper in his work clothes, looking older, looking tired, pushing a fussing toddler in a cart full of diapers and fish sticks. Here the fluorescent glare of routine held him exposed, emasculated; I recall the surprise of my own embarrassment at the indignity of it.

Early on, I discovered the potential of barrooms to conceal and transform, to bedevil and redeem.

Still, I could not have predicted that I would someday want to tell a story about a bar and the people who made it home, so insular and natural was the world it offered, so redemptively tautological its architecture of signifiers. Not until I entered graduate school and learned about the game of interpretation would I understand the barroom as a place where people lied to reveal their truths, where the most stunning truths about the my own social world lay just below the surface of the lies they told. The bar whose story I tell here is as unique as it is representative. As institutions, bars bespeak, in the language of local truths, the categorical imperatives of working-class experience in America. The Smokehouse is, at once, agreeably metonymic and forcefully singular.

The experience of class in America is impossible to explain, difficult to render, and dangerous to address. It rests uneasily in the space between performance and evocation. My interest is in understanding how people at the Smokehouse not only experience but express interpretations of class experience, to themselves and to the world. It has often been remarked that all Americans, from welfare dependents to corporate executives, think of themselves as middle-class—and the ways Smokehousers speak of their own socioeconomic affiliations further confirm this observation. That there seems to be no conventional language that allows Smokehousers to name their sociopolitical situation as working people is precisely the point, for what is unresolved in Smokehouse "theory" is taken up in practice—in, as I will argue, the practice of argument. And although the population of the bar is not homogeneous with respect to material capital—clearly, some people at the Smokehouse have more economic power than others—the prevailing cultural ethos derives from shared values and assumptions linked to the practice of "real life," and emerge from a set of attitudes about the meaning, value, and place of work in everyday practice. Though some Smokehouse "regulars" have become owners of small businesses or have jobs that might be considered "white collar" (usually clerical or service jobs), the residual orientation to *work* as a core cultural value is central to the processes through which Smokehousers define themselves.

My own ambiguous class position has meant that the problem of "class culture" has compelled me for a long time, though until I got to graduate school I could not articulate the problem *as* a problem, no doubt for the aforementioned reasons. When I entered graduate school and discovered class *theory*, I was thrilled to be vindicated in all the arguments I'd had with people in my neighborhood by such figures as Marcuse and Adorno, who helped me to console myself with explanations of why other people didn't get it and I did; only later did it occur to me that my vindication was the source of such critics' appeal (through them I could take comfort in knowing that I had cleverly managed to escape the working class, as my more enlightened view of things would attest). My original interest in ethnography was to trace the mechanisms by which others had fallen victim to hegemonic forces of domination and the serendipities that had allowed me to escape such a fate. But anyone who has done ethnography knows that it is difficult to sustain such illusions for long. So I began the project with the intention of setting myself apart (so easy to do through anthropology); before long, I was motivated by the urge to tell the truths that cultural critics, by virtue of their own self-righteous and elitist positions, would never attend to. Neither motivation is a felicitous one; I have long since modulated my arrogance on both counts: my more modest goal, now, is to narrate a small part of a cultural process.

In producing "auto"-ethnography, my purposes are at once critical and celebratory. I would like to think that this work follows in the tradition established by such exemplary students of culture as Jose Limon, who, in his remarkable ethnography of South Texas Mexicanos, articulates a dual goal-critique *of*, and critique *through*: "I also came to know . . . my people's capacity to culturally critique and bedevil those who have dominated the working-class Mexican people of the United States. I would, however, add a distinctive theme in these pages, and that is the capacity of my people to bedevil themselves, always under the constraining conditioning of the sociocultural Other" (1994:x).

Though I offer taxonomic structures as heuristics for understanding tensions in Smokehouse theory and practice, I should make it clear that I am ultimately less interested here in developing a taxonomy of semantic categories or in delivering an anatomy of the "ways of seeing" of this community (as one might be inclined to do with a historically and geographically bounded cultural group) than in considering the social and rhetorical predicaments that make taxonomies and categories of experience impossible (or, perhaps more optimistically, unstable). Part of my case here is that "class culture" names a site of sociopolitical contradictions, and it is the meaning of these contradictions that I wish to explore. I propose that argument is the principal expressive modality through which Smokehousers manage the contradictions of class culture; in argument one might observe a product and process of culture, the pull of tradition and the energy of invention. Any culture bears these processes; I am suggesting that class culture, existing as it does between the material and the symbolic, foregrounds them.

There are so many—Smokehousers, colleagues, friends, family—to whom I am deeply grateful for helping me find ways to tell this story. First, I want to thank everybody at the bar—especially L.L., C.S., S.S., R.R., R.G., M.C., and R.P.—for teaching me so much about the important stuff. I would like to thank the Foop especially, who offered friendship and demanded honesty. I also want to extend my thanks to friends and mentors at the University of Illinois at Chicago, who have read versions of this draft and have in so many ways supported this project: David Seitz, Gloria Nardini, Daiva Markelis, Jeanne Herrick, Rich Gelb, Raul Ybarra, Eve Weiderhold, Rashmi Varma, Anita Dellaria, John Huntington, Elliot Judd, Greg Matoesian, and, in particular, Marcia Farr and Bill Covino, whose mentoring was so essential in helping me to put together the first version of this manuscript. A very special thank you goes to Anne Flanagan, whose imagination I have tried to plagiarize at every moment in this writing, and whose friendship continues to inspire me. Several colleagues at the University of Southern Mississippi deserve thanks as well. I am grateful for the support and friendship of Ellen Weinauer and Jonathan Barron, whose wise and patient counsel helped me to muster the emotional and intellectual energy a project such as this requires. I am indebted as well to Lisa Langstraat and Genevieve West, who with grace and forbearance read the succession of monstrous drafts I foisted upon them. Their talents as critics and editors have been more helpful to me than they can imagine, and their wisdom and friendship have done a good deal to sustain me in the latter stages of this work. Thanks should go to Adam Clay and Jon Forbus who worked so hard to help me get the final manuscript into shape. Also, I am deeply grateful to Aaron Fox at Columbia and Penelope Eckert at Stanford for their insightful readings of, and enormously helpful commentaries on, earlier versions of this manuscript. Many thanks as well to Peter Ohlin at Oxford University Press for his ongoing support of the project.

Most of all, I must express my gratitude to my family for their unconditional support of and unwavering faith in me in all my efforts. To my grandparents, Nils and Alma Lindquist, I can only say *tusen tack för allt*. The wisdom and influence of my mother, Doris Lindquist, is manifest in every line I write: she has been my best teacher. Thanks as well to my favorite uncle, Rolf Lindquist, whose wit and intelligence continue to inspire me. Love and thanks go to my husband, Richard Hallstein, who made impossible sacrifices of his own time and energy so I could complete this manuscript, and whose loving encouragement made this work possible. Finally, I am grateful to and for my beautiful boy, Jonas, who illuminates everything.

Contents

A Place to Stand

1

Rhetorical Practice
and the Ethnography
of Class Culture

The problem with you is that you ask so many questions that
sooner or later, a guy runs out of answers.

Smokehouse regular Walter Penske,
to me, in an argument at the bar

At the Smokehouse Inn,[1] a neighborhood lounge in south suburban Chicago,
the talk flows as freely as the Old Style on tap. The bar at the Smokehouse
is a place where working men and women congregate daily to seek sanctuary
from the world of work and, with their words, forge an alternative space. Those
who work behind the bar at the Smokehouse are in the business of producing
leisure; those who play there spend what time and money they can afford to
consume it. But for both producers and consumers, the real currency that
drives the social economy of the Smokehouse is talk.

Although there are several reasons why I have chosen to write about the
language and culture of those who frequent the bar at the Smokehouse—many
of which have to do with my own prior commitments to the group—this
ethnography of working-class rhetoric is largely motivated by the need for
ethnographic research into a problem that continues to animate conversations
in fields ranging from sociology to cultural studies: namely, the problem of
how working-class identity is formed in relation to perceived material conditions, on the one hand, and to local practices, on the other. I am interested in
documenting Smokehouse "expressive practices," rhetorical phenomena that
emerge from the lived experience of class culture.[2] In particular, I mean to
show how *argument*—as an expressive modality through which Smokehousers
express class-based loyalties at the same time that they define the limits of these
loyalties—is central to this process of identity formation. In describing this
project as an "ethnography of rhetoric," I mean also to situate the practice of
argument in the constellations of discursive purposes and practices that constitute the dynamic contexts of specific communicative events. I assume that con-

ceiving expressive practices as rhetorical events is one way to understand these practices as cultural products of social processes.

In keeping with Kenneth Burke's view of rhetoric as what happens when "individuals examine their identities to determine what they are and how they fit into groups with others who share those identities" (Heath 1986:202), I examine "Smokehouse rhetoric" as a process of identification and locate argument in the repertoire of strategies people at the Smokehouse use to position themselves in social space. Because at the Smokehouse people practice argument not only to identify themselves socially but also to participate in the invention of public belief, it becomes necessary to map some of the social processes through which cultural realities are invented, affirmed, and revised. To study the rhetoric of a given social group is, also, inevitably, to consider how that group establishes relationships between language, culture, and truth. One can hope for only a glimpse of these processes, however, for it is never possible to isolate contiguous streams of meaning into measurable units.[3]

One of the issues related to understanding argument in its capacity as a process of invention and identification is the question of how argument participates in persuasion. If the process of persuasion is treated as a private matter—that is, as something that happens in individuals to change the deep structure of belief—it becomes an operation not readily observable, something best left to theorists. But if persuasion is regarded as a teleological process in which the ends are social as well as the means, and if these ends are highly contingent on identity configurations within social networks and on contingent material conditions, then it becomes clear that ethnographic research in particular scenes is a productive way to apprehend the dynamics of persuasion more generally. To understand the particulars of persuasion for a given culture is to understand how that culture establishes itself *as* culture—how it invents and sustains its mythologies and what circumstances must obtain in order for these mythologies to change—as well as to recognize that shifts in public belief are contingent upon their value in the local marketplace of ideas. Attention to the particulars of rhetorical practice enable such understandings. My strategy to treat constructions of culture as moments of persuasion derives not only from my interest in rhetorical theory but also from my interest in class culture and the problematics of applying phenomenological inquiry to political structures and social processes.

Regardless of its motives, scope, or focus, all ethnographic research begins and ends with the problem of culture. My interest in telling an ethnographic tale of the society at the Smokehouse is in learning something not only about what it means to be working class but also about how language works to create, manage, and situate culture. Because ethnography approaches social interaction heuristically, any interpreted account of behavior presupposes a theory of culture. Though it constitutes the assumptive ground on which ethnographic studies are built, the concept of culture has been, and continues to be, the subject of much discussion and debate across disciplines. One set of problematics has to do with the relative stability of culture. To what extent culture is a mechanism for containing and managing systems of meaning, and to what extent it names a process of generating new forms, is a point of contention among scholars of social processes. Peacock (1986), for instance, defines culture as "the taken-for-granted but powerfully influential understandings and codes that are learned and shared by members of a group" (7). Spradley (1979) emphasizes common knowledge and ways of interpretation, describing culture as "the acquired knowledge that people use to interpret experience and generate social behavior" (5). More recent conceptions of culture, informed by trends in postmodern philosophy, deemphasize what is coherent and unified and conceive of culture as a dynamic, often contentious, process. In this view, culture is, as James Clifford maintains, "a hybrid, often discontinuous inventive process" (1988:10).

In addressing the problem of how to reconcile the tension between the static and the dynamic in organized experience, Jerome Bruner contends that culture is both invented and managed by stories: "While a culture must contain a set of norms, it must also contain a set of interpretive procedures for rendering departures from those norms meaningful in terms of established patterns of reality" (1990:41). For Bruner, as for Clifford Geertz (1988), narrative is the synthesis of poetic forms and social relations into culture. Kathleen Stewart (1996) defines culture as the phenomenological realm in which symbolic tensions and structural contradictions may coalesce, through narrative: "In such a space, culture itself can be seen as nothing more, and nothing less, than what people say" (38). To assume the narrative constitution of culture, then, is to assume tensions between the individual and the social, the conservative and the inventive. To think of culture as a fabric of stories (as an "assemblage of texts," to borrow Clifford's phrase) is useful in attempting to understand how the Smokehouse group can constitute a "culture," because that group is defined largely by its points of contention, and is bounded by group members' willingness to engage in conventional speech genres, the better to manage those contentions by marking consensus tacitly, through less explicit levels of practice.

To understand culture as a narrative formation means that it cannot be regarded as an isolated, or isolable, entity. It must be understood as relational as well as distinctive, as a site of action and reaction. Such a dynamic conception of culture makes it possible, in turn, to understand cultural practices as creative local formations that emerge from the tense relation between the exigencies of particular sites of immediate, embodied experience and the larger political economy—an understanding of culture that is critical to the study of "class culture," the subject of this ethnography. Implicit in my claim to take as my subject "working-class culture" is the assumption that shared cultural experiences (and the narrative processes and products of these experiences) are linked to material conditions, that what happens at the local level manifests what is structural and systemic.[4] In presuming to describe "class culture," I am assuming that everyday experiences and predicaments are structured (if not determined) by the larger political economy, that quotidian practices are synchronic enactments of diachronic processes.[5]

Yet the idea of social class is no less theoretically problematic than the concept of culture. Generally speaking, however, "class" can be said to refer to the systemic products of a social hierarchy sustained by unequal access to resources. For Marx, these resources are material; in Marxist economics, social classes are "positions within the productive relations of the economic structure of capitalist society" (Grimes 1991:12). Later social theorists such as Weber and Bourdieu assume these resources can be symbolic as well as material. In acknowledging the extent to which culture and society interact dynamically, Bourdieu (1984) has claimed that the practices of a given social group are motivated by its place in a larger system of relations in the socioeconomic hierarchy. But although Bourdieu maintains that cultural practices are embedded in a complex structure of social meanings, he does not investigate the specific cultural "marketplaces" in which these meanings are generated, mediated, and sustained: Bourdieu's treatment of cultural practice is grounded in quantitative data; thus it focuses on the relations between social systems rather than on the internal workings of any one of these systems.

To do ethnography of working-class rhetoric is to commit to the idea that class is a function of culture, and culture, a function of class.[6] How, then, does one gain access to the phenomenology of structural relations? Douglas Foley (1989) addresses this question, identifying the central problem as the conflicting identification of working-class culture as a political culture, on the one hand, and as an anthropological one, on the other. In the first case, the working class counts as a "political culture" to the extent that it can support an ideological "project" connected to its position in the social structure; in the second, the working class qualifies as an anthropological culture, to the extent that is a coherent historical culture distinguished by shared knowledge and traditions. The anthropological idea of a historical culture speaks to what is social and shared, passed down more or less intact through history; the history it engages is its own, not a larger history of social struggle. Foley observes that in anthropological linguistics, speech communities are seldom treated as part of a larger context of social relations: though the field is "rich in empirical studies of distinct cultural groups," it has avoided viewing speech communities as "emerging class cultures" (153). Neither conception of "working-class culture" sufficiently theorizes class culture and accounts for the specificity of its forms and practices: Whereas reproduction theories have overdetermined cultural forms, anthropological investigations of communicative behaviors have paid little attention to the structural determinants of culture.

In this formulation, the ethnography of working-class practices should engage the interplay of these political and anthropological definitions of class culture. Of the handful of critical studies of working-class culture produced in the last couple of decades, Foley identifies Paul Willis's ethnographic study of British working-class youths as a example of this synthesis. According to Foley, Paul Willis "is often celebrated here in America for putting subjectivity, voluntarism, that is people, the heroic working class, back into class analysis from the structural determinism and functionalism of 'reproduction theorists' such as Bowles and Gintis (1976) and Bourdieu and Passeron (1977)." For Foley, Willis's ethnographic work is exemplary because it interprets class culture as a process that emerges from material conditions, showing marginalized cultural groups inventing distinctive cultural forms counter to the dominant ideology.[7] Similarly, Ortner (1991) cites Penelope Eckert's research (1989) on adolescent social structures as an example of ethnographic work that manages to walk the line between treating adolescent social groups as traditional cultures (as social organisms that provide order and unity) and understanding them as sites of class reproduction (167).

Still, the relation between "ideology" as a structural product and local practice remains problematic. How is it possible to account for the material in the symbolic in the invention of cultural forms? How do social structures produce the exigencies of, or conditions for, expressive practices? Following from a synthesis of Habermas's conceptions of communication in the public sphere with Goffman's emphasis on strategic miscommunication, Foley suggests seeing "class culture" as the repository of "alienated communicative labor"—a move that would view expressive practices as emerging from structural realities while steering the investigation of class cultures away from the subject of "ideological hegemony" toward the practical construction of class identities (143). Such communicative labor can become the object of ethnographic study.[8] The ethnography of working-class rhetoric, then—though it clearly cannot provide an expansive, *etic* view of the socioeconomic mechanisms that drive the distribution of resources—is concerned with examining how the meanings attached to resources are produced locally, though the *emics* of cultural practice.[9] On one level, this entire project can be read as an argument for the validity of working-class culture as an ethnographic subject. As problematic as such a project is in theory and method, I believe that such work is essential in delineating social processes that have all too often been left to theorists to worry about. The problem of how everyday practices emerge from—and work against—ideological systems remains thorny, but I take up Foley's challenge to locate class dynamics in "expressive practices" and to emphasize the role of performance in public constructions of class identity.

This project relies heavily on Bourdieu's metaphor of culture-as-marketplace but departs from his methods in that it aims to understand the meanings that members of a specific social group attach to cultural practice—in this case, language. To see working-class culture as the site of inventive production is to see it as an ongoing process that operates in the spaces of structural contradictions and is not always predictable in its synthetic forms. I approach the data in the following chapters in the hope of understanding arguments not solely as indices of their referential "content" but rather in terms of what they *mean* and *do* for those who engage in them; in that sense, this work is theoretically undergirded by the fundamental sociolinguistic assumption (e.g., Hymes 1974) that studies of communicative practice reveal most about the way language works to create and sustain cultural realities when they look deeply into the social contexts in which communication takes on meaning. Whether or not "performance" is framed as an analytical category, sociolinguists and folklorists are generally interested in the cultural work of performed discourse. Some, like Hymes, are interested in what language *does*; others, like Bauman (1977, 1986, 1992), are concerned with verbal art, a style of speech framed as performative. My own work looks to how language (and in particular, argument) "performs" in both these senses—that is, how it establishes the terms of social interaction more generally, as well as how it functions dramatically to activate local ideologies.

Yet the instability and indeterminacy of both the processes of class culture and of ethnographic inquiry make it difficult to take "class culture" as the a priori subject of ethnographic interpretation. To put it another way, the application of one narrative epistemology to another makes such ethnographic projects representationally problematic. As Aaron Fox (1994) explains, what makes the ethnography of class culture especially difficult is the experiential and rhetorical problematics that ethnography and class culture hold in common—that is, each is the site of conflicted identities and rhetorical motives and affects/effects. Class ethnography is, in Fox's words, "a collision between a non-methodological method and a non-objective object" (1). This problematic of meaning and significance leads Fox to conclude that the ethnographic study of class culture should be understood only as an "ironic" enterprise, aiming to theorize (and thereby stabilize) a dynamic and conflicted process of invention and signification.[10]

The problem of approaching class culture ethnographically once again returns us to the uses of rhetoric as a conceptual frame. It is in this interpretive domain—that is, in the space between class and culture, between the structural and the phenomenological—that "rhetoric" is activated as a key term in what might otherwise appear to be a traditionally sociolinguistic approach to communicative practice.[11] Whereas this study follows from the methods and assumptions of linguistic anthropologists (such as Dell Hymes) in emphasizing contexts of use as arbiters of linguistic meaning, those working within such a tradition tend not to describe linkages between linguistic forms, social motives, and processes of identification as "rhetorical." Though "rhetoric" is a construct more traditionally associated with humanistic approaches to culture, I find it useful here to foreground processes of conflict and identification and to describe tensions between the poetic and hortatory in accounting for these processes.[12] "Rhetoric" helps us to account for how the Smokehouse conceives of itself as political culture, implying strategic positioning, public presentation, and persuasion. To suggest "rhetoric" as a heuristic allows for the agonistic as well as the consensual in culture. It encompasses what is contested as well as what is shared, emphasizing the performative and conflictual nature of discursive activity. If narrative is the "stuff" of culture, and culture is (to some extent) a product of class, then a project in the interpretation of class culture necessarily entails attention to the performative and conflictual.[13] To locate microprocesses of social change, one must look at occasions for, and of, persuasion.[14] To this end, my interpretation of Smokehouse culture is inflected by lexicons of classical rhetoric, because this language offers a way to describe not only tacit ideologies but also processes of strategic discourse. I find the conceptual language of classical rhetoric especially useful for describing the cultural logics of argument, for it proceeds from the assumption that truths are probable and that *facts* are less important in assessing arguments than the social arrangements that obtain in communicative situations. The terms that inform my interpretation here are drawn from classical rhetoric, specifically, from Aristotle's description of persuasive strategies in the *Rhetoric.*

To account for the complexities inherent in instances of argumentative rhetoric, I refer to Aristotle's *pisteis,* or stock of persuasive appeals. The philosophies of language and social psychology on which the pisteis rest have been widely debated, but Covino and Jolliffe (1995) offer a useful and succinct explanation of how they work: "In his *Rhetoric,* Aristotle discusses three sorts of textual appeals: to the authority of the rhetor (ethos), to the emotions or 'stages of life' of the audience (pathos), and to systems of reasoning (logos) that the rhetor and the audience share" (15). The pisteis, in other words, account for relations between ideology, authority, and rights of participation. The authors point out that although these appeals are treated separately in the *Rhetoric,* "examining their operation clearly shows that they intersect and interact" (15). This conceptual apparatus not only provides a way to isolate components of a given speech event while preserving the contextual embeddedness of the event but also places the issue of *authority* at the center of analyses of persuasive discourse. One way, then, to discover how persuasive discourse operates at the Smokehouse is to examine how different kinds of authority "intersect and interact" in arguments.

Of the pisteis, I find the concept of *ethos,* which names a relationship between an individual speaker and his or her cohorts, especially useful for an analyses of socially situated acts of rhetoric. As Karlyn Kohrs Campbell explains, "Ethos does not refer to your peculiarities as an individual but to the ways you reflect the characteristics and qualities that are valued by your culture of group" (1982:122). To put it another way, ethos specifies the nature of a speaker's right of participation in hortatory discourse. A rhetor can establish ethos either by creating a character to suit the occasion or by calling on his or her reputation in the community: that is, either by *inventing* ethos or by referring to his or her *situated* ethos (Crowley and Hawhee 1999:108). Thus authority can be either constructed or conferred; the notion of ethos encourages an examination of rhetorical authority as a dialectic between social role and communicative practice.

While Aristotle's pisteis enable description of the appeals operative in particular acts of persuasion, they cannot adequately account for what the practice of argument—and in particular, performed argument—means for Smokehouse arguers. But taken together with Bourdieu's grand metaphor of culture-as-marketplace developed in *Distinction* (1984) and elaborated in his later work (1991), this combined lexicon describes the relationship, always at work in acts of persuasion, between social assumptions, speaker authority, and communicative strategies. To understand the cultural values attached to genres of discourse, and to discover how they accrue to these genres, one may assess these values in terms of the "marketplace" in which they operate. Bourdieu (1984) holds that cultures are analogous to market economies, such that cultural artifacts and practices are defined by their values as cultural "capital." Although Bourdieu ultimately posits a social hierarchy in which the most powerful cultural groups determine the workings of the entire social "economy," he does point out that local interests have an immediate stake in prevailing values in local markets. As Bourdieu goes on to argue in *Language and Symbolic Power* (1991), one of the cultural practices that takes on value in response to "market forces" is speech. The theory he elaborates in that work makes a place for the essentially performative nature of speech acts: according to Bourdieu, whether and how a given speech act performs successfully depend on the established set of stable social relations (the *institution*) that not only sets up criteria against which the act must be judged but also invests speakers with authority to create or assess it.

Though I believe that the most productive way to understand connections between linguistic meaning and use is to study language as it happens "naturally," in actual social settings, to call this project a rhetorical enterprise foregrounds its status as an *act* (as well as a study) of rhetoric. In other words, I affirm that questions of meaning cannot be addressed empirically without influence from the very social pressures and cultural imperatives that are the subject of study. At every stage in creating an ethnographic interpretation of Smokehouse communicative practices, issues of method and representation—that is, my own communicative practices as ethnographer—are themselves subject to query and interpretation.[15] I do not claim to offer a neutral, scientific, or somehow "unauthored" account of the people and events at the Smokehouse but, rather, to tell a particular kind of story—a story grounded in ethnographic methodologies, but a story, nonetheless—of Smokehouse communicative practice. My story of the Smokehouse is really a story about stories, for it treats not only the stories Smokehousers tell about themselves to me in interviews but also the stories they tell about themselves, to themselves, in argument.[16]

I became interested in the bar at the Smokehouse as a site for the empirical study of rhetoric several years ago when, as a graduate student, I was hired as a bartender at the Smokehouse. What immediately struck me then about my new place of employment was how central to the social life of the people there—employees and customers alike—arguments about "politics" seemed to be. Though the working-class background and associations I shared with others in the bar meant that I was regarded (and that I regarded myself) as an insider in many ways, my political views set me apart from others at the bar. My position as both insider and dissenter put me, time and time again, at the center of barroom debates. Though I take the communicative behaviors of the Smokehouse group as my subject, this study is auto-ethnographic in the sense that much of my interpretation of Smokehouse culture shares the social and epistemological implications of my own participation in Smokehouse rhetoric. Some may object that all studies are auto-ethnographic, but this one foregrounds not only my own subjectivity but also my active participation in performative events.

My own place in Smokehouse life presupposes a rhetorical stance and has had profound implications not only for the way I introduced my study to others and how I went about collecting data but also for how the ethnographic tale unfolds. It is important to understand, furthermore, that this position emerges from the context of interaction with other Smokehousers as well as from my own (historically) conflicted position in working-class social life. Though I spent only three years actively "doing ethnography"—observing, participating in, and writing about arguments at the bar, I have come to understand that the story of class conflict and cultural identity I tell here has a narrative strand that really begins quite some time before I was introduced to the Smokehouse Inn. A colleague of mine, hearing about the many ways my relationship with others at the Smokehouse is marked by conflict and emotional stress, wanted to know why I continued to feel a sense of commitment to the group and why I chose the bar as a research site—if in fact I had such an agonistic relationship with the people there. It was a fair question, one that left me wondering if the particular kind of antagonism I felt at the Smokehouse might be, after all, the very source of its appeal to me. The more I reflected on the kinds of cultural events that have shaped my own history, the more this conclusion made sense: looking back on my experiences at home, in the community, and in school, it occurs to me that I have always seemed to find myself in the role of dissenter. It is a role I learned, over time, to play well.

The confrontations I describe here with Jack, Walter, and others at the Smokehouse constitute the most recent episode in my history of contentions with working people in my own community. Yet until I was well into my graduate studies, I never imagined that differences I had always perceived between me and others—in my community and later, at the university itself—had anything to do with anything as systematic (or at least, as architectural) as culture. I had always thought of myself as "different"—unique, perhaps, on a good day, and socially inept, on a bad one. Then, I was certain that any social failing was an indication of some essential lack on my part, that my chronic maladjustment to my environment was perverse, idiosyncratic, and intractable. I don't mean to claim to be sole heir to such feelings of social estrangement—in fact, I suspect my history will sound all too familiar for many who have come to academe from working-class backgrounds. But I do suggest that because my particular brand of alienation was in many ways a product of how my own values and assumptions conflicted with those around me, my ethnography of Smokehouse rhetoric is a product of this history. Whatever else it takes as its subject, an ethnography cannot help but be "about" the ethnographer herself.[17] Undeniably, my own history in the larger community of which the Smokehouse is a part, and with working-class ways in general, has informed every choice—in the field, and on the page—I have made in developing this work. It narrates an ongoing tension between location and dislocation, between passionate alliance with, and deep alienation from, others in my home community. I offer a piece of that history here as a way of telling where the story begins.

The circumstances of even my earliest associations meant that I would never fit seamlessly into the social fabric of our suburban working-class neighborhood on Chicago's southeast side. The first of these associations was my mother, who was different from those around her in everything, it seemed, from lifestyle to education to politics. The most immediately obvious difference between my mother and the mothers of anyone else I knew was that mine was not married. In most American communities now, unwed motherhood is virtually unremarkable, but in the late sixties and early seventies—the time during which I was doing most of my growing up—it was an anomaly, if not a scandal. I remember endlessly explaining to incredulous playmates just how it was that I could exist at all without a legitimate set of parents to beget me. "Is your mom divorced?" they would ask. "No," I would say, knowing what came next. "Is your dad dead?" would follow. "No," I would respond, impatient. "I just never met him." "But how could you be born?" On one occasion, after having explained to a particularly dogged inquirer just how I *could* have been born, my mother got a call from an angry parent demanding to know how she could allow her daughter to go around putting such things into other children's heads.

If my mother wasn't the typical neighborhood mom in her domestic status, she was no more normal in her tastes, values, and habits. She didn't smoke. She didn't drink. She didn't listen to popular music, dance, or socialize with the neighbors. For entertainment, she read books. She disapproved of displays of racism and prudishness. Other kids from the neighborhood found her remarkable because she let me stay out late, didn't beat me, didn't seem to mind if I swore, and insisted on being called by her first name. I myself used to think that because my mother had gone to college for three years she knew everything. I would ask her an impossible metaphysical question (how big is the universe? what does God look like?) and then complain when she couldn't answer: "But you went to college!"

But unlike my friends, who told me my mother was cool, I didn't think my mother was cool. I was sure she was perfect in every other way, but I did not think she was cool. Some of my friends' mothers painted their nails and wore jeans and high heels; some even had long hair. The mother of Robby, the kid next door, was the coolest mom I knew. Robby's mom had long black hair and wore rings on all of her fingers. She smoked and drove a two-door Chevy Impala with the radio loud. She and her husband had a tricked-out Harley-Davidson, which Robby would sometimes get to ride.

My mother, by contrast, maintained a careful distance from our neighbors. Given the likelihood that any conversation would turn casually and conspiratorially racist, she found it impossible to socialize with others around her: any encounter she might have with any neighbor on any topic would eventually, inevitably end with the neighbor assuming her complicity in attitudes toward race. The community's profound suspicion of minorities, and of blacks in particular, was so pervasive that anyone who wished to express racist views could assume, quite correctly, that his or her audience would wholeheartedly share those views—unless, that is, the audience consisted of my mother. So she, not knowing how else to avoid the racist rhetoric she felt surrounded her at every turn, simply kept to herself.

Though I shared my mother's views, I did not share her strategy for dealing with others in the neighborhood. As soon as other children understood that I did not intend to show solidarity with them by expressing contempt for blacks, they discovered that they could defeat me by making a point of using racist language, by calling me "nigger lover" (an epithet that, I soon learned, named the worst possible deviation from the norm). I found myself embroiled in so many confrontations about matters of race that I began to wonder when I was speaking from moral principle and when from an urge to defend my own integrity. And, yet, I saw the options that were available to me: I could maintain the moral high ground by resigning myself to isolation in which my mother lived, or I could cultivate friendships and keep on arguing. I was convinced that I could change people's minds about this (or any other) subject through reasoned argument, via skillful dialectic, though I rarely saw evidence that it worked. Besides, I wanted to have friends.

Until I was thirteen, we lived with my grandparents, in their house. Both of my grandparents had come over from Sweden at the turn of the century and cultivated their ethnic identity with the same intensity as my mother rejected it. They were not religious, but retained old-world Lutheran habits and sensibilities. They didn't drink or smoke. They never went to restaurants or to the movies. They were scandalized by anything loud, colorful, or spicy. Yet I was fascinated with my grandparents' Swedishness, by the wealth of traditions they carried into their talk, diet, and social life. Their friends were Swedish. They spoke Swedish often and (having long since given up on my mother) encouraged me to speak it. We ate Swedish food and listened to Swedish music. Because I didn't have to assert my difference from my grandparents as my mother felt she had to, I was free to embrace the language and traditions she rejected. And because I experienced the authority of my grandparents in a less direct way (they took care of me while my mother went to school and worked but usually deferred to my mother on questions of child rearing), I was freer to challenge their prejudices and enjoy learning what they were uniquely equipped to teach me.

As I was growing up, my grandmother occasionally alluded to the mystery of my origin by asking me whether I ever intended to find my father. My grandfather, on the other hand, never discussed the matter. A pragmatic man raised on a farm and conditioned by a long life of hard work as a housepainter, he didn't put much stock in sustained discussion. He had a well-defined philosophy: don't waste time indulging in philosophy; it only gets in the way of getting things done. And he was, as I recall, able to *do* just about anything.

My mother and I moved out of my grandparents' house when I was thirteen. We moved into an apartment in the next town. We lived there for a year and then moved into a tiny house a couple of miles away. When my mother finally gathered the resources to leave town altogether, we moved to California, where we could invent a life apart from the one invented for us by the neighborhood. My mother sold the house, and we packed what we had—some clothes and a dog—into our rusty Vega and drove to Los Angeles.

Though I had always thought of myself as different from others in the neighborhood, this new place made me feel a surprising sense of nostalgic solidarity with these same others. My mother loved L.A. and the freedom from community censure it promised, but I was lonely. Home in the neighborhood, I had a huge network of friends—"burnouts," like myself—who generally agreed that school, and upward mobility in general, *sucked*. An intensely conservative group, my friends the burnouts distinguished themselves in part by their refusal to participate in anything that could be construed as trendy, progressive, or upscale. At North Hollywood High School, I was surprised to discover that I was the only one still wearing bellbottoms.

I met Andrea (the first Jewish person I'd ever known) in my biology class. We got to be friends and moved in together. We lied about our ages, got jobs as waitresses at a nearby coffee shop, and set up house. I found myself having to work more and more hours on the graveyard shift in order to keep up with the expenses; eventually I simply quit going to school. Andrea, whose father was a university professor, was shocked at my decision to give work priority over school. She kept going to school, even though it meant giving up sleeping. She expected to become a lawyer, like her brother.

My mother and I stayed in California for a year, until we ran out of money. My mother, reluctant to move back in with my grandparents, rented a studio apartment. We slept on sofas my mother rescued from the alley. But I was glad to be back in town, among friends.

Social relocation, however, meant educational dislocation. The local high school decided that because I had missed so much, I should be held back a year. I was indignant: couldn't they see that I was smart? Here I was, someone who had held a job of her own and had maintained a household—who had *worked* for a living—only to be treated, to be classified, as a child! I could not imagine that an institution that knew so little about my life in the *real* world should have anything worthwhile to offer. Less than a month into the semester, I dropped out. Leaving school did not seem to be an unreasonable decision. My closest friends had already quit, and they had jobs and seemed to be getting along okay. When I quit, the dean told me that I was making a huge mistake, that I'd never "go anywhere" in life. It was then that I decided to earn a PhD, though I hadn't the first idea of what I had to do to get one.

After I quit high school (a decision my mother, herself frustrated with the inflexibility of the school administration, did not try to reverse), I enrolled in a course called Introduction to Philosophy at the local junior college. After the first day of classes, I already knew that I loved college. I marvelled at the freedoms it offered (now here was a place where they treated you like an adult—you could even smoke, even with the teachers—the *faculty*—watching). I loved philosophy and was seduced by the thought that you could actually *play* with ideas (and even more remarkably, that there were institutional rewards for such games). When I wasn't in class, I wandered the halls of the college, aimlessly purposeful, drinking coffee and smoking and feeling smart and important. I knew then that I wanted to be an intellectual. I would continue going to college until I completed the requirements to become one.

But I did not, in fact, stay in school. My newfound freedom to come and go as I pleased, combined with the social pressure to get a job, eventually got to me. My mother tired of paying my tuition only to see me drop class after class after the refund date. After a year of unrelenting dabbling, I decided I might as well go to work full time. My mother told me of an opening at the advertising agency where she worked. I applied and was hired as a receptionist. Working "downtown," I found myself surrounded by people in suits. Nobody I knew ever wore a suit (unless there was a wedding or something, when the suits themselves became the subject of joking commentary). That people at the agency wore suits made them appear intractably different from anyone I really knew. I remember being invited to lunch by an account executive and wanting very much to go but turning him down because I had no idea what I would say to someone in a suit. At that time, though I was not yet of legal drinking age, I began to go out to local bars for after-work and weekend recreation. These cramped and smoky rooms were the social center of the community, and everybody knew that the real reason to "go out to the bars" was not to get drunk (drinking could, of course, be done anywhere) but to announce to the world that you had come of age.

After two years of working as a receptionist, I understood that I would never be anyone important (like the copywriters or account executives), so I decided to go back to school. I had every intention of getting a degree in English and returning to the agency to get a job writing ad copy. I wanted to be a copywriter because copywriters were obviously "creative" (something I was sure I was) and didn't have to "dress up" for work. I was driven by my desire to prove that you didn't have to wear a suit—didn't have to leave the neighborhood—to be important.

But when I got back to the junior college and started taking classes there, I began to think that maybe copywriting wasn't really where it was at, after all. Who really wanted to be a yuppie—a phony—suit or no? I decided I liked the idea of becoming a music major but discovered that I didn't have any particular talent. After that, I tried chemistry (the experiments were fun) but found that math confounded me. Then I went into psychology to "figure out how people think," but an English teacher told me psych was for science dropouts (how did he know?), so I abandoned that plan, too. I continued my general ed coursework without having any idea what it would amount to and was finally awarded an associate's degree. The English teacher who had disparaged psych majors told me that I was a good writer, so I thought I would get a degree that reflected my talents, if not my background. But before I could graduate from junior college I learned that I had to take a general equivalency diploma (GED). I passed the GED, and went "away" to a regional university, where I declared English as my major.

After only a semester at Northern Illinois University, (I'd found it too difficult to be away from my boyfriend and friends from the neighborhood for days at a time), I transferred to the University of Illinois at Chicago. At UIC, I declared a major in creative writing. I liked the idea of being a writer; it hadn't occurred to me that I'd have to spend so much time writing to become one. I earned the BA without a clue about how writers really worked or what their lives were like. As I was still interested in how language worked, I decided that my next degree would be in linguistics, though I had only a vague idea of what linguistics actually was. Outside of school, I spent much of my time trying to explain what, exactly, I was doing in school studying something nobody'd ever heard of and seemed to be more or less useless in preparing for any kind of a real job.

I spent the second year of graduate study in linguistics waiting for someone to tell me what to do. I knew I had to write something called a "thesis," but I had no idea that *I* was supposed to be the one to plan it. I suppose I would still be waiting, had it not been for an encounter with a relative who happened to come over at Thanksgiving and, in an attempt to make the kind of conversation that happens between people who see each other only at Thanksgiving, had asked me what my research involved. Research? I had responded, puzzled. I wondered: how should I know? They haven't told me yet. The strangeness of this conversation convinced me that there was something I didn't know about what I didn't know. I had always been able to get by (even to excel) as an undergrad by completing assignments according to the requirements and submitting them on time. The expectations of graduate school, on the other hand, mystified me.

One thing was sure: because there were no teaching assistantships available for me as a grad student in theoretical linguistics, I would have to find work somewhere else. I found a job at a bar close to my house; when the owner fired me for stealing money he himself had taken to buy cocaine, I got another bartending job, through a friend of a friend, at the Smokehouse. When I arrived one afternoon for an interview with the boss, he looked me over, gave me a list of drink prices to memorize, and told me to report for work the following evening.

There was much I didn't know about the Smokehouse at first, but at least I understood the rules there. At the bar, at least, I knew what I didn't know. Though the Smokehouse was in a neighborhood several miles away from my house, the people who worked and gathered there were very like the people I knew from my own neighborhood: they worked as laborers or craftsmen or in service jobs; they were politically conservative; they had married young and were raising children; they either lived in the same area in which they had grown up or had moved from a Chicago neighborhood when it had "changed" (the word connotes racial integration and connotes an attitude somewhere between contempt and resignation).[18] So when I began working at the Smokehouse, I knew what kind of society I'd likely find there and could predict what its members were likely to believe and value. Still, I was intimidated by the extent to which people at the bar seemed to claim membership in an impossibly tightly knit social network of people who shared not only mugs of beer, but also lived histories.

With a couple of notable exceptions, anthropologists have not claimed bars as sites for research into the practices of postindustrial urban cultures.[19] Still, bars remain an understudied site of American cultural forms, especially communicative practices. Among those who have treated them as settings for ethnographic investigation, the potential for bars to offer microcosmic glimpses into social dynamics at work in the larger society has been duly remarked. In an ethnography of speaking in a black middle-class bar, Michael Bell (1982) maintains that Brown's Lounge, as a bounded geographical space in which collective activity is foregrounded, offers an ideal opportunity to observe the kinds of African American cultural norms and practices that obtain in the wider social milieu. He explains that the world of Brown's, the environment and complex of human activities that make it up, exists in order to permit the patrons to see themselves and their actions while they are in the bar as consistent with their own definitions of what it means to be black and middle class. Within the complex world of its symbols and social communication, within its walls, its geography, its time, its ordinary occurrence, its dreams, and its harsher facts will be found images of self and community. . . . Moreover, these images will not isolate the patrons of Brown's from the urban African-American community but will connect the bar and its patrons to the wider aesthetics that prevail in black America. (9)

In a study of gender politics in a college-town tavern, ethnographers Spradley and Mann (1975) make a similar claim about the status of bars as microcosms of larger social and cultural patterns. They hold that bars "offer a unique opportunity to study certain values and norms in American society," and explain that precisely because obvious markers of social status are perceived to be absent within bars, individuals tend to "express those deeply held and often unstated values on which the social order is based" (9). Just as observations of the social life of bars can provide insight into social and cultural imperatives governing race and gender, so too can barroom ethnography illuminate dynamics of social class.[20]

Despite the relative dearth of anthropological information about the society of working-class bars, the place of bars in the society of the working class has attracted the attention of social historians, who have documented the evolution of the role of bars in working-class life. Roy Rosenweig (1991), for example, links bars to the singular situation of the worker in claiming that neighborhood drinking establishments arose in the middle of the nineteenth century in response to shorter working days, when on-the-job tippling was displaced into leisure space and time. He says that bars as social centers came to be expressions of working-class resistance to the values of the dominant culture, specifically, "resistance to individualism as well as acquisitiveness." Going to the saloon, Rosenweig explains, "affirmed communal over individualistic and privatistic values" (1983:247).

That neighborhood taverns offer patrons a way to seek sanctuary from mainstream society can be seen in the characteristic tendency of the local bar to represent a space out of space, and a time out of time. In order to function effectively as "alternative" space, a bar must, moreover, carefully maintain its boundaries. Local bars can be culturally exclusive territories, as Philipsen (1992) observed in his study of language patterns in a blue-collar community he calls "Teamsterville." Philipsen writes of his experience upon first stepping into a neighborhood tavern:

[L]ike other Teamsterville taverns, this was not merely a public place open to anyone, but an enclave in which some but not other personae were welcome, and I was an intruder. There was no sign outside the tavern, because "everybody" knew who belonged there and those who needed a sign to welcome them were not among that circle of insiders. (3)

Even though I (unlike Philipsen) felt more or less at home among working people, the Smokehouse scene itself initially struck me as similarly prohibitive. In those first couple of weeks at the bar, the closeness among customers and waitresses seemed to me as stifling as the smoky, windowless little barroom itself. From my newcomer's perspective, it seemed that each person there knew every other person, and always had. The men had fun with me, the "new girl," by giving me misinformation about drink prices, calling each other by the wrong names in order to confuse me, and feigning indignation if I failed to remember what brand of beer they drank. The women—and, in particular, the waitresses—regarded me with suspicion and, occasionally, with outright hostility. I remember the men at the bar—the same "regulars" who so enjoyed having fun at my expense—making a show of "protecting" me by telling me to "watch out for" Roberta, a veteran waitress. "She can be a mean one," one man warned. "But she don't mean nothin' by it. Don't let her get to you."

After a few weeks, I knew all the waitresses and customers by name and was beginning to feel like a part of this small and (I had believed) impenetrable society. The closeness that had once struck me as claustrophobic and exclusive was, I now felt, the best thing about working at the Smokehouse. A day spent working behind the bar was a day spent participating in the ongoing drama of shared stories, lives, and histories. The Smokehouse was the setting of an unfolding narrative; the talk that went on there was dialogue between familiar dramatic characters. Even I, who had at first felt so much like an outsider, had a role to play.

My role, it became clear, was that of antagonist. As soon as it became public knowledge that I was a college student and a "liberal," I was drawn into performed debates. Though I had often found myself at the center of political arguments with others in my community, at the Smokehouse my philosophical differences from others constituted a public display, even a social ritual. When there were others at the bar who shared my "liberal" views, they were generally not cast into a scripted, performative role to the extent that I always seemed to find myself.[21] It was a role, I now understand, I did not attempt to undermine, as much as it vexed me: it gave me a way, at least, to find a place among others.

Although this study of the expressive practices of a small network of working people is primarily concerned with understanding something about the relationship between rhetoric and social class, it will no doubt become obvious that gender relations constitute the background against which internal power dynamics are writ large; unquestionably, cultural expectations about how men and women should speak and behave govern every aspect of working-class life.[22] Further, bars celebrate an image of masculinity that defines the ethos of working-class culture and is certainly relevant to an understanding of Smokehouse social organization and cultural practice. Yet I wish to emphasize, here, that my decision to relegate gender to the background has everything to do with my decision to move *class* to the foreground and nothing to do with any assumption that gender would not be a rich and important subject for scrutiny.[23] Ironically, the contradiction inherent in my role as friendly antagonist was, to some extent, mitigated by my gender: were I a man with middle-class and academic associations, my differences from and transgressions against Smokehouse conventional wisdom would, I suspect, be less likely to be tolerated—partly because of the tacit rules that dictate that *doing* is masculine and *saying* is feminine and partly because, as a woman, I was more likely to be perceived as harmless—that is, I am likely to be seen as lacking the rhetorical authority that would allow me to threaten cultural norms seriously.

Undeniably, my ethnography of the Smokehouse has been a highly emotional, as well as intellectual, process. Those at the Smokehouse are a group of people about whom I feel unequivocally ambivalent. Sometimes the bar is a place where I feel centered and at ease; other times I leave feeling distinctly alienated and profoundly troubled. At best, the bar is a place that offers, in its communal spirit and rituals of solidarity, a real sense of relief from social imperatives that exist "outside;" at worst, it is fertile ground in which the worst cultural manifestations of working-class alienation and despair can germinate and thrive. At times I have felt grateful to have the opportunity to know Smokehousers and to participate in their lives; at other times, I have been left to question what on earth would compel me to want to have any part of the scene at the Smokehouse. In the "field," this tension has as an analogue the (perverse, or so it has always felt) fact that some of my most useful "data" have come from situations that have left me feeling the most emotionally drained and psychically defeated.

I hope it will become clear to the reader that I do not intend to either valorize the Smokehouse as a repository of pure and essential folk wisdom or to deprecate it is a backward, anachronistic fortress. It is not my place to redeem or to condemn, only to offer a sense of how Smokehousers perceive their social predicaments and how these perceptions—and, to some extent, the predicaments themselves—are matters of rhetoric. In truth, the people who work and play there are simply trying to "get by" and to make sense of their lives. Some are abusers of alcohol, some are not, some have gone to college, some have not, some mistreat women, some do not, some are clearly racist, some are not, and so on. Taken as a whole, what Smokehousers seem to want is what everybody wants: to figure out how the world works and to understand their place in it. Many are manifestly philosophical and use the barroom as a forum in which to collaboratively invent and publicly test their ideas. I do not claim to offer either the big picture or the last word, only a few pages in the script of on ongoing social drama.

In the course of this study, I have learned something not only about the people in my own community but about my own place in it. As for the latter, two things in particular come to mind: one, that I am more working class than I thought I was, and two, that I am more middle class than I thought I was. In the interpretation of data to follow, I make the case that Smokehousers "need" me to forge their own identities: in the same way that Geertz's Balinese men practice cockfighting in order to learn what it means to be Balinese, people at the Smokehouse ritually pit themselves and their mythologies against me— and the middle-class and academic mythologies I represent—to learn what it means to be working-class. But that much was clear to me early on; what was not so clear was the extent to which I needed *them*.

There is power in claiming the authority to speak for an entire group of people. At the Smokehouse, I enjoyed the privilege of speaking for the "intellectuals." Here at the bar at the Smokehouse was a culture in which I was always sure of the rules (unlike in academe, however much I claimed to profess its views); still, I could enjoy whatever status and power (I thought) the university conferred by association. But even if my participation in academic affairs did not always earn me the appreciation of my barroom cohorts, my identification with the academy left me room to invent myself. In the process of working on this ethnography, I learned to comprehend the extent to which others were just as busy inventing *me*. Viewed from one perspective, this ethnographic study of the Smokehouse is an account of how competing rhetorics provide the heuristic background in terms of which (or against which) each might invent itself. In a sense, this portrait of the Smokehouse bar frames a moment in a culture in transition, a moment in its struggles to contend with dilemmas posed by competing forces of tradition and change.

Each of the chapters to follow has its own theoretical and interpretive focus. The chapters should be read individually as a series of ethnographic tales and collectively as a contiguous assemblage of views and interpretations of Smokehouse culture, language, and life.

Chapter 2, "A Place in the Middle," is what Van Maanen (1988) would call an "impressionist tale." As such, it is a narrative account of people and place told from my vantage point as bartender. I present such a tale here not only in an effort to orient the reader to the particularities of place and personae but to affirm the truth that narrative is in some ways best suited to render phenomenological densities, to show how a field of signification shot through with contradictions coheres as a cultural text. Though this particular narrative is a text woven from actual events I have recorded as field notes through long-term participation and observation, it is a synthetic story of people and events, a story deliberately constructed to convey both the complex and the predictable in Smokehouse life.

Chapter 3, "A Place to Be," draws the parameters of the rhetorical situation in which arguments emerge as social practice and are represented as ethnographic data. It establishes the Smokehouse as a white working-class institution and suggests how the barroom setting not only contains but *constitutes* patterns of social interaction. It describes the social structure and interpersonal dynamics of Smokehouse society and considers rhetorical implications of my position (as Smokehouser and as ethnographer) for ethnographic fieldwork.

Chapter 4, "Across the Table: Walter, Joe, Arlen, Maggie, and Perry" attempts to further apprehend the textures and limits of the rhetorical situation of the Smokehouse by taking Smokehousers *out* of the bar—at least symbolically—for a time. It introduces some of the key players in Smokehouse society in a space removed from the sociable nexus of public interaction. To foreground the rhetorical imperatives of the bar as public space, it presents Smokehousers as something other than an aggregate public, as a collection of differently situated and motivated individuals. Though these five are introduced in terms of their private interactions with me in one-on-one interviews, the point here is not to suggest what Smokehousers are "really like," in private—rather, it is to displace them into a different rhetorical situation where their narratives might work together to explain the social imperatives that give expressive practices their distinctive shape and meaning.

Chapter 5, "A Place to Tell It," focuses on relationships between narrative, culture, and ideology. It includes excerpts from interviews with the five Smokehousers introduced in the previous chapter and attempts to map the logics of identity encoded in the views they express on themes that emerge through everyday rhetorical practice. My goal in this chapter is not to draw easy comparisons between individuals' performative selves and their more "private" selves; more precisely, I aim to consider attitudes that individuals *profess*, in a rhetorical context removed from the public arena in which arguments are scripted and performed. I do this in the hope of constructing an interpretive problematic that attends to the different publics to which Smokehousers address themselves as they narrate the themes—of race, class, work, education, and politics—that function as rhetorical *topoi* in the Smokehouse logos. I include this collection of narratives not only to suggest how themes and topics organize a *common logic* but to indicate individual positionings with respect to this logos.

Chapter 6, "A Place to Stand," examines speech genres and events that organize Smokehouse social life and looks in particular at the shape and meaning of argument as performed genre and cultural event. To interrogate the shifting location of rhetorical authority in argument, I give special attention to the relationship between ethos and logos, or the relation between the cultural logic and the social positions established by claiming or conferring rights to speak for that logic. The overarching purpose of the interpretation of the data presented here is to explore what the special kind of rhetoric in which those at the Smokehouse participate—that is, what assumptions undergird acts of communication as well as what persuasions are at work—might suggest about the group's own "theory of practice." I suggest, finally, that argument as it happens at the Smokehouse is a "class act," an event that emerges in response to tensions in Smokehouse logics of class identity.

Chapter 7, "A Place for What If," draws together the meanings of performance, persuasion, and class identity at the Smokehouse to suggest how each term delimits the others. My aim in theorizing the practices of Smokehousers is to make sense of how *they* theorize, or give meaning to, their own rhetorical practice. Here I conclude that the practice of argument at the Smokehouse bar represents cultural processes of class identification vis-à-vis the unnamability of class culture, as well as of domination of local forms by rhetorical marketplaces in which abstraction from local experience is the preferred currency. I argue for an understanding of *persuasion* as a manifestly public process, one highly contingent on how acts of persuasive discourse are meaningful as cultural performance and which happens incrementally over time. I conclude that rhetoric—as both a way of knowing through language and as persuasive discourse—is meaningful only in terms of particular cultural contexts and that culture can be understood only as a rhetorical process.

2

A Place in the Middle

Behind Bar at the Smokehouse

Two o'clock on Friday afternoon: I am scheduled to work the bar tonight. My shift begins at 3:30, but there is plenty to do before then. I pick out my work clothes: a short denim skirt, sleeveless blouse, sneakers and socks. Or should I find a long skirt to wear, maybe? I know tonight will be busy, and a longer, fuller skirt will be easier to move around in. I look into my closet once again and see only blue jeans. Perry, the bar owner, has forbidden us to wear jeans at the bar, insisting that if we *must* wear pants, they should be "dress pants." But the boss's dress code is less rigid than his gender code: for jobs tending bar, he hires only "girls."

I finally decide in favor of the denim skirt, recalling the boss's repeated injunctions about how important it is for *you girls to keep the guys at the bar interested.* (When I was first hired at the Smokehouse, Perry had assured me that he was flexible about what bartenders wore. He had explained that he asked only that his girls look nice: "If you got good legs, wear a short skirt; if your assets are elsewhere . . . you know, do whatever works.") I pull my hair into a high, tight ponytail—it looks better down, maybe, but I know I'll be working hard, and I want the hair out of my way. The battle in getting dressed for work is always a fight between competing ideals of sex appeal and utility. As far as the boss is concerned, a good bartender is one who knows, above all, how to be attractive to her male patrons. But what any bartender knows is that it is hard to be a good bartender by any definition in painful shoes. A Smokehouse bartender's first dilemma—something sometimes harder to resolve than bar quarrels—is how to reconcile the private self with the public one.

I can't seem to figure out what to do with my hair. The ponytail makes me look less like an English teacher than like a teenage gymnast. But, really, there's no time to mess around—I want to get to work in time to get lunch at the carry-out across the street before I start. If I eat too early in the afternoon, or if I skip lunch, I'll be hungry later—I know I probably won't get another chance to eat until my shift is over, 1:00 AM at the earliest. A bartender is allowed one "free" meal per shift—an appetizer or a sandwich—but she doesn't get any kind of official break, and it's almost impossible on a Friday night to eat and work at the same time. The food always arrives from the kitchen at precisely the wrong time, and as soon as I lift a bite to my mouth, somebody wants something and I have to stop and rush over. Furthermore, the cooks, often harried and overworked, do not take kindly to "extra" food orders. (It can be so difficult to get food from the kitchen that often bartenders don't even bother, or they talk one of the regulars into running out for fast food.) I could probably convince Arlen to sneak back into the kitchen to fix something after closing, but I don't really want to wait that long—sometimes the last customer doesn't leave until after 2 AM.

I resign myself to the ponytail and examine with ill-focused dissatisfaction the overall effect of the look in front of a full-length mirror. After stuffing some extra Band-Aids for my feet into my purse, I hurry out. As I climb into the car, I notice a long run in my stocking, but it's too late to go back and change. Ah, well, I think, no matter; the bar is dark, the run won't be noticed. I could go broke buying pantyhose—they never stand up to more than a day's wear behind the bar.

The drive to work takes me past a limestone quarry, an asphalt plant, and finally into forest preserve area as I get closer to the Smokehouse. I enjoy the drive to work, especially during the fall when the trees are bright with color. Now, in the summer, the way is densely green and shady. Greendale, a heavily wooded town of big trees and little houses, is the hometown of the Smokehouse Inn. The Smokehouse itself is a shabby, rustic-looking structure with several dimensions of wings, landings, and awnings. A red neon sign advertising the name of the restaurant stands in odd contrast to the carefully stylized old-world look of the building across the street. Another marquee proclaims "Senior Citizen Specials" and urges pizza-lovers to "Try the Brick Oven Difference."

The Smokehouse building was first built a century and a half ago to be used as a hiding place for slaves escaping from the South. Since then, its boundaries have expanded in all directions. The overall effect is that the building has grown somehow organically, that it has without human intervention sprouted off at random. It looks—for all its tendencies toward what is old and traditional and rustic—vaguely unstable, as if it were at any moment preparing to burst forth with a new wing, a new appendage. Since its birth in 1876 as a simple four-walled brick house, it has, little by little, encroached upon the space surrounding it.

I park in the lot across the street and stand at the curb waiting to cross. (I can tell by the latest addition to the marquee that there's a wedding going on tonight. The sign reads CONGRADULATIONS KELLY AND STEVE!!!!!! When banquets are in progress, Perry ropes off the parking lots closest to the restaurant for wedding guests.) Traffic is heavy on Friday afternoons at this time—workers coming home from work; trucks conveying their last loads to the limestone quarries; mothers driving kids to afterschool activities. There is a feeling of busy Friday anticipation. The long week of work is over. The week is over, that is, for all but the workers at the Smokehouse, for whom the weekend signifies work's beginning.

After what seems like several minutes, a giant dump truck slows and its driver motions for me to cross. As I cross in front of the truck, the driver gives a booming blast on his horn, the sound of which sends me scurrying for the curb. I look back at the driver in annoyance, but he looks amused at my reaction. He smiles and waves and continues heavily on his way to the quarry. I stand in front of the Smokehouse door looking after the truck, wondering if the driver is somebody I know. Is he one of the bar regulars, maybe?

I try the front door to the building and am surprised to find it locked. For a moment I consider the possibility that perhaps the janitor has been sneaking booze again and has forgotten to unlock the door for me, but then I remember that Perry, the owner, is "remodeling" again. I recall now that Perry intends to convert the front entrance and vestibule of the building into an "office" (in which to conduct interviews, reprimands, firings, and the like) and to redirect customers through the doors leading to the banquet room. When the banquet room doors become the only way to gain access to the restaurant (Perry has explained), customers will be compelled to see and admire his banquet facilities. This, he has concluded, will lead to a better banquet business, which has, he has come to admit, been dropping off lately. But Perry's remodeling has, in the meantime, inspired much grumbling among inconvenienced bar customers, who feel as if their needs—as Perry's most faithful patrons—should come first.

I try the banquet room doors and, to my annoyance, find them locked as well. Maybe Willie *has* been hitting the booze, after all. Byrd, the maintenance man, swears that he has seen the old janitor sneak behind the bar early in the morning. But glancing at my watch, I am surprised to see that it is only 2:45— I'm early, no wonder the doors are still locked. The side door, the door leading directly into the lounge, should be open even now, though, I am sure. That door swings open heavily, and I step inside the cool dark of the bar.

As many years as I have worked here, still I am surprised at how utterly disorienting it is to enter the bar's womblike darkness from the daylight outside. Customers—even regulars—seem also to be surprised, for they often trip over the step from the vestibule to the bar. When they do, I pretend not to notice. If the tripper has noticed that I have noticed, I reassure them: "You know, that happens to just *everybody* who comes in. Hard to see, isn't it?"

As my eyes adjust to the dark, the lines and shapes of the room fuzz into place. There is an old bar, of the type that grew out of the austere excesses of the early 1960s—dark, glossy, varnished wood, backed stools covered with brown nubby fabric, a clunky mechanical cash register. It strikes me that the room itself bespeaks the status of barrooms prior to the social changes brought by the enactment of civil rights, the rise of feminism, and the sexual revolution. Then, bars such as this one became hideouts for men seeking refuge in the company of others, like themselves, seeking refuge. There are windows along the south wall, but they have long ago been bricked up, as if in a conscious effort to keep the outside, always threatening to push in, out.

The room is warm, close, insular. It is in fact part of a much larger and busier institution and has the feel of a kind of shelter within the shelter of the restaurant itself. A pair of swinging saloon doors leads from the bar into the foyer of the restaurant; during busy hours, the doors are in constant motion as waitresses hurry in and out ordering drinks for their customers. A person entering the room via the swinging doors is greeted by the sight of twin video-poker machines along the opposite wall; after restaurant hours, these machines will be manned by businesslike waitresses, sipping pink wine from tall glasses with long straws and smoking as they feed the night's tips into the machines. (There was originally only one machine, but the great popularity of the video-poker machine soon inspired Perry to add another; now, that corner of the room looks like a bit of that favorite vacation spot of many of the Smokehouse crowd, Las Vegas.) To the right of the poker machines, three sets of tables and chairs and a jukebox line the wall. The tables are weakly illuminated by "Victorian" hanging lamps brightly decorated with old Coca-Cola iconography. Now, the light from the lamps reveals ash-strewn tabletops, which last night's bartender has apparently forgotten to wipe down.

This is my favorite time at the bar. There are no customers, but the place hums with the anticipation of the night to come. The waitresses are just beginning to gear up for a busy night. They walk purposefully from bar to kitchen to dining room, setting tables, stocking ice, making coffee—smoking, smoking, smoking. The barroom itself has, before opening on Friday afternoon, the portentous emptiness of a room waiting for a party.

"Hi, Pollyanna," calls Roberta, one of the Smokehouse's two veteran waitresses. It is her usual way of addressing me these days. I have learned that for Roberta, acceptance is always marked by a teasing just on the edge of hostility—so I know she likes me. I am sure the name derives from my associations with college and, consequently, with what is perceived to be a kind of supercilious propriety. But I like Roberta and am glad to see that we'll be working together tonight.

"Boy, am I glad you're working the front bar tonight," she says, stopping at the bar long enough to light a Newport. "That Valerie doesn't know her ass from a Manhattan. Last night she had waitresses waiting three deep for draughts. For beers! That's what everybody needed. I could see if we all wanted Grasshoppers or something, but . . . have you met her?"

I tell her I haven't. Bartending, like waitressing, has a heavy turnover. Except for a faithful few, most bartenders last only a couple of weeks, or even days. The "new girl" may well be gone—complaints to Perry will get her fired, or she'll simply stop showing up—before I ever have a chance to meet her (a lot depends on how the customers—and the waitresses—take to her). Or perhaps she will have trouble at home—babysitter trouble, or, even worse, man trouble. In the few years I have known the Smokehouse, it has lost many a good bartender to an irate husband or boyfriend who doesn't think *his* woman should be doing this kind of work.

"Who's working the Pit tonight?" Roberta asks. The Pit is the restaurant's service bar, open on Friday and Saturday nights when it's likely to get busy. "Or don't we have a Pit again tonight?" Lately, business has been slow. I check the bartenders' schedule, an auto-shop calendar on which Perry has penciled in the bartenders' shifts for this month. A bartender's working days change from month to month; often, they change from week to week. Sometimes a bartender will get several working days; sometimes next to none. It all depends on what Perry decides.

"You're in luck," I tell her. "Valerie's on again tonight for the Pit. I guess I'll get to meet her, after all."

"Oh, that's fucking wonderful. So much for making any kind of money tonight. Customers tend to get a little pissed when they get their martini with dessert. Well, I guess you'll be seeing a lot of me tonight. Aren't *you* the lucky one!" Waitresses aren't supposed to come to the front bar for their drinks when there is a pit bartender. But the front bar is often manned by a more experienced bartender, so they do it anyway. I know that Roberta, a fast waitress, will not tolerate a slow bartender.

Roberta hurries off toward the kitchen. If she gets her prep work done before the restaurant opens, then perhaps she'll have time to sit and have a smoke or two before she gets her first table. If it gets busy, she may not get another chance to relax until the last table is gone. As soon as she is gone, Nelda, the Smokehouse's "salad lady," enters the bar. Her job is to do the cooking that doesn't actually involve *cooking*—that is, Nelda is responsible for making salads, relishes, garnishes, condiments, and the like. Now, she leans heavily on the bar, her fleshy brown arms folded under her chest.

"Hi, Julie . . . how you doin' today? Seem like I just got here, already my ankles killin' me. Hot today, ain't it?"

I am surprised to hear Nel complain, but only because she does it so rarely. It's not that she doesn't have cause for dissatisfaction: she is in her sixties and must stand on her feet in the kitchen for eight hours, sometimes more. The kitchen is, I know, unbearably hot. In the summertime, I dread even to go back there just long enough to order food for the bar. Once, on a day just like this, I asked one of the cooks what the temperature was in the kitchen. He had glanced at a thermometer mounted near the open back door and said, "A hundred and ten, now. But it'll get worse."

Nelda pushes a large plastic cup toward me over the bar and I, knowing what she wants, fill it with orange juice. Perry has again decreed that kitchen help are not to get juice—only water or pop—but the boss isn't in yet, so I give the salad lady what she wants. She doesn't say anything at all, because that would make her guilty of the crime of stealing orange juice; a bartender can bear the responsibility for this sort of transgression much more easily. Kitchen help, it seems, are always under suspicion for something.

After the bar opens for the day, Nelda probably won't be able to get any more juice, because she'll have to ask someone else—maybe somebody less willing to break the rules—to go to the bar for her. None of the kitchen help except for Arly, who is distinguished by his "managerial" status—as well as by his whiteness—is allowed to walk through the dining room during dinner hours.

It is now 3:00. I go into the bathroom to see how my ponytail has withstood the breezy drive here; when I come back into the bar, Arlen, the Smokehouse's resident (he lives in a room above the bar) all-purpose cook, accountant, and bar manager, is seated at the far end of it. The closing music from *General Hospital* blares from the television, but Arly is, as usual, engrossed in a crossword puzzle. I turn down the television and approach him from behind the bar. He doesn't look up from his puzzle.

"Hello, Foop," I say to the top of his head.

"Hello, Foop," he says, still without emerging from the puzzle. Arlen and I almost always call each other some version of the one nickname we have between us. The name came about as the result of a hazy early-morning conversation, the subject or import of which nobody can remember, and out of which only a nonsense word escaped into the present: "Foopa." But the word has become part of the bar's regular lexicon; most of the regulars know that it refers either to Arlen or to me. Only rarely does anybody ask where the word actually came from, or what it really "means."

"Foop," I persist, "I'm gonna go next door and get a taco. Do you want one?"

"Yyyyeah," he concedes after a moment, as if *he* were the one doing *me* the favor. "But only one. No hot stuff." Arlen doesn't eat much these days. I guess putting down a case of beer a night doesn't leave him much room for anything else.

When I return with the tacos, Arly is still hunched over the puzzle. He takes his taco without looking up and polishes it off in three businesslike bites.

"A Jewish head-covering," he thinks aloud. "Eight letters."

"Yarmulke," I offer. "Y-A-R-M-U-L-K-E."

"You think you're so smart," Arlen observes. "Just because you been in school your whole life—." He pushes the finished puzzle aside and finally looks up at me. "There's about five shows I wanna see this week. Think you can fit me into your busy schedule? Or do you need to check your appointment book?"

Arly and I often get together on our day off to go to the show. He loves movies—knows all the film history, can name all the actors. Together we sit at the bar reading the latest reviews, until I notice the time and jump up, crumpling the greasy taco sack.

"Shit, Foop, they'll be coming before I get anything set up." But it's too late—someone has left the side door open, and Tom, one of the telephone guys, appears in the vestibule. Squinting, Tom stumbles over the landing. "You know," I say, "just everybody does that. Hard to see, isn't it?"

Though the bar doesn't officially open for another ten minutes yet, I apologize to Tom for not being ready for him. He shrugs and sits in his usual seat. I open a Stroh's, the brand of beer he drinks. People always ask how I can remember what to make and what to serve to whom, but the truth is that bar customers probably have the most predictable habits of any group (save, perhaps, for gamblers) I know. People don't just *prefer* a drink, they *are* that drink; it's part of their style. When Tom stops drinking Stroh's, I'll know he's working toward becoming a new man.

While Tom sips his beer, I rush about readying the bar to open. How does it always happen, I ask myself, that I leave the house early, arrive in plenty of time, and still manage not to be ready when the bar opens? I light a cigarette, even though I don't have time to smoke. Suddenly I'm overwhelmed: there's so much yet to do, I can't seem to decide what to do next. Finally I decide to go downstairs to the cellar to get ice. That would be a good idea, because everything else I could do behind the bar even while customers are there. I haul the five-gallon bucket from behind the bar and plop it on top of the bar. Tom looks up, shaken from his reverie by the noise.

"Need ice?" he asks. Tom always offers to get ice for the bartenders. "I can get it for you." I thank him and decline his offer, even though I'm in a hurry and could use the help. Tom works as a telephone lineman and could probably use a little rest—and anyway, I know he offers because he feels obliged to be polite.

The cellar of the Smokehouse is a room that proclaims its history, despite its clutter of present-day restaurant and bar paraphernalia. It feels as if something historic might have happened here a century ago; but I already know from Smokehouse lore that this cellar is where fugitive slaves once huddled en route to the free states. Layers of history seem to coat the damp walls down here; whenever I come down for a routine task, I am struck, and a little chilled, by the narrative richness of the place. But the mythology at the Smokehouse is that the cellar is haunted—to be sure, it looks as if displaced spirits crouch in the dark places. Waitresses and customers alike delight in sending teenage busgirls down for ice or wine, snapping the cellar light off from above, and listening for the inevitable screams. But the history of the cellar is not told as part of Smokehouse history; nobody at the bar mentions the building's historic role as part of the Underground Railroad. The building that houses the bar still serves as a kind of hideout, to be sure—but of a much different sort, for a much different set of fugitives.

Next to the ice machine—the kind you sometimes see standing outside the offices of roadside motels—is a stack of five-gallon plastic buckets. Some advertise "Open Pit Barbecue Sauce, Restaurant Recipe"; these are still stained red on the inside. I often wonder why Perry doesn't mind us carrying ice around in buckets that reveal his rib sauce's unglamorous origin—he for whom food must be claimed to derive from either "secret family" or "old Italian" sources. Realizing that I've left the bucket for the bar upstairs, I fill two of the buckets from the stack with ice, scoop by scoop, and make my way up the stairs.

Now, from the perspective of the cellar, the barroom looks brilliantly lit. Light filters down through the open door to the bar; I can just make out the outline of the top stairs. This part of the ice-fetching operation always makes me a little nervous—it takes all my strength to muscle the buckets up the stairs, and the stairs themselves are treacherous. One waver on the step, and I'd tumble backward down the stairs and into the cellar. But as far as I know, nobody has actually fallen, and I am reluctant to solicit help from—and perhaps obligate myself further to—the guys at the bar. I brace my shoulders and muscle the buckets up.

As I hoist the ice buckets up onto the bar, I notice that another customer, Roy, has arrived and is drinking a beer. I see that Tom, too, is on his second beer; the empty bottle has been pushed to the outer ledge of the bar.

"Oh, hey, sweetheart," says Roy. "I saw you were busy, so I just grabbed us a coupla these." He holds up his bottle and then indicates a pile of bills on the bar. "Here, take out for 'em." But I apologize for my absence and tell him the beers are on me. "If there's one thing I like," remarks Roy, "it's a woman that got legs like that buys me beer." It is a common practice for bartenders to "buy" customers drinks to amend some error or indiscretion, or when the customer has proven his loyalty as a patron by spending most of his roll at the bar—but it seems as if lately, Roy, a regular customer, says the same thing every time I buy him a drink. I am told that he makes the same remark, over and over again, to all the bartenders. The phrase has come to characterize Roy as much as, say, the St. Louis Cardinals cap he always wears to proclaim his disdain for the Cubs, Chicago's yuppie Northside team.

Perry has been having the bartenders keep a record of the drinks we've given away in a little log book at the side of the register. The rule is that we're supposed to account for everything and not to exceed the limit of six "freebies" a night. This limit is difficult to maintain, for often male customers will come in packs of five or more and buy several rounds. You buy one group a round, and you're up to your limit for the evening. Perry instituted the "six-drink rule" after learning of the results of a lie-detector test, which he insisted that Maxie (a bartender and lifelong friend of his) and I take in order to merit a 25-cent-an-hour raise. The test showed that each of us (Maxie and I) "frequently stole" over five dollars a day by giving away too many drinks to paying customers. Still, the six-drink rule is regarded by the bartenders as something of a joke: they simply write the first six freebies down and don't mention the rest.

So I give away my first two drinks of the night. I go to the notepad to record them. I enter: "2 Stroh's bottles, 1.25 each; 2.50." I initial the entry and date it. As I'm writing, I hear the door swing open again. This time, Ed Baines appears in the doorway. He is a mammoth of a man—a former high-school gym teacher—and he greets me with a mock scowl. "Oh, it's YOU," he growls, "when does the bar down the street open up? Maybe I can go drink there until the shift change." His face sneaks into a smile; he laughs. "Hi, honey. How're you doing? How's school?" I chat with Ed, but I don't bother asking him what he wants to drink; I already know. I reach for his usual glass (a big tumbler) to fill with his usual Vodka and Seven-Up, but he grabs my arm in mid-reach. "I don't use that glass anymore. Where ya been?" He indicates a brandy snifter the size of a baby's head: "I got tired of that other one." The snifter looks as if it'll hold even more than the tumbler; Ed's strategy is to have his drinks put in bigger and bigger glasses without paying more per drink. I don't even bother to try and charge him more; I know he'll make a fuss. He's a loyal customer, and, as any bartender knows, the important thing is to keep the regulars happy.

Another customer—this one new to me—has now claimed the stool next to Ed Baines. The new guy and Ed smack each other on the back, and the newcomer drops a pile of bills onto the bar. "Back up the coach, here, willya?" I clap an empty shotglass down in front of Ed to show that his next drink has been paid for. (Often, when several groups of guys are in at once, I run out of shot-glasses and have to remember who paid for which round when. But by and large, the regulars abide by a kind of barroom "code of honor": they'll tell me if I make a mistake, even if the mistake is in their favor.) I begin to go to check on the phone guys, but Ed calls me back over. "I'd like you to meet a former student of mine. This is Steve. Helluva ball player." I extend my hand to the man. He is much younger than Ed, looks to be about my age or even younger. The guy looks surprised at my outstretched hand; instead of shaking it, he grabs it and kisses it with a loud sucking noise. "I wouldn't do that if I was you," Ed tells him. "She's one'a them femi-nazis." The guy just stares at me. "Not only that," Ed goes on—I can see he's on a roll—"she's a pinko, too." He laughs. Steve grins. I sigh. "Yes," I say to the younger man. "It's true, I'm a communist. I guess that means I have something in common with Ed."

The big man makes a big show of his outrage: "Say, WHAT?"

"Ed doesn't believe in the U.S. Constitution, either," I explain to Steve.

"Hey, hey, whaddaya mean?" roars Ed.

"Well, you know, you don't believe in freedom of speech," I tease. "You know, the First Amendment. . . ?"

"Who says?" Ed is getting suspicious; he knows I'm up to something. "I do, too. Who says I don't?" The younger guy, Steve, is looking back and forth, not yet sure how to read this exchange.

"Ah," I say, savoring the moment. "So you DO agree with me about the flag thing." I know it is dangerous to allude to the "flag thing," but I decide—the phone guys are at the other end of the bar and seem not to be paying attention—to risk it. At that moment, I wonder vaguely why I can't resist saying things that I know will get me in trouble around here.

The "flag thing" happened once when I was working a very crowded bar, late on a Friday evening. The phone guys—a group of regulars, and veterans of the war in Vietnam—were in that night and had been talking excitedly about a "so-called artist" at the Art Institute who had, as part of a display, placed an American flag on the floor and invited visitors to the museum to step on the flag. I knew better than to get into this one and had consciously tried to avoid being drawn into the conversation. But Will, one of the regulars, had indicated me to his friends and said, "Now, take this one, here. I bet she's one of them that thinks it's okay to walk on the flag." Sensing the potential for real trouble, I didn't respond to his accusation. Still, Will had persisted: "I'll bet you that *she* thinks it just don't mean nothing to wipe your feet on the American flag." Then: "Isn't that right, Julie?" Though (for once) I made a real effort to remain neutral, I was quickly made aware that my silence was read as confirmation of Will's accusations, as tacit approval of the artist's actions. Soon I was being shouted at from all sides of the bar; I was at the center of swelling voices, pounding fists, pointing fingers. I finally broke my silence in an effort to explain my position, to say that believing that the artist in question shouldn't be arrested didn't necessarily mean I agreed with the rightness of what he did. But the point was, it seems, lost in the fracas.

Since then, that particular argument—though it happened in response to a point of view I never actually professed—has been canonized as the text in which our differences are clearly inscribed. It continues to be potentially volatile and is therefore often alluded to in jokes *(Hey, Julie, walk on any flags, lately?)*, but I now know better than to give the topic too much room to grow, or to make it the subject of real public debate.

"Sonofobitch," says Ed Baines, shaking his head. "Are you gonna get my friend here a beer, or are you gonna stand there yappin' all day?" I smile, knowing I've won. I say to Steve, "Hey, was Mr. Baines that cranky as a gym teacher?" I hear Ed Baines to his friend as I move away: "It's so goddamn easy to push her buttons."

I go down the bar to fetch another round for the phone guys. "Hey, what is this shit? Put on Channel Five." Two of the waitresses are standing at the bar, waiting for their first customers of the day, smoking. The three of us protest; today's episode of *Donahue* is on date rape and is now featuring a young woman's tearful testimony. But the men at the bar persist. I change the channel, knowing that the waitresses never really expected to have things *their* way, anyway. Smaller conversations around the bar die out; all attention is focused on the television and Alex Trebek's game-show-host voice announcing the rules for *Jeopardy!* As the questions are asked, the men at the bar compete to see who can be the first to yell out the answer. In the "Final Jeopardy" round, they up the ante by agreeing to buy a beer for the guy who gets the question right.

As the regulars are shouting at the television, I take the opportunity to slip out to the kitchen to visit Arlen. Arlen stands in a ragged, dirty T-shirt, sweating, slapping barbecue sauce on slabs of pork with a big paintbrush. *Jeopardy* blares from a small black-and-white TV mounted on one of the kitchen shelves. "Hey, Foop, " I say, poking him in the side. "Shh!" he says, staring over my head at the TV. "All right, fine," I say, feigning offense. "I'll go away. Too hot back here, anyway." Hattie and Pearl, the other two cooks, glower, sweating, from their respective posts at the grill and steam table.

Back at the bar, I see that two new customers have come in. For a moment I savor the irony that the minute I leave the bar for a second, someone new comes in wanting speedy service. But then—to my surprise and dismay—I see that the customers are middle-aged women. The men at the bar stare briefly at the newcomers and then go back to the game show. The women, feeling the stares, lean closer to each other, chatting furtively. In spite of myself, I anticipate an ordeal. These women look ornery, and I have a feeling they'll be difficult. One woman looks around impatiently, the other scrubs at a spot on the bar with a cocktail napkin.

The phone guys have also been joined by two others; now, they look eagerly down the bar to get my attention. But the women have come in first, and I have to serve them first, even though I am sure their drinks will take longer to make. If the women happened to be regular customers, they would probably order the easier "male" drinks, since women who hang around the bar regularly tend to drink like men. But these are new, and I can see that they don't look quite at home sitting at a bar without male accompaniment.

I ask the women for their orders, and my fears are confirmed. One asks for a Brandy Alexander; the other wants a strawberry daiquiri. I glance down the bar; the phone guys look impatient, but they have heard the women's drink order and reassure me to take my time. I tell the Brandy Alexander Woman that I need to run back to the kitchen to get the ice cream to make her drink and ask her if she would like it made with regular cream, instead. "No," she says, even though she can see that I'm busy and that there are others waiting for drinks. "I want it with ice cream." I go to the back freezer to get the ice cream, only to find it frozen so solid that it takes several minutes to scoop out even a little chunk. I race back to the bar, where I hurriedly plop the ice cream into the blender with some brandy and creme de caçao. "Use the other kind of caçao," instructs the woman. After the Alexander is blended to the woman's specifications, I give it a squirt of canned whipped cream and start on the daiquiri. Behind me, I hear Steve remark to Ed Baines, in reference to the Brandy Alexander Woman's weight: "She looks like she really needs THAT, eh?"

After the women are taken care of, I rush to fetch beers for the phone guys, who by now have been waiting several minutes. My hands are sticky from the ice cream and the daiquiri mix, so I have trouble counting out change. "Just keep it," says Roy, even though he'll surely leave another tip when he leaves. I thank him and put the three ones in my tip jar. When I make my way back to the other end of the bar, I notice that the women have already gone, their half-finished drinks abandoned. There is no tip.

I feel a sudden pinch of annoyance at the women: damn them, I think. But then, just as suddenly, I am struck by the powerful irony of Ed Baines's "femi-nazi" remark: I realize with dismay that even though male customers can often be leering and pushy, I generally prefer to wait on men. But (I explain to myself) I know when I approach a male customer that he will likely be content to order a beer and will reward my efforts with a tip. Any kind of shit I get from a man will certainly be predictable and will probably be negotiable. Female customers, on the other hand, are likely to order almost anything and never seem to want to compensate a bartender for the time and effort it takes to prepare those elaborate girly drinks. It comes down, I conclude, to simple economics: waiting on women simply means more work for less money. It occurs to me that the men at the bar sense—and appreciate—my impatience with female customers.

In spite of these revelations, I am glad that the two women are gone. Soon the restaurant will be busy, and waitresses will want fancy drinks for their own tables. If—as is the case tonight—there is a new bartender in the Pit, serving the overflow of waitresses will slow me down considerably.

I look up from wiping the bar—still sticky from the whipped cream from the Brandy Alexander Woman's drink—to see Roberta standing in front of me, leaning into the waitress station.

"Hel-lo," she warbles, waving a hand in front of my face. "Earth to Pollyana."

"Oh! Sorry. I'm here. I just spaced for a second. Whaddaya need?"

Between drags on a cigarette hastily lit, she begins to sound off her drink order, loudly and mechanically, like an automatic rifle.

"Three drafts, a Tom Collins, and a Bloody Mary. Sorry, Julie, but Valerie doesn't know how to make a Tom Collins—can you believe it? I thought I'd just get whole order from you."

I see that the phone guys are again looking for a round. Even though I know they understand that the waitress station has priority, I feel a pang of guilt for having made them wait so long earlier, when the Brandy Alexander Woman came in. I look at them, shrug, and turn back to Roberta.

"Can I?"

"Okay, go ahead," she agrees, but she looks a little annoyed. Her annoyance annoys me—I think, she shouldn't be at this bar in the first place. But I don't blame her for wanting to do whatever will make her some money. Roberta works hard (like most Smokehouse waitresses) and supports her children, alone (like most Smokehouse waitresses), on what she makes here. My annoyance at her turns to annoyance at myself—why the urge, always, to serve the men first?

After I bring the phone guys another round, I jog back over to the waitress station. I make the Bloody Mary first, because I know it's the one drink that won't "go flat" as it sits. I run a lime around the rim of the glass and then grind the lip of the glass in a tray of celery salt. Then, in goes the vodka, mix, celery, olives, and another lime. I fetch the draughts and blend the Tom Collins. By the time I finish with the Tom Collins, the beer has lost its head. Holding her cigarette tightly between her lips, Roberta uses a straw to whip up some foam in the beer with one hand and thrusts a drink ticket at me with the other. I ring up the drinks on the ticket and hand it back to her; she hurries off carrying the full tray aloft, her stringy bicep taut against the white frill of her sleeve.

I look around the bar and see that everybody looks satisfied, so I shake a cigarette out of my pack and light it. But just as I feel the first delicious drag swirl down to fill my lungs, the heavy door squeaks open and the carhaulers—the whole gang of them, six in all—enter, loudly laughing and hey-heying. The carhaulers claim the entire far side of the bar and call me over: "Hey, darlin'. We're thirsty. How 'bout a round of draughts?" I suggest to them that maybe a pitcher would be a better buy, but they insist on separate glasses, because each has his own brand of beer. The three brands of beer on tap at the Smokehouse are similar; all are light domestic brews—but the haulers refuse to deviate from the brands to which they have proclaimed their loyalty.

"We could get a pitcher of Stroh's," one suggests.

"Are you kidding?" another wants to know. "You can drink that crap, but I'll stick to Old Style."

"Old Style!" rejoins the first. "Talk about pisswater!"

Even though the men do not drink beer from clearly labeled bottles to display their beer preferences, they nonetheless manage to convey this information. I fill the six glasses, one by one, and set them in front of their respective owners.

"Take it out of here," commands Carhauler One.

"No, no, I got it," insists Carhauler Two.

"Don't even think about taking their money," warns Carhauler Three. "It's my round." I look from One to Two to Three, weighing my options. I decide that no matter what I do, one of them will get pissed off—at me, for failing to decide the contest in his favor. I take the money from One's pile of twenties, ignoring the protests of Two and Three. "Sorry, guys," I say. "He called first."

I have little patience for the carhaulers' wars—the group is perceived, by all the bartenders, to be troublesome, obnoxious, and cheap. The group—thinned out some, since Perry barred it from the Smokehouse after restaurant customers complained of shouted obscenities—almost always, since its recent return, comes into the bar after work at this time. The carhaulers drive trucks loaded with new cars to be distributed to dealerships, and the haulers use their leisure time to come to the bar to complain about work, women, and minorities, in that order of priority. Often, they try to show off for each other by belittling the bartenders and ordering them about. Of all the men who come to the bar, they are by far the worst tippers—the entire group might leave, say, two dollars on the bar after leaving the bartender exhausted and the bar a mess.

With the arrival of the haulers, the noise level in the bar increases tenfold. It is usually a relatively quiet bar, but the haulers yell insults at each other, laugh, and pound on the bar. The others at the bar glare at them. One of the haulers gets up to play the jukebox. The voice of Reba MacEntyre swells into the room. I turn down the volume on the TV set, much to the annoyance of Ed and Steve.

I chat with Ed Baines, with the phone guys, with Ed Baines again. A few other regulars come in; I make conversation with each as he arrives. John asks me what he can do to keep his wife from "wigging out" every time he stays out late. Mike tells me of a Rottweiler puppy he just bought: one hundred percent pure Rott, he assures me. William, a solitary RV salesman and amateur philosopher, wants to know what I think of Maslow's hierarchy of needs. William sits smoking long cigarettes, head elevated and legs crossed. The others greet him but do not engage him in conversation. "But really I find the Idealists more interesting," William remarks as I serve Ed, who is seated next to him. Ed looks over at William now and then, with pointed distaste, as if he were the source of a bad smell.

By about seven, the first shift of regulars is gone. If this had been a weekday, the bar would have cleared out much earlier: many of the early regulars have jobs that require rising well before dawn and so must go to bed early. The evening for such working regulars begins late in the afternoon after work, around 3:00 or so. But on occasion an early regular will come in early in the afternoon and stay until the bar closes, even on a weekday. Lately, though, the Greendale police—the ones, at least, who do not themselves come to the bar to drink—have been vigilant. When the police are known to be *bad*—when word gets around that there have been more than the usual number of drunk-driving arrests—the crowd in the bar thins out. Many of the regulars who live in the neighborhood now walk or ride bicycles to the Smokehouse, not daring to drive their cars.

At 8:30, the bar is empty but for a night regular who has come in early. Wendell sits at the end of the bar, drinking beer from a brown bottle. (The seats at the near end of the bar are, since the bar is narrowly horseshoe-shaped, roughly equivalent in spatial meaning to the seat at the head of a long banquet table: those who occupy these seats are highly visible and can talk most easily with those sitting on either side of them. When the bar is empty, regulars tend to seat themselves at the "head" first; when the bar is full, those who are most central to arguments are usually those seated at that end. The head of the bar is thus a place of privilege and signifies insider-ness: generally, only well-established regulars occupy this space.) Wendell is telling me of the trouble his Local of the labor union is having deciding which presidential candidate to back in the primary. So far, he says, support has been split.

"It didn't used to be like that," he tells me. "The unions always knew who to stand behind. There was no question about it. You went for the guy that was pro-labor. Now, you don't know *who's* gonna do you any good. The Republicans are for big business, and the Dems wanna give everything away to everybody else. At least the Republicans don't believe in handouts. . . . I just don't know what's gonna happen."

Another time, I might have argued, might have pointed out that Republicans seem to have little interest in working people, might have demanded that Wendell please define "handout." But now I listen and nod politely. There is no audience, no need for either of us to perform. Had we not been alone at the bar, Wendell and I would likely be the most virulently oppositional contenders in an argument. Since the flag incident—in which Wendell proved to be the most aggressive critic of my "liberal" views—there has been little love lost between us; but we never did get along very well even before that incident. Recently, Wendell asked me, in the presence of several of his friends from work: "You still in school, Julie?" Then he had turned back to his friends: "She's the only one I know gonna be collecting social security from a goddamn college!"

But now, alone in the bar, there is no malice between us. Wendell speaks softly and earnestly about The Situation of Labor Nowadays. I ask interested questions and don't interrupt to challenge his claims.

A hearty summer rain is falling on the world outside, and the sound of the rain and thunder penetrates even the thick cocoon of the bar. The only other noise now is the low yakety-yak of the television. I sit inside the bar's elbow on a little wooden stool, drinking a leftover Tom Collins and smoking a cigarette. I am grateful for the rest, glad for the sound of the rain and the easy conversation.

Lurene appears in the waitress station, suddenly. Lurene has the economy of motion so characteristic of the veteran waitresses I've known: she moves quickly and silently, with stealthy efficiency. Now, her usually implacable face—small-featured and impossibly finely lined—is excited.

"There's a tornado warning; you heard? They sighted one 'bout 10 miles west. Low funnel, they say. Comin' this way pretty quick, from what I heard. Two Manhattans rocks, please. Extra sweet." She speaks quickly and economically, the way she walks. But her voice still has the South in it, the vowels long and flat.

Lurene hurries off with the Manhattans, but immediately returns to stand at the bar and smoke. Even the restaurant business has dropped off now: the storm has kept all but the most determined customers away. The three of us chat and smoke, finding in each other's company the special kind of primal intimacy that happens when there is the subtle threat, but not any real promise, of danger. Every now and then we go outside to look at the sky, for there are no windows in the bar. The tornado never comes, and we are almost disappointed.

At about 9:30, the night regulars clamor in, just as I finally get the order of tomato bread and fries I ordered hours ago. I take a bite and then pour a drink, chew and make change, wipe my fingers, and fetch a beer. Before I have eaten half the meal, the bar is again full. The whole crowd is here tonight, despite the rain: Jim and Wayne, a pair of thirtyish practical jokers; Walt and Daniel, two elderly widowers who have just come in from the dining room; Ricky and Paul, owners of a local car repair shop; Laurie and Donna, a couple of newer wait-resses on their night off; and Jack, the bar's most regular regular and longtime boyfriend of Roberta.

Jack drapes himself over the bar, at the head. Jack always stands, some-times for several hours at a time. He never sits, never removes the Greek fisher-man's cap from his head. Jack is, according to Arly, a "creature of habit." His quirks and rituals are a source of amusement to those who know him well.

Jack now sees I am busy. He feigns thirst, clutches his throat. I glare at him, but wait on him first.

"Thank you, baby. You know, I think you broads just don't know how to *move*. I keep tellin' Bertha, she gon' turn to stone, she move any slower." He laughs. Bertha is Jack's name for Roberta and is short for Bertha Butt. (Roberta, who is almost preternaturally energetic, is slim and wiry at age 45.) Jack always teases the women at the Smokehouse—tells them they're fat, that they have *big butts*. He has a reputation as a prankster and a tease but is seen as no match for Roberta herself. (Lurene likes to tell a story about a time when Roberta took Jack out to his favorite German restaurant for his birthday. It seems that Jack had, after washing down his dinner with several mugs of German beer, taken to loudly professing a philosophy of male superiority to anyone who would listen. "When the Herr wants a cold beer," he had been declaiming, "then it's the job of the Frau to go fetch it for him!" To which Roberta, unimpressed, had re-sponded calmly, "Frau Roberta thinks you've had enough beer for one night. Hand over the keys, Herr Brain.")

I lean against the bar in Jack's corner.

"It's quite a privilege to wait on a real man's man like you. I want to prolong the experience," I tell him. "That's why I'm so slow. You understand, I'm sure."

"Oh yeah, baby, that makes sense. Makes sense. That ain't normal, comin' from you."

We both laugh. Jack and I have an understanding: we can insult each other, but only in public—and not, of course, about anything really "true." Whenever Jack comes in while I'm working the bar, the others know he'll try to "push my buttons" and that they can expect a good argument. Often, Arly will raise po-tentially volatile issues to try to provoke an argument between Jack and me. Occasionally these arguments will become hostile, but these hostilities usually resolve themselves into jokes. The line between war and play, thin as a hair, is often approached, if infrequently crossed. Only once, when I was new to the bar, Jack had argued with me in a way I could not interpret to mean anything but outright hostility. When my injured feelings became apparent, Jack had chuckled at my distress and tried to hug me: "It's okay baby, I didn't mean nothing by it, you got to stop taking this stuff so seriously." Maggie, a fellow bartender who had heard about the argument from Arlen, later told me not to "take it personally." After all, she had said, "He's not against you, he's just against what you say." At the time, I told her I didn't quite see the difference. But now I think I understand the point she was trying to convey: an argument (and it doesn't matter how deeply the arguers "believe" in the truths they profess) is always a performance, a public event. So what is said therein has little to do with what is private, or "personal."

Now, Jack is trying to bait me into a new argument. He is leaning over the bar, beer in fist, confiding to Wendell in a too-loud-to-be-confidential voice: "Them Dems don't know their ass from a hole in the ground. If only they could shut up the Libs." Wendell is nodding in agreement, but Jack is watching me out of the corner of his eye. I decide not to gobble the worm this time: I'm too busy; the "audience," too unpredictable. But another time, I might have gotten into character and taken up my part at Jack's cue.

Later, the crowd thins. By 11:30, Jack, Walt, and Danny are the only regulars still here. Arlen and Roberta, who have finished their work in the kitchen, have joined them at the bar. Roberta sits next to where Jack is standing, sipping Tia Maria through a straw. Arly, standing on the other side of Jack, is hunched over a crossword with a flashlight. Walter and Danny are next to Arlen and are arguing about reform in the Catholic Church. I am at the sink washing glasses, and over the whir of the glass-washing machine I hear Dan say to Walter: "Aahh, you don't know what the *hell* you're talkin' about." I know Dan is speaking to Walt, because the two men have built a relationship on disliking each other—they disagree on most issues and enjoy insulting each other's views. Lately, the two have been inseparable.

By the time I finish with all the glasses dirtied during the rush, Dan and Walt are discussing capital punishment and are reluctantly agreeing this time. They approve of the death penalty. Hell of a topic shift, I think. I turn up the volume for the jukebox; for the fourth of fifth time this evening, Garth Brooks sings about corner saloons and ivory towers. Tonight Garth delivers a solo performance, but sometimes, late at night when the beer is flowing and people are feeling loose, Garth is accompanied by a chorus of voices from around the bar: "Oh, I've got friends . . . in loo-ooow places!" Now the lyrics, which I know by heart, are occasionally drowned out by an especially loud declamation from Walt's corner.

Perry stands over the jukebox feeding "red" quarters (money he has allocated for use in bar machines and marked with a stripe of red) into the slot. Nobody else seems to want the music on, but Perry insists that it makes for a more lively atmosphere and so makes it his business to keep the jukebox going. After he finishes with the music, Perry comes over and stands at the head of the bar between Arly and Jack. He has heard the subject of the debate and is speaking out against the death penalty and sipping white zinfandel from His Glass, a small snifter. (After all, he is saying, how are we any better, if we murder the murderers?) Lurene sits at the poker machine, an empty glass and a full ashtray on the barstool next to her.

Before long, I find myself drawn into the argument. Jack jerks his thumb in my direction and says, with much dramatic emphasis: "Now this one here, she feels soooorrrryy for the bastards." I try to clarify my position, but Jack interrupts, demanding to know how *I'd* feel if someone raped *my* mother and cut her to ribbons. Even though Perry is on my side of the issue, Jack's challenges are directed only at me. Arly occasionally looks up from his puzzle to offer support for one of Jack's points; Lurene is silent, transfixed in front of the poker machine. Even with all the shouting, she never turns her head. "You don't know shit from Shinola!" Walter tells me and slams his empty beer bottle on the bar to drive the point home. Jack winks at me and laughs just under his breath.

By 11:30, Jack and Roberta are preparing to leave. Jack is performing his usual routine, declaiming about what a woman's place is, how females should act, a man's right, etc., etc. A newly arrived stranger in a black leather vest overhears and is gravely nodding his approval. But the rest of us laugh at Jack's theatrics. Roberta rolls her eyes and removes her car keys from her purse. "Ready to go?" she demands. "Keep talking, and I'll send you to bed without any supper." Jack holds his mug aloft and implores, "Just one more, hon, whaddaya say?" Roberta looks at him, her face comically intractable. Jack shrugs, throws a wad of bills on the bar for a tip, and trails with exaggerated humility out behind her.

At 2:15, Arl and I are finally alone. I clean and stock the bar, haul cases of beer up from the basement to refill the coolers, and punch out. I pour myself a glass of Chianti and sit down to count my tips, feet propped on an adjacent barstool. I count out eighty singles, two fives, and five dollars in change. About average for a Friday shift.

Arly goes off to the office with my stack of money; after a few moments, he returns with four twenties, a ten, and a five. "I taped *Star Trek*," he reports. Often, Arl and I will sit together for an hour or two after the bar closes. It is Arly's only real leisure time: he must start work in the kitchen in midafternoon, oversee things at the bar at night, count the bar's bank at the end of the night, and make new banks for the bartender and waitresses for the following day. As for me, I enjoy sitting down for a while to relax before the long ride home. After working so many hours, my mind is as awake as my body is exhausted.

We sit side by side at the bar working a crossword and watching *Star Trek: The Next Generation*. After a while, Arlen goes into the kitchen to sneak us a snack. He returns with a plate of fried cheese sticks, and we devour them as we talk of the events of the day.

"Oh," says Arlen, changing the subject suddenly. "You better make sure all your glasses are clean before you go. Last time you worked, Gina was complaining that you left everything dirty."

It is a commonplace among bartenders to complain about the upkeep of the bar: because one bartender must rely on another to do her share of the cleanup work for a given shift, there is often disagreement about what counts as "cleanup work," and what counts as a "share." But bartenders rarely confront each other directly: typically, the word *gets back* to a bartender that she is being complained about by another; the complainee then makes sure that the word goes out that she, the complainer, is a liar. For a bartender to complain directly to the boss would be a clear violation of the tenuous solidarity that exists among the bartenders, despite their system of covert complaints and accusations.

"Don't ask me what's going on," Arly shrugs. "You females are always bitching about something. I think you just like to complain about each other."

Around 3:30, I decide that I should be leaving, but I still don't feel like getting up from the barstool. "Going so soon?" Arly wants to know. For him, it's early. Arlen will stay up for several hours yet, watching television, doing crosswords, and enjoying his private time in the bar. Because he sleeps in the upstairs apartment, the bar is, in effect, his living room. Only late at night, after the bar has closed and before the maintenance crew arrives in the morning, is Arlen's house his own.

Arly unlocks the side door and walks me out to the car. It is a humid summer night, and the garden—a landscaped outdoor area mainly used for summer wedding receptions—looks cool and inviting with its fountains and Italian lights. Maybe I can talk Arlen into sitting outside next time, I think, instead of watching TV in the bar. As I get into the car, I again notice the message on the big marquee: "Taste the Brick Oven Difference!"

"Foop, what does that mean?" I ask, puzzled. "I didn't know we had a brick oven."

"Brick oven? We don't." He shrugs. "I don't know what the hell that's all about. Who knows? I guess if you wanna taste the brick oven difference, you gotta go down to Lorenzo's. They got a brick oven."

I say goodnight to Arly, and we make plans to go to a movie the following day—provided, of course, that neither of us gets called in to work. Because Arlen lives at the Smokehouse, he is always the obvious choice for a replacement in case someone else is unable to come in to work. Even though he is officially a cook, often he will be told to tend bar if there is a shortage of help. I know Valerie's scheduled to work the front bar tomorrow; but often as not, new bartenders simply stop showing up after a night or two of work. They are intimidated by the disapproval of the waitresses or see the bar society as impenetrable.

"I'll call before I leave the house," I tell Arlen.

The drive home is a long one. It is utterly dark in the woods at night. I flip on the radio and kick off my shoes as I drive. I am glad tomorrow is my day off: two 11-hour days in a row are too much. After spending that much time behind the bar, I sometimes begin to feel as if I've been locked away in solitary confinement, with a crowd.

3

A Place to Be

The Smokehouse as Local Institution

A Place among Others

People come to the bar at the Smokehouse to drink. But more important, they come to drink among others. The bar is a place where one can arrive and immediately find a place in the structured chaos of serious play, in the comforting rhythms of planned spontaneity. The Smokehouse is a utopian place outside the uncompromising routines of work as well as the everyday center of things where *what is real* reveals itself to those who share investments in its authenticities. It is a place of concentrated leisure, where the coarse textures of sociality are pressed into relief. It is the place of a dense and busy social imaginary.

Any account of Smokehouse rhetoric must begin with a consideration of the relation between those who are "doing" the rhetoric and the institutional site of its production. The cohort of white working-class adults I'm calling "Smokehousers"—a network of people who either are employed by or are regular customers of this south suburban Chicago restaurant and bar—functions as a small community as its constituents share lives, histories, and ways of making sense of both. Yet that "community" is also constituted by its location in a fixed and bounded geographical space.[1] The bar both collects people out of their usual routines and exerts its own distinctive pressures on social practices and arrangements. Smokehousers have lives beyond the bar, though it is with respect to its authority as institution that they come together in a collection of personae—as a distinct, if circumscribed, "public."

The "working-class bar" has achieved something of a mythical status, both as a preserve of residual folk culture and as a xenophobic, anachronistic bastion of neighborhood lore. Its ability to function as a place of sociable leisure apart from everyday routines and obligations has made it the focus of nostalgic desire for a more richly communal past, as well as a target of voyeuristic interest in more "authentic" spaces supposedly existing apart from the (bourgeois) mainstream. The local barroom is imagined to be the home of a dubious political underlife, a site either of nascent reactionary movements or defensive indifference to politics "outside." Although such images of barroom culture (in both academic and popular imaginations) can occlude more productive understandings of the specificities of life in bars, they do spring from a seed of truth about the importance of bars in working-class life. Scholars of working-class culture both in Britain and the United States have affirmed this truth: Stanley Aronowitz, for example, writes that that the barroom survives as one of the "traditional markers of working-class culture," where "waves of male industrial workers have congregated to share their grievances against the boss, their private troubles, their dreams of a collective power and individual escape" (1989:229). Likewise, John Clarke explicitly links bars as institutions to the culture of working people, holding that "the pub has held a central position in the local articulation of working-class culture as a sort of 'colonized' institution which, though not formally owned by the class, has been internally moulded by the class's custom" (1979:245). The bar is a working-class *institution,* a historical place where logics of identity and common sense are enacted in every moment of leisure.

The centrality of the bar in working-class community life can be attributed to its potential to protect traditional social arrangements and lifestyles against modern forces of commodification and "embourgoisement." Historians of industrial communities and "the saloon" alike have noted that bars have traditionally mediated between home and public spheres; this role has remained more or less intact as patterns of industrial labor have changed and urban demographics have shifted (e.g., Dius 1983; Slayton 1986). Others have suggested that working-class bars invert the normal social order: local values of reciprocity, sociability, and vernacular speech forms are asserted over their bourgeois counterparts of competitive consumption, social mobility, and standards of linguistic propriety (e.g., Rosenwieg 1991). For residents of Greendale and surrounding communities, the Smokehouse is a highly visible social institution, so much so that patrons who live in surrounding towns sometimes declare their intentions to visit the Smokehouse with the metonymic announcement that they are going "to Greendale."

In a study of the working-class population of a Midwestern bar he calls "The Oasis," E. E. LeMasters assures us that "[T]he Oasis is not a neighborhood tavern. Its customers arrive in cars, not on foot, some of them from several miles away" (1975:11). LeMasters's criterion of proximity notwithstanding, I would insist that the Smokehouse *is* a neighborhood tavern, for it clearly functions as the social center of a community, albeit a community scattered by a changing social and economic landscape. The suburban site of the Smokehouse, Greendale, has an attenuated, quasi-rural geography that presents a marked contrast with the multiplex, urban density of traditional Chicago working-class enclaves such as Cicero or Bridgeport.[2] But though many of its patrons drive several miles to get to the bar (as I do), the Smokehouse nonetheless maintains its status as a public center for private (or local) interests. Indeed, if the Smokehouse could be described as any kind of social configuration, it could be said to be a kind of provisional neighborhood. One might venture to say, even, that the bar is all the more important as a social institution now that its community of patrons has been "displaced" from its historical urban "homeland."

Of the four genres of barroom in the area—corner tap, dance club, strip joint, and restaurant lounge—the Smokehouse is the latter. It is a *respectable* place, a place famous for its steaks and barbecued ribs, a place where you can bring your kids from time to time (and some patrons occasionally do bring their children along with them to the bar, parking them on adjacent barstools and entertaining them with popcorn and kiddie cocktails). The family-style restaurant to which the bar belongs is not a *fancy* place, but a *nice* one. Young men who live in the area bring their girlfriends "out to dinner" at the Smokehouse: wine can be ordered by the bottle, and there is a pleasant bar where the couple can relax and wait for a table (he'll have a Heineken, she'll order an Amaretto stone sour or a strawberry daiquiri). The bar's proximity to the dining room enforces a level of decorum to which the patrons of an exclusive corner bar would never be expected to submit (men drinking at the bar during restaurant hours are admonished by the owner to "watch the language" so as not to offend diners and others not privy to the codes and rituals of masculine sociability). Yet the bar has a well-established life of its own, even if its excesses are modulated during dinner hours.

Although Smokehousers have social connections and commitments outside the bar itself, the barroom at the Smokehouse serves as the institutional nexus of leisure activity where Smokehouse employees and customers regularly gather to drink, to talk, to commiserate, to court, and to play. Many Smokehousers spend a great deal of leisure time at the bar, sometimes as much as several hours each day. As bartender, I expect to encounter the same "regulars" daily. Some drive straight to the bar from work in the afternoon and stay there until the bar closes.[3] I have often unlocked the door to admit a customer when the bar opens at four, only to urge him out of it again at closing time. A regular at the Smokehouse can come in anytime during the week and expect to satisfy his or her hopes of finding someone in whose company to pass the hours. It is really the social stability and accessibility of the bar that make it such an attractive place to spend time for Smokehouse regulars.

Because of its ability to mediate between public and private space, the barroom at the Smokehouse acts both as an open public forum and as a local backyard, as a place where political debates may take place beyond the judgmental gaze of "outsiders." The ambiguous status of the bar as both public and private space is significant to its discourse: whatever power the barroom itself may lack to enforce the boundaries of the group is taken up (as will be shown in chapters to follow) in generic speech codes; in this way, the social setting of the Smokehouse constrains the cultural practice of its small society.

A Place Apart

Although the fact of the barroom setting shapes the kind of relationships and communicative practices that take place there, Smokehousers often get together outside the bar to organize group activities such as softball games, trips to the bowling alley, pool parties, and even ski trips. People commonly share rides to and from the bar, help each other move, and look after each other's children. These outside commitments indicate that the Smokehouse network is defined only in part by its physical environment: although employees who do not spend free time at the bar tend to be peripheral members of the group, not all bar customers (including some regulars) can be considered real "members" of the group either. As a group that coheres round time spent at the bar itself as well as by frequent social contact in other settings, it is the kind of social organization network theorists describe as *multiplex:* its members occupy more than one social role and tend to interact in several contexts (e.g., Milroy 1980).[4] In fact, those who constitute the group would probably question its classification as a discrete social unit, precisely because the network *is* multiplex. Moreover, people experience a sense of group solidarity through conventional speech events (such as argument). Smokehousers establish themselves as a network through the specific practices in which they engage; at the same time, the *right* to engage depends in part on showing cultural solidarity in other ways, such as by working or spending leisure time drinking.[5]

The Smokehouse cohort is composed of employees as well as regular customers; however, the employees who make up the core of the group can be considered to be regulars, as well.[6] Many of the Smokehouse's waitresses and bartenders come there to socialize on their days off and will remain at the bar to talk to regulars after they finish their shifts. On the job, waitresses often go into the bar area to sneak a smoke between tasks, sandwiching intermissions of playful banter with regulars between trips to and from tables in the restaurant. It is common for men who are regulars at the bar to date waitresses; in the past few years, I've seen several of these waitress-regular unions result in marriage. Most live in the neighborhood surrounding the bar, but it's not unusual for neighborhood regulars to drive long distances to maintain ties to the bar even after they've moved away (I still see one regular at the bar on weekends even though he has lived, for several years now, in Fort Wayne, Indiana).

Even if the bar is a place that celebrates the practice of leisure, residues of the working life appear everywhere.[7] The demographics of the bar population are attuned to the rhythm of the work day, so that the entire network of social relationships at the Smokehouse halve into two "shifts," which roughly correspond to the hours during which each congregates at the bar. These shifts do, of course, overlap, but populations remain fairly consistent with respect to time of day. I have come to expect to see the same group of regulars at the bar at any given time (except, perhaps, for during the "transition" hours of the evening, roughly between 7 and 9, when the afternoon crowd is thinning out and the night crowd is filtering in). Often, there is an hour or two of "dead time" in the evening between the shifts. The two shifts of regulars parallel the work shifts into which Perry has recently divided some weekdays: the early shift (3 to 8) and the late shift (8 to 1 or 2).[8] A bartender scheduled to work only night shifts, then, would have contact with a different population of regulars than would a bartender working only days.

For all its commitment to leisure, the quotidian life of the bar assumes highly predictable routines. Established regulars do not use the bar sporadically or spontaneously; on the contrary, they show up at the bar at the same time day after day (or night after night). The likelihood of a regular customer coming in during one or another shift has to do as much with work schedules as with social ties: regular bar patrons fit leisure time into whatever hours are accessible. Regulars will sometimes "tie one on" and stay from the day until the night shift, but the mass of the bar population divides fairly cleanly. In this structure, waitresses are positioned as links between people at the temporal extremes of the network, as their hours (roughly 4 until 10 o'clock) overlap both shifts; however, they are more likely to act as social ties to regulars in the second shift, because these are the people in whose company waitresses tend to spend time after having punched out. Bartenders, because they tend to work alternately early in the day and late at night (and sometimes both shifts in the same day), get to know both crowds but often have different relationships with each. Sometimes bartenders prefer one kind of weekday shift over the other, because they prefer to socialize with that particular group of regulars.

In both early and late groups, my own role is the same. I am the antogonist, the "liberal," the egghead always on the other side of an argument. Yet it is significant for the story I tell here that I'm only peripherally connected to the daytime regulars, whereas I have a more central role in the night group. It is among this latter group that I have conducted most of my research: the particulars of my analysis are based on taped conversations and interviews with people who tend to be at the bar during the night shift. But although my arguments about Smokehouse rhetoric emerge from data on episodes of discourse from this subset of the larger Smokehouse network, I believe that my conclusions about the meaning and uses of this rhetoric apply to the group as a whole. The finer points of my analysis—the real "-emic" perspective—derive from the night crowd (it is from this group that my data from arguments with Jack, Walter, and others have come), but my observations about social dynamics and discourse practices at the Smokehouse have been a product of my interactions with people at all points in the Smokehouse network.

You could say that the bar society is exclusive or that it is egalitarian; in both cases, you would be right. Anyone can come into the Smokehouse and commandeer a barstool, yet some people clearly have a more distinctive *place* in Smokehouse society than others. Jack, for instance, claims a highly visible place at the end of the bar. His position at the bar is analogous to that of a patriarch at the head of the dinner table (or, perhaps more appropriately, a speaker at a podium). Jack's claims to this territory are honored by his cohorts, as well: I have seen others who had been occupying Jack's spot vacate it apologetically at his arrival. For Jack to relinquish his place would be as improbable as it would be for a woman to successfully persuade the men at the bar to switch the television from sports to daytime drama.[9] Although there seems to be room within the structure for pockets of resistance to what (or who) is authoritative in the terms of the hierarchy, apparently it is the very *fluidity* of social constraints regarding status and authority that allows for the status quo to be comfortably maintained. Smokehousers compete for status in the group (as the following chapters will show), yet they tend to assume that the society of the Smokehouse is essentially communal and that "outside" ways of determining status do not prevail inside the private universe of the bar. This perception of immunity from the forces of the larger symbolic marketplace is, clearly, one reason why the bar functions as a refuge for those who spend time there. But even though mainstream values seem not to hold at the Smokehouse, status positions are forever negotiated in talk at the bar: through rhetoric, and often through the rhetoric of argument (as will be shown later), Smokehousers invent themselves as authoritative members of the group.

You might say, as well, that the bar crowd is heterogeneous—it is, after all, a collection of *types*—albeit uniformly so. The Smokehouse is a working-class bar; but just as importantly, it is a *white* working-class bar. With one exception—Larry, a mixed-race regular who identifies in the company of other Smokehousers as white—the Smokehouse crowd is racially homogeneous, even though the surrounding neighborhood—as well as the Smokehouse staff itself—is racially integrated. The preservation of this homogeneity is important in terms of Smokehouse politics of solidarity—racial boundaries are significant, if sometimes difficult to locate precisely.[10] Hiring policies at the Smokehouse are a particularly telling indicator of attitudes about the place blacks and whites should occupy in social space. The restaurant employs bartenders, cooks, waitresses, dishwashers, and maintenance men: all the kitchen staff (with the exception of Arlen, who is also bar manager) are black; all the "front help" (i.e., employees in positions accessible to the public)—waitresses, bartenders, hostesses, and busgirls—are white. The owner of the Smokehouse, Perry, considers himself to be politically "liberal," but admits that blacks are not hired in high-visibility positions because of the danger that the Smokehouse would lose the business of many of its white customers. Outside the workplace, black and white employees rarely socialize, and none of the black workers can be said to be a member of the Smokehouse cohort. Although racial tensions are rarely expressed in confrontations between blacks and whites—I have never seen (or heard about) an incident of racial harassment at the bar; on the surface, at least, black and white employees are friendly to one another—rarely do black and white employees often sit down at the bar and drink together after work. On the few occasions I have seen one of the kitchen workers at the bar, he or she has sat alone, and conversation with regulars has been on such neutral ground as sports, weather, or restaurant business. The politics of race is often the subject of arguments among whites at the bar, and Perry frequently uses the example of his own reluctance of hire blacks as evidence that racial discrimination does in fact exist. Race relations are always at issue at the Smokehouse not only insofar as they shape the social landscape there but also as they are voiced in arguments.

A Place to Drink

No account of Smokehouse life would be complete without mention of the omnipotent *presence* of alcohol. Quite apart from the alcohol consumption patterns of individuals, the social mechanisms of drinking are the center of barroom interaction. Talk about drinking—its logistics, its consequences, the loyalties and entanglements it engenders—is produced in greater quantities, perhaps, than alcohol itself is consumed. But alcohol consumption by individuals does not alter existing social tendencies as much as it magnifies them: when the parties involved in any given interaction have been drinking, the stakes are higher. Alcohol consumption both defuses and heightens whatever tensions would otherwise be present—assuming that one could imagine the social life of the bar apart from the relationships that the very routines of drinking help to establish.

The drinking habits of Smokehousers range from excessive indulgence to total abstinence. Some people regularly drink too much by all but the most committed tippler's standards; on the other hand, it is fairly commonplace for regulars who happen to be "on the wagon" to spend long hours at the bar sipping cola or ginger ale. For some, alcoholism is a very real problem. Others seem to drink regularly with little consequence to their home and work lives. Despite individual propensities, drinking routines and rituals are an important part of the social life of the Smokehouse, inasmuch as they enact virtues of egalitarianism, reciprocity, and masculine camaraderie. Smokehousers typically engage in such time-honored and well-documented bar rituals as buying in rounds, competitive drinking, and participating in toasts. Because alcohol (usually beer) is so much at the center of social interaction at the bar, Smokehousers observe tacit rules of propriety regarding its social uses. It is important to participate in drinking rituals such as buying rounds and drinking toasts, yet it is equally important to be able to *hold your liquor*—as much as you will be obligated to participate in drinking routines (unless you are on the wagon, in which case your abstinence will normally be respected); it is equally important that you don't appear to be too *loaded.* You may show up the next day publicly complaining about your hangover (a condition that will earn sympathetic affirmation from others), but your drunkenness must not be a public liability. You are permitted to become garrulous and sentimental, but not aggressive or rancorous. The point of drinking is to produce conviviality, not to disrupt it. It is, furthermore, the bartender's role to see that this function is served. She is expected to facilitate drinking games and rituals—to, for example, keep track of whose *round* it currently is and be quick on the draw with a bottle of booze if someone is buying shots. But she is also expected to *cut off* a person who has had too much and is interrupting the stream of sociability.[11]

A Woman's Place

By a wide margin, most Smokehouse regulars are men, though the bar does have its share of female regulars. You might say that the Smokehouse is a place for women as well as men, though you might just as legitimately conclude that women have their place. As many observers of bar tavern have noted, bars have traditionally functioned as male enclaves, as places where attitudes, behaviors, and sensibilities associated with male identity are celebrated without challenge to their authority (Halle 1983; LeMasters 1975, Rosenwieg 1983; Spradley and Mann 1975). At the Smokehouse, this "male ethos" is most obvious in the division between customers (mostly male) and the employees who serve them (inevitably female). The assumption that women should serve and entertain men is immediately apparent in the restaurant's policy to hire only women as bartenders. Female employees, and bartenders in particular, are expected to dress and to act in such a way as to attract and to cultivate the attention of male customers. That women should present themselves in a manner that will comport with male standards of femininity is an assumption generally shared by male and female Smokehousers alike. Even when women are present at the bar—which is most of the time—the Smokehouse barroom is indelibly marked by masculine styles of sociability, and it functions, above all, to foster camaraderie among men.

The implicit belief that men should control the activities, environment, and discourse of the Smokehouse is so essential to the social order that it rarely surfaces in discourse unless framed in a genre marked as self-referential speech, such as joking or play. Although the group can tolerate differences in opinion in talk of other subjects concerning power relations such as race, class, and ethnicity, the sociality of the bar is threatened by overt challenges to assumptions about gender roles. Once, in a discussion about the popularity of sports in America, I suggested that maybe the pervasiveness of sports culture was evidence of sexism in our society and went on to say that I didn't think it should be a *given* that we should show sports on the bar television. I *went so far as to say* that any women present at the bar should have more of a say in whether sports should be shown at a particular time. This proposal met with such furious resistance that in a rare moment, I felt truly ostracized. Argument about gender relationships is pragmatically different from argument about other issues, because arguments about the kind of authority men and women have (or don't have) threatens to chip away at the very foundation of assumptions on which the social structure is built. Whereas arguments about politics or even race (given that usually only whites are present) can be safely relegated to the realm of the "merely theoretical," debates about gender roles inevitably encroach upon the domain of practice.[12]

At "Brady's Bar," the site of Spradley and Mann's study (1975) of gender roles in a college bar, the position of bartender could only—given the high-visibility and high-status nature of the position—be occupied by a man. But the relationship between bartenders and social status at the Smokehouse is more complex: while women hold positions as bartenders, the contradiction created by placing a woman in a potential position of authority over men—or, at least, in a position of equal authority—is resolved at the Smokehouse by granting female bartenders status as "honorary males."[13] That is, bartenders are privy to, and can participate in, social interactions typically reserved for men. Male customers don't alter their behavior to accommodate the presence of bartenders the same way they might if other females (customers or waitresses) happened to be present. On several occasions, I've heard men admonish friends not to "swear" when "ladies" are present at the bar; however, I have seldom heard this injunction delivered with the intent to protect the "lady" *behind* the bar.

Because she takes on aspects of the male role, a bartender has the authority, despite male control of bar discourse, to provoke, manage, and legitimate arguments. This role often requires a good deal of diplomacy; a bartender must somehow remain "outside" the bar discourse, even as she participates in it: that is, a bartender must appear to be committed enough to a stance to appear to be sincere, while at the same time deferring any commitment that threatens to alienate those participating in the discourse. Here the analogy to ethnography is patent: the bartender, like the ethnographer, must maintain a stance that is both central and peripheral to social action. The rhetorical dilemma of the bartender parallels the paradox of the participant-observer—each must carry on social intercourse with the group, but must also remain uncommitted to the interests of that group long enough to assess the meaning of these interests.

Generally speaking, the hierarchy among Smokehousers can be described as follows, beginning with those enjoying positions of high status: male regulars, bartenders, waitresses, male (nonregular) customers, female regulars, and female customers. But within the terms of this structure—and perhaps because of the terms of this structure—the Smokehouse network is, in a sense, egalitarian: status distinctions that prevail outside the bar tend to have less direct power over Smokehousers *at* the bar. The bar itself can be said to have a kind of "leveling" effect: within the confines of the bar, there seems to be surprisingly little competitive tension among Smokehousers with respect to personal appearance, material assets, age, physical capability, and so on. The darkness of the bar, combined with the solidarity that comes from the ritual sharing of vice, makes it a place where the old and poor can pull up a barstool and speak, on more or less level ground, with the young and prosperous. Unlikely friendships develop between grouchy old men and optimistic young women, between middle-aged grandmothers and college jocks, between policemen and petty criminals. When I've attended Smokehouse activities outside the bar (a Sunday softball game, for instance), I have been struck by the effect of this displacement on relationships constituted by the imperatives of the bar. Outside the bar, the Smokehouse group seems like an incongruous bunch, like an unlikely fellowship of types. Talk outside the bar is harder pressed to deliver the conviviality promised by the transformative power of routine: easy joking relationships become more guarded, ritual insults are put on hold. In fact, it seems to be the felt presence of the social hierarchy within the bar that relaxes other kinds of cultural restrictions governing social relations.

A Place in the Field

You might say that my role behind the bar has always been to stir up trouble as much as it has been to mix drinks: whether I am working behind the bar at the Smokehouse or just "hanging out" at the bar, I expect—and am expected—to argue. My arguments with others are invariably about "politics," and the positions I advocate are almost always in opposition to those of others. Whether or not I'm willing to participate in a given argument, I am urged—even pressured—to offer my opinion to incite debate. I learned from Arlen—who delivers news of quotidian dramas to me like so many wrapped presents—that my point of view has even been invoked in arguments at the bar when I haven't actually been present. When I visit the bar on my day off, I often encounter regulars who, upon telling me all about an argument I'd missed, demand to know, "where *were* you last night?!" When I show up at the bar in the midst of an argument in progress, my presence is immediately acknowledged as the arrival of the dissenting point of view, and I am urged by others, on the spot, to offer up my opinion for public use. It would be inaccurate, however, to claim that I am always the "victim" of these disputes: I frequently solicit opinions about topics I know from experience have the potential to provoke argument, and Smokehousers no doubt call upon me to argue because *they* know from experience that I'm usually willing to get involved.

The contentious nature of my relationship with others at the Smokehouse has been central to the entire ethnographic enterprise—not only to the conclusions I have drawn about how Smokehouse culture is invented through expressive practices such as argument but also to how I have chosen to go about working in the field. My ethnographic endeavor consists in attempting to understand the culture produced at the Smokehouse, but it is also true that the culture that prevails at the bar has defined what it means to "do ethnography" there. Though I knew from the outset that I would obtain my data using methods of interviewing and participant observation, I could not at first have fully anticipated the kinds of arbitrations that would become necessary in the course of my research. The process of negotiating a research role at the Smokehouse has taught me something not only about what people there think about who I am and who *they* are but also about rhetorical processes of identification more generally.

The research position available to me at the Smokehouse has been established by the ways in which my participation in the culture at the Smokehouse is circumscribed by cultural norms and expectations. As I explain in chapters to follow, my attitudes and opinions are often seen as coming from a position of nonparticipation in the *real world:* as a "career student," I am perceived as not having experienced the everyday travails of the world of work. For those at the Smokehouse, I seem not only to speak for but to *stand for* a viewpoint prevalent in mainstream society that is antagonistic to the values, convictions, and concerns of working people. Yet even though I am the voice of middle-class ignorance of or disdain for working-class concerns, I am also one who, by simply treating them as worthwhile topics for discussion, validates these concerns.

Paradoxically, my role as dissenter defines the nature of my solidarity with Smokehousers, and the fact of this paradox has had implications for the ethnographic strategies feasible at the Smokehouse. As a Smokehouser whose social job is to critique cultural values, my "natural" place is at the fulcrum of a scale that balances insider-ness against outsider-ness: as insider-participant, I am in a position to engage in—even to generate—the very phenomena I wish to study; as outsider-observer, my task is to observe and to make sense of these phenomena. This precarious position points to a familiar anthropological and epistemological dilemma: how to be both subject and object at once? And, more important, what is at stake in operating at this juncture?

This subject-object dilemma is, in a sense, also the point at which the anthropologist becomes the rhetorician. Because my role *in* what some ethnographers have called "the target culture" is characterized by its marginality, conducting an ethnographic study at the Smokehouse has demanded that I display skill as a rhetorician, for such a project consists in persuading individual Smokehousers not only that they stand to gain something by participating as subjects but also that *I* should be the one to represent their interests to others "outside." My first consideration in developing a research approach, then, had to do with figuring out how to orient myself to those who were to be the "ethnographed." But here it might be helpful, in considering the problems of rhetoric and method that confronted me in the bar-as-field, to elaborate some rhetorical issues implicit in the vexed and vexing encounter that is fieldwork.

Traditional ethnographic methods of fieldwork, rooted in Enlightenment ideas of truth and objectivity, demand that the ethnographer maintain—or at least strive for—objectivity. Fetterman (1989), for example, has advocated a "nonjudgmental" attitude toward the "target culture," suggesting that the researcher should be careful not to evaluate the beliefs and practices of that culture in her own terms. Clearly, such a stance may be useful as a safeguard against the practice of cavalierly constructing authoritarian narratives that ignore or dangerously misrepresent the point of view of the culture under investigation. But just as clearly—putting aside for the moment the question of how appropriate (and feasible) such a position would be in the study of one's own culture—the assumption that culture is an empirically knowable, stable pattern of social interaction undercuts the role of interpretation in the collection and representation of ethnographic data, relegating the ethnographer to the position of gatherer/recorder of observed "facts."

In recent decades cultural anthropologists have begun to question the idea that ethnographic research can be conducted according to the paradigms of natural science. This skepticism has been motivated by trends in philosophy and rhetoric and has called into question the assumed relationships between culture, researcher, and social meaning.[14] A consequence has been an increasing emphasis on the disorderly and conflictual nature of culture and discourse. Adler and Adler (1987), for instance, explain that in contrast to the orderly and observable social world posited by anthropologists working in the tradition of the Chicago school, subscribers to existential models of social interaction reject a view of the "cooperative social world and cooperative research subjects" in favor of the idea that social meanings are more complex and covert than they may appear to someone outside the group. In this view, a social group is characterized in part by relations to other groups; thus, its members are necessarily conflicted over their status in complex structures of power. A group will, say existential sociologists, present itself to outsiders in such a way as to protect its status and identity, as social interaction is driven in part by the need to "manage the impressions given off by others" (24). A field approach derived from such a conflict model of social interaction suggests that the only way to get at social meanings is to *be* an insider and to cultivate relationships with those who can offer insights into the meanings members of a group attach to cultural practices.

Unlike ethnographic methods that look to the principles of positivist science to make sense of cultural phenomena, such ethnomethodological approaches move beyond investigations into observable behavioral patterns in social groups and focus instead on how meanings are negotiated when one embodied consciousness confronts another. Accordingly, researchers wishing to understand the connection between meaning and consciousness in a given setting must fully participate in social contexts in which these meanings are given life; they must consider the identities, histories, and intentions of the people whose meaning-making process they wish to understand. To do this, researchers must abandon prior theoretical and methodological alliances to avoid constituting/interpreting the research community in terms of these alliances. In short, fieldworkers must "become the phenomenon" they describe (Adler and Adler: 27–28). They must, that is, abandon their own cultural logic (or conventional logos) and submit to the terms of the logos of the culture under study.[15]

Yet even the most sincere cultural "conversion" can't escape the rhetorical problematics of fieldwork: ethnomethodology may apprehend the phenomenological meaning attached to behaviors and events unavailable to fieldworkers of a more positivist orientation, but it can never truly succeed in abandoning other cultural logics. For this reason, Adler and Adler advocate a method that would give the fieldworker an "active yet honest" role in the community and suggest that she adopt a "membership role" in which she is regarded by the group to be studied as a fully enfranchised member of the group, research affiliations notwithstanding. Only in this way, they write, might she achieve an "inside perspective" while retaining a theoretical ground for interpretation. Such a divided subjectivity is possible, say the Adlers, because social life is by definition a process of negotiating competing alignments (32). Such an approach brings to the foreground the rhetorical dimension of fieldwork: here the fieldworker must be a skilled rhetorician, one who remains alert to the motives, interests, and demands of different publics.

Sociolinguists have long held that speech communities are held together by tacit assumptions about the appropriateness of linguistic utterances (e.g., Hymes 1974). If it is true that such communities are set off in social space by shared interpretive habits, then it's possible to understand the difference between community member and nonmember as, in effect, the difference between one who may judge the beliefs, practices, and values of others in the group and one from whom such judgments will be regarded as inappropriate. By these criteria, I am a "member" of Smokehouse culture. Given the nature of my role as "friendly antagonist," impartiality as described by Fetterman is particularly problematic: whereas the social commitments I share with others demand that I value Smokehouse culture on its own terms, it is also true that whatever "membership" I claim *depends* on my "devaluing" certain practices and beliefs. Effecting a posture of neutrality would entail a radical repositioning of my place among Smokehousers, for they regard me as one whose role is, precisely, to make—and to express—judgments of their beliefs/values/lifestyle. Smokehousers expect me to perpetrate—or, at the very least, perpetuate—ritual conflicts *about* the appropriateness of certain cultural values. Because at the time I began my research I had long since been identified with a particular rhetorical stance, I could not, on beginning the research project, pretend to be neutral.

That an ethnographer functions as a translator of social realities from one kind of rhetoric to another means that just as it is impossible to be objective in describing the practices of one's own community, it is equally impossible to be entirely, radically subjective. Although "going native" in the manner described by ethnomethodologists and radical ethnographers would seem appropriate for the study of a group of people who see academic ways of knowing, at best, irrelevant and, at worst, condescending, it is essential to acknowledge the impossibility of displacing oneself into a new cultural domain without bearing traces of the old one. To complicate things further, how does one "go native" when one already *is* native, and when one's status as such derives, in a sense, from one's truck with what is nonnative? Postmodern critics of anthropology such as James Clifford (1988) have suggested that the idea of "pure culture" becomes impossible in a shrinking, postcolonial world; hence, the idea of "nativeness" is problematized.

The idea of field memberships that specify degrees of phenomenological involvement is a product of efforts to name the research relationships possible in a world of unstable cultural boundaries. The Adlers have called ethnographers who investigate communities in which they have prior membership "opportunistic" researchers and have pointed out that although such opportunists have access to the group they wish to study, they "may, ironically, have problems in being accepted by group members in the new role. Although they are committed to the group already, outside interests set them apart" (1987:756). In my own field experience, this mediation between roles has required a process of careful negotiation: even as I have always been perceived as one who functions as a kind of "cultural critic," I have had to be careful not to invoke the authority of the academic community in condemning Smokehouse values and beliefs. For me as a researcher to have done anything that could be interpreted as intended to show how the group is "wrong" in its beliefs for the purpose of "proving" some theoretical construct would surely (even though I commonly critique these beliefs in my role as fellow Smokehouser) be regarded as an act of betrayal. It was essential to begin instead from a position of inquiry that did not imply that working-class culture in the form it takes at the bar is deficient: I made it clear that if any deficit would be assumed, it would be on the part of the middle-class academic culture. This kind of mediation, it seems, has been crucial to maintaining the particular dynamic by which arguments are generated in keeping with the motives and identities of the arguers.[16]

When I began to actively collect data, I explained that I intended to do a study of how people develop their political views and that I wanted to understand what causes them to change their minds. I said that I had decided to use the Smokehouse group as the site of the study because it was obvious that people there had strong political opinions, had developed these views from "real life" experiences, and were willing to express them. With this as the stated purpose of my study, I was able to interview several core members of the group about such matters as orientation to media information, attitudes toward literacy and education, reading and writing habits, political beliefs and affiliations, and opinions about the nature of persuasion.

Because of the agonistic relationship between academic and working-class cultures, I have had to be careful about presenting my research goals in an nonthreatening way (although the process of negotiating these goals has taught me much, in itself, about the conflicts and antagonisms between the two cultures). I know—from countless dealings at the bar with people who, on learning that I am an English teacher, either implore me not to criticize their language, or else simply fall silent—that these are people who have experienced the world of academics as one in which they have little cultural capital, against the standards of which they expect to come up short. Because those at the Smokehouse are only too aware that any scrutiny of their language is likely to be accompanied by a judgment, I had to be careful about the language in which I introduced the project. To have characterized my work as simply a "study of argumentation" would have had the effect of privileging the ways of arguing practiced in the academic community and would have implicitly devalued the practitioners of that rhetoric.

With all of this in mind at the outset, I initially thought that it would perhaps be best to take on what Adler and Adler call a "covert" membership role and to conduct my data-collecting activities (that is, to record public speech) surreptitiously. On the one hand, it seemed to me that even though the Smokehouse is technically a public space, this kind of nondisclosure was fraught with ethical problems; on the other, I could see no way around the problem of how to introduce a tape recorder (an essential bit of technology, given the speed, intensity, and spontaneity of the most interesting arguments). Finally, I decided that the only way to resolve the dilemma in a way that was both methodologically feasible and ethically sound would be to be explicit about the fact of my study and to refrain from calling attention to specific data-collecting episodes: that is, I would make most employees (those likely to hang out at the bar) and most regular customers aware that I was doing a study and that I was using a tape recorder as a way to help me to remember how arguments went, so that people would understand that certain discussions might make it onto tape. Nevertheless, I have found it impossible to present the study to everyone in the group in precisely the same way. I found it easier to reveal more about my research to some people in the group than to others: some, like Walter and Arlen, took an active interest in my study (and were enthusiastic subjects for interviews), others seemed merely indifferent to whatever I was up to, and still others struck me as potentially risky. I did not, in any case, record conversations that were assumed to be private or talk among people who were peripheral to the core group of Smokehousers represented here (and who had no knowledge of my research).

More specifically, I collected data on natural speech by switching on a small, hand-held tape recorder I kept behind the bar as episodes of narrative and argument happened. This approach wasn't ideal—much was buried under the din of clanking bottles and the noise from the glasswasher—but it enabled me to amass a sizable corpus of usable data. Fearing that such an announcement would disrupt the flow of spontaneous conversation, I did not declare my intentions to record particular conversations, though people would occasionally ask if the recorder was on. At times, the tape recorder itself became the subject of small performances—Arlen, who always knew when I was recording conversations, would occasionally stick his head over the bar to where he knew I kept the recorder to shout expostulations intended to affirm (what he presumed to be) my stereotyped view of Smokehouse politics: "Kill 'em all! Ronald Reagan forever!" Jack, similarly, would refer to the tape recorder by delivering canned reactionary polemics and switching into his best faux-Southern dialect. In such instances, the data-collecting technology was neither irrelevant to nor prohibitive of the process of "collecting data," but instead became a kind of prop, an accessory to the dramatic interplay of Smokehouse personae. Most of the time, however, the recorder was forgotten and ignored. On a couple of occasions I was directed by someone at the bar to turn off the tape recorder; naturally I complied with such requests. Though many at the bar told me that they were supportive of my efforts to write something that might be read by people who didn't know what things were like "in the real world," my field research was seen as something of an eccentricity, as yet another piece of evidence confirming their suspicions about the peculiar habits of "college types." This ambivalence is perfectly in keeping with Smokehousers' general attitudes about gestures toward upward mobility: You should never stop trying to *make something of yourself,* but please try not to get *weird* about it.

Although I have been observing and taking part in arguments at the Smokehouse for several years, I actively "gathered data"—that is, took notes and tape-recorded arguments—over a period of about a year. In order to gain access to the position I thought would be most conducive to collecting good data, I explained to the owner that I wanted to "do a study of political opinions" at the Smokehouse and asked him if I might "fill in" at the bar if anyone needed a day off. He agreed, and I was able to work several shifts, during which time I recorded many arguments. It might be said that a bartender is a kind of naturally occurring ethnographer: this is indeed the case with a bartender at the Smokehouse, who both observes and participates in the events that happen all around her in the course of a day's work. This in-and-out-of-things position is highlighted by the geography of the field site itself: the bar at the Smokehouse is shaped like a tight horseshoe, so that the bartender is literally at the center of social life—half of which, at any given moment, is going on behind her back.

As much as the rhetorical situation that prevails at the Smokehouse is a function of group dynamics with respect to class identification, it is also shaped by attitudes about gender. Because the bar is a highly gendered territory, the social roles and relationships of Smokehousers are in large part defined by expectations about gender. This means that the sphere of influence and range of motion a woman has at the Smokehouse is constrained not only by gender politics in the more abstract sense but also by cultural perceptions about the physical characteristics of her body. As Carol Warren puts it, "At the heart of male and female roles in any culture, shaping the adoption of response to particular dress, perfumes, and hairstyles, is the issue of sexuality" (1988: 29). Inevitably, the contours of the relationship between the ethnographer and the community under study are drawn by issues of sexuality. Whatever else the fieldworker might be to those in the research community, she is, first, someone in a body.

Although women as a group generally have less social power than men at the Smokehouse, in accordance with cultural norms about gender, some women may, under certain circumstances, exercise the power conventionally associated with female sexuality. This is particularly relevant in the case of women who work behind the bar at the Smokehouse, where the body is "on display" as a matter of course.[17] As an ethnographer who is also a bartender, I operate in a social sphere in which my body, as well as my language, operates as signifier. Carol Warren articulates the issue of body-as-sign in the ethnographic relationship as follows:

> What is presented to the host culture is a body: a size and shape, hair and skin, clothing and movement, sexual invitation or untouchability. The embodied characteristics of the male or female fieldworker affect not only the place in the social order to which he or she assigned, but also the fieldworkers' and informants' feelings about attractiveness and sexuality, body functions and display. (1980, p. 25)

As a woman whose appearance is generally perceived by Smokehousers to conform to cultural standards for feminine presentation, my body operates in yet another rhetorical domain; as such, it may, in certain situations, exert its own persuasive force. Though as a woman I generally carry less authority than a man, whatever sexual attractiveness Smokehousers attribute to me may, ironically, have worked to my advantage among male "subjects," who might otherwise have been less willing to tolerate my questions, challenges to their authority, and generally antagonistic behavior.

What I have come away with after participating in and observing Smokehouse rhetoric over the course of a year is a collection of data comprising 30 hours of taped spontaneous discourse (public conversations, narratives, and arguments), 10 hours of taped interviews, several notebooks filled with field notes documenting the contexts and idiosyncrasies of particular instances of argument, and bits of random dialogue and observations scribbled on cocktail napkins. The exemplary data that appears in the analysis to follow have been

taken primarily from arguments about candidates in the 1992 presidential election, political parties, and race relations, for these seem to me to be the most
coherent and sustained examples among the recorded data. To be sure, that I
have selected and included these data and not some others is itself a rhetorical
act, intended to illustrate my argument about how argument happens and
what it means at the Smokehouse.

4

Across the Table

Walter, Joe, Arlen, Maggie, and Perry

A ny consideration of the how and why of arguments at the Smokehouse must, given that an argument is always *about* something, include a careful consideration of the *what.* This "content" derives from the form arguments take and the purposes they serve for those who engage in them—and is therefore impossible to isolate as a cultural text—but if (as I will go on to show) arguments play a role in the public construction of knowledge for the Smokehousers, then it is useful to clear alternative spaces where one might see how this knowledge is thematically configured.[1] To create a rhetorical situation that might work heuristically to offer another perspective on the ideologies authorized through, and activated in, public discourse, I spoke one-on-one, in "private" interviews, with five Smokehouse regulars and employees: Walter, Perry, Joe, Maggie, and Arlen.[2] What emerges from these conversations, finally, is a narrative backdrop against which to illuminate the *how* and the *why* by foregrounding the *what* as a production of the *who.*

But let us note from the outset that interviews do not constitute, or even participate in, an uncontested, "objective" ethnographic space. They are, rather, a discursive contrivance, a rhetorical strategy.[3] Interviews are motivated, and substantiated, by my own rhetorical position on the margins of Smokehouse life, as well as by my aims as researcher. They do not presume to uncover, through systematic questioning about the cultural semantics of social phenomena, the "deep structure" of categorical meanings that make up the "worldview" of Smokehousers.[4] As a Smokehouser, I myself can claim to act as informant for the group's *practice;* I can look to my own working-class experience, my own cultural competence, to understand "what it takes" to be a Smokehouser. But because I do not share Smokehouse assumptions about how

Smokehouse (and working-class) culture is situated in larger structures of social relations, I cannot therefore claim to speak for Smokehouse *theory*. To put
it another way: I can't look to myself to find the "whole truth" about what it
means to be a Smokehouser because "meaning" is—as a social process—precisely what is at issue in argument. Interviews invite demonstrative theorizing:
in sitting down with Smokehousers to hear them voice their views and narrate
their stories, I hoped to gain access to a view of knowledge-in-production that
is not, given my role in performed arguments, available through scrutiny of
"naturally occurring" speech genres. I met with individual Smokehousers in
the hopes of carving out a new rhetorical place where I might position myself
as uncritical consumer of narrated ideologies, where I might hear what Smokehousers *feel they must say* in order to catch flashes of insight into what they
think they think. In so saying, I am not presuming to extract the truth about
motives about which Smokehousers are themselves unaware—to root out examples of Smokehouse "false consciousness"—only to suggest that there are,
inevitably, levels of mediation between private belief and public engagements.

More specifically, holding private conversations with Smokehousers outside the context of public debate forces, through narrative displacement, a sanctioned ironizing that casts into relief not only the narrated productions but the
motivated subjectivities of the talkers. By inviting people to speak, in a place
that is not the bar and in a genre that is not argument, about their investments
in issues that affect their lives as working men and women, I wanted to know
how these five narrated themselves as social and political agents.[5] Their collected narratives hold up a hermeneutic lens that both refracts individual differences and permits a reading of a socially produced and sanctioned cultural
text, a text that inscribes features of an ideological system in stasis and flux.
Thematic divergences and narrative disjunctures say as much about the shape
and limits of Smokehouse conventional wisdom as do neat parallels and predictable correspondences, for it is ideologies that are contested, at stake, in the
ritual confrontation of narratives that is an *argument*.

Just as it is important to look at the place of argument in the communicative repertoire of Smokehousers, it is useful to regard interview data as the
products of a communicative event that has a particular place, qua event, in
Smokehouse rhetorical practice. At the Smokehouse, the interview is not a
"naturally occurring" speech event.[6] That the interview—an artificial situation
contrived to elicit answers to previously determined questions—is not something Smokehousers "just do" is certainly true, but neither are the five people to
whom I spoke in interviews wholly unaccustomed to sitting down with me and
proffering either stories or philosophy. Smokehousers are used to telling stories, and they are used to telling them to me. There are occasional "dead times,"
times when the bar is virtually empty (as on some Saturday or Sunday afternoons); on these occasions, I might spend hours in the company of a lone regular (such as Joe or Walter) or fellow worker (such as Maggie, Perry, or Arlen).
When there is no larger audience for whom to perform, spinning stories and
working out theories about people and things is a way to pass the time, not
necessarily to pass muster. More often than not I find myself in the role of lis-

tener rather than that of active narrator; this dynamic is partly an expectation of the role of bartender and partly a function of the cultural frames of reference I share (and don't share) with other Smokehousers. So the interview—though contrived for, and mediated by, the purposes of my project—is not entirely unprecedented as a communicative situation.

Before interviews, I prepared a set of general questions ranging from simple questions about school and work histories to requests for theories and information about social and political processes. I developed this repertoire of questions because it seemed to me that they touched on topics and issues—work, education, race and ethnicity, class, language and literacy, politics—that arose again and again in the arguments that mediated between constructions of identity and conventional wisdoms.[7] Yet even in response to pointed questions, these five frequently took to rendering their philosophies narratively, asserting positions that were then elaborated, contextualized, and authorized by stories. It is precisely this habit of chronic "narrativizing" that leads me to believe that one may gain access to ideologies through a series of discrete, contrived communicative events with a handful of informants. The richly textured relations between narrative and ideology have been widely remarked: Jerome Bruner (1990), for example, argues that of all the possible products of culture, *stories* are the richest and most dynamic repositories of cultural meaning, inasmuch as they function "to find an intentional state that mitigates or at least makes comprehensible a deviation from a canonical cultural pattern" (50). Bruner explains that the study of narratives is the best way to understand the ideological fabric of culture (or, in his own terms, "folk psychology"), because narrative "deals with the stuff of human action and human intentionality. It mediates between the canonical world of culture and the more idiosyncratic world of beliefs, desires, and hopes" (111). Stories, in other words, are a vital expression of the possibilities, and the limits, of a social ideal.[8]

Represented here are voices of a bartender-waitress, two regulars, a cook and bar manager, and the owner of the Smokehouse. I chose these five interviewees to gather a colloquy of voices representative of the shared dimension of social experience and of its diversity. It would have been easy to select informants whose professed views overlap more seamlessly than these. But these five—Arlen, Walter, Perry, Maggie, and Joe—are at the organic heart of the group, and in some sense define its rhetorical boundaries. Each invents a distinctive public self, each is a sometime participant in arguments at the bar. That is not to say, however, that this group represents the five "best," or even the most active, arguers.[9] I wanted to seek out people with different relationships to argumentative contexts, performance, and style; I deliberately sought a "diverse" group to interview because I was interested in interviewing each person as a point on a map of the rhetorical territory that spans the space between identity and difference. Hence, this group of five illustrates, *qua* group, points of tension between individual and group identity and between the gravitational pull of conventional wisdoms and the entropic influence of other, alternative systems of knowledge.

Whereas ethos in argument is constructed largely through rights of participation and oratorical style, rhetorical authority in an interview situation is, to a great extent, a given: it is granted by the interviewer, a priori, to the interviewee. This is, of course, not to say that the interviewer does not have an agenda, only that she provisionally *consents to be persuaded* of the interviewer's point of view. As speech event, the interview serves a metacommunicative function in which the person being interviewed is invited to show that he or she has a "private" persona different from the public one—or, perhaps more accurately, that the barroom persona isn't the whole story, that there is something more to be communicated, to yet another public. In telling Smokehousers that I was writing a book for those who, like many academics, had no firsthand knowledge of how things are for working people, they were invited to envision an audience beyond me, an audience of others with an entirely different relationship to language, work, and community. Whatever truths emerge in interviews, they are inescapably a product of what happens when people on either side of the tape recorder come into contact as positioned rhetoricians negotiating a narrative reality for an audience of imagined others. What emerges in the "private" space of interviews is, then, a collaborative production for the benefit of a larger audience.

The following is a composite of narrative snapshots, profiles of Walter, Joe, Arlen, Maggie, and Perry. They suggest not only each person's cultural history and place in Smokehouse society but also my relationship with him or her and how he or she negotiated the rhetorical situation of the interview itself. In introducing these five, I present them not only as constituents of an organic social body but also as a collection of distinctive voices.

Walter Penske

At the Smokehouse, Walter Penske is one of the most visible—and vocal—regular customers. He is in his seventies, a widower, and often comes to the bar seeking company, comfort, and conversation. He and another regular, Daniel, frequently share rides to and from the bar: although these two are known to have something of an agonistic relationship, it seems that, despite their differences, they need each other's companionship. Walter and Daniel have been compared by others to the two cantankerous, warring old men on *The Muppet Show*. Walt and Dan regularly engage in arguments at the bar, but Walter has a more clearly defined and fully developed persona as arguer and is perceived to "have an opinion." Although it sometimes seems to me as if Walter seeks *me* out as a foil for his argumentative rhetoric, I have been told by others at the bar that he is usually happy to strike up an argument with anyone who happens to be around and is willing to have a go. Although Walt is regarded as something of a crank by the others—he is sometimes seen as unusually stubborn and inflexible in his political views—he is generally liked and welcomed at the bar, even so. When Walter's wife died a couple of years ago, several people from the bar— waitresses, bartenders, and regulars—attended the wake, even though none of us had met his wife. After the funeral, Walt brought his son and daughter-in-law back to the bar to meet the rest of his "family" from the Smokehouse.

When I asked Walter for an interview, I told him that it was pretty clear to me that the two of us disagreed on important issues and that I often found myself wondering why each of us thought as we did. I explained that I wanted to find out something about how people came to have their opinions and that I was curious about how political views developed. I told Walter that I perceived him as someone who had strong, well-developed points of view and that for this reason I thought he would be someone good to talk to. Walt responded by saying that he thought I was pursuing a very difficult, but important, question. He told me he had often wondered the same thing himself and agreed enthusiastically to the interview.

I spoke with Walter one sunny summer afternoon at his house, the two of us sitting around the kitchen table drinking—he Scotch; me Pepsi. We were alone in the big ranch house, save for a big grey poodle named Pepe. Before the interview began, Walt showed me around his house, gave a little history of each room, told me where he spent his time, and remarked on what he liked to do. He indicated books he had either recently read (the novels of J. R. R. Tolkien) or was in the process of reading (*Richard III*).

Walter appeared to be entirely comfortable with the purpose and genre of the interview and was forthcoming throughout our conversation about information and events in his life and about his interpretations of these events. He spoke for long, impassioned turns, weaving anecdote into reflection, reflection into philosophy. An hour into our conversation, he exclaimed, "Hey, this is fun! I don't mind this at all!" During the interview I felt—even though I was the one asking the questions—as if the story were *his,* as if he were the one in charge of it. I had the sense that the interview provided a rare opportunity for Walt to contemplate events that had shaped his life, that he was attempting to explain himself to himself, as well to me. I had always perceived Walt to be one who cultivated a persona as a no-nonsense, up-by-the-bootstraps conservative; however, removed from the barroom pressure to perform, Walt attempted repeatedly to persuade me of his own political "openmindedness": he insisted, well into the interview, that he really had a "lefty" side, too.

My interview with Walter lasted over 3 hours, after which time I stayed and chatted for another hour or so. On several occasions after the interview, Walt approached me at the bar to say that he had been doing more thinking about a question I had asked and that he wished to tell me more about something he had said during the interview. On one occasion, several days after we spoke at his house, Walter told me at the bar that he had been thinking about a question I had asked about why some people become liberals and others end up as conservatives and that he had concluded that people develop political perspectives as a result of wanting to conform to their social environments. "It's peer pressure," he said. "Like wants to be like like."

At 73, Walter is the oldest member of the Smokehouse group. He now lives in Greendale, but grew up in South Chicago, where he lived for the first 40 years of his life. He moved to the suburbs when his neighborhood began to "turn" and has lived in Greendale ever since. He has one son, who is grown and is, as Walt himself puts it, a "yuppie." He himself is a first-generation American; his own parents emigrated from Eastern Europe: his father from Lithuania, his mother from Poland. But although Walter clearly wants to maintain ties to his ethnic heritage, he does not hesitate to assert his Americanness: "I'm an American," he insists. "Born American, bred American, gonna die an American death."

Walt is not college-educated; he quit high school to go to work in his junior year. Nonetheless, he takes great pride in his ability to educate himself through reading and dialogue with others. When I see him at the bar, he loves to talk about the latest book he has read, and he often attempts to engage me in a conversation about the book's meaning and merits. Lately he has shown great interest in the plays of Shakespeare and said that he found *Richard III* to be "one of the best books" he had ever read.

Retired now for 15 years, Walt worked most of his life as a product engineer for a major manufacturer of farm equipment. His work life has consisted of exclusively blue-collar jobs, many of them involving unskilled labor: "I labored, when I was a kid, on construction . . . on rooves, and siding, and all that grubby type of hard, dirty work." Although he speaks with impassioned pessimism about his early life as an unskilled laborer, Walt assured me that he found his job as a skilled craftsman with the farm equipment manufacturer profoundly satisfying. "I loved my work," he explained. "I loved my work. . . . I wanted to do that work all my life, when I finally got myself into it."

Although Walter has always been a working man and wishes to be seen as just that, he seemed to want me to know that this identity has been hard-won, not just adopted uncritically or by default. He made a point of displaying his awareness of the dynamics of social class and of his own place in the social structure. And though he repeatedly emphasized the importance of maintaining a critical awareness of what goes on the world, Walt was equally emphatic about the necessity of understanding the truth of "common sense." Walt unquestionably wants to be perceived as one who is intelligent—not, quite clearly, as an intellectual, but as one whose insights have been born of interpreted experience, rigorous self-education, and the struggle to survive.

Joe LaRue

Unlike Walter Penske, Joe LaRue is generally not regarded by others at the bar as one who might be defined, above all, by his love for argument. He is perceived as an easygoing guy, a quiet guy, a guy who "keeps to himself." He usually comes into the bar after work, alone, to drink beer and to "unwind" from the pressures of work. Although he does participate in arguments, Joe tends not to go out of his way to initiate them, and his argumentative persona is notable mainly for its lack of style and drama. Joe's reluctance to adopt a performative style in argument is invoked by others, like Walt, as evidence that he is more "honest" than his more dramatic counterparts.

I chose to interview Joe not only because of his status as a regular Smokehouser but also because Walter recommended him as an ideal subject. Walt insisted that even though Joe wasn't a big shot at the bar, he was "very bright" and insisted that I stood to "learn something" from him.[10] I found Walter's admiration of Joe's ideas as somewhat surprising, given that Joe is a much different kind of rhetorician than Walt: although Joe and Walter agree on many political issues, Joe seems to take argument less seriously as an opportunity for self-definition through public display: "A lot of times if people try to start a debate with me, I'll just say, kinda, Yes, yes, and kinda blow 'em off, you know?" Joe explained to me. "And there's other times when I don't mind goin' toe to toe with some people around here."

When I approached Joe with the idea of his doing an interview, I reminded him that I was in the process of observing political arguments at the bar and said that I was interested in learning about how people came to have the views they expressed in arguments. I explained to Joe that I had noticed that he wasn't ordinarily one of the biggest "loudmouths" and that I would be interested in having him talk, in a nonargumentative setting, about some of his views on social education, politics, and "life." When I mentioned that Walter had recommended him as someone who seemed to know a lot about these kinds of issues, Joe seemed surprised and flattered and agreed to the interview. He repeatedly asked me what exactly I wanted to know and said he wanted to know what I would ask him so he could "think about things." I told him not to worry so much about getting things "right," that the kinds of things I wanted to know didn't necessarily have correct answers and that he could always change his responses later on if he wanted to. This seemed to satisfy him, and we set up a time to meet at the bar for the interview.

On the day of the interview, Joe met me at the bar in the afternoon on his way home from work. I found him sitting alone at the end of the bar, drinking a bottle of beer and nervously puffing on a cigarette. He seemed anxious about what would happen during the interview, although he insisted that he did want to go ahead with it. What did I want him to say? he wanted to know. Weeks after the interview, Joe approached me once again wanting to know how he had "done" in the interview. I assured him that the interview had been a good one and asked him why he was worried about it. He said he thought he hadn't given very smart answers to the questions, because he was "a working man, not a scholar." He wanted me to understand that he didn't have the luxury of spending time contemplating abstractions: "I do what I need to do to survive. It's not cerebral like what you do," and then quickly qualified this defense by adding, "It's not important." Joe's insecurity about his authority to speak on "cerebral" matters resurfaced again and again in his repeated assertions that he could have been "smarter" if he had had the opportunity to further his education. Joe wanted me to know that even though he hadn't gone to college, he liked to consider important issues and that a teacher friend of his liked to say that he was "a diamond in the rough."

During the interview, Joe and I sat at a table in the part of the dining room closest to the bar, with the tape recorder, an ashtray, and Joe's bottle of Miller Lite between us. Joe's answers to the questions I asked tended to be short, vague, and sometimes even defensive in tone. Joe responded directly to the questions I asked, rarely presuming to interrogate the meaning or significance of the question, and without providing many examples derived from his life experiences. Unlike Walt, Joe seemed to see the interview less as an opportunity to tell his own stories and more as a test. Because Joe's responses to the interview questions tended to be terse, my interview with him turned out to be significantly shorter than Walt's, lasting only about an hour. At one point during the interview, we were interrupted by the bartender on duty that night, who had come over to the table to find out what was going on. Having noticed that I was asking Joe questions from a printed list, the bartender, Gina, had paused for a second before asking, "Joe doesn't get a grade on this, does he?" In so saying, I suspect she spoke Joe's own anxieties.

Joe grew up in a lower-working-class suburb just outside of Chicago, but now lives in a more affluent suburb adjacent to Greendale. He is 40 years old, divorced, and has two children, 14 and 12. He has worked for the past 4 years for a company that repairs construction equipment but has had many other jobs in his life; these have been, he says, "strictly blue-collar." Even though he is and has always been a working man, he considers himself to be "middle class." He has no clearly defined ethnic identity; he is, as he puts it, "a mutt." "I've had ancestors that came over on the Mayflower; I had ancestors that were here to *meet* the Mayflower," explained Joe. "Talk about an American! I am not any generation, I am . . . the slag on the melting pot, I am the mixture, you know, a conglomerate . . . English, Irish, French-Canadian, Indian . . . German, you know, a whole hodgepodge."

After he was graduated from high school, Joe went into "the Service." He had been awarded a music scholarship to the University of Illinois for his trumpet playing but was unable to go because he had not taken any of the aptitude exams required by colleges for admission. Joe told me that he wished he had gone to college because then, he went on to speculate, "I'd probably be teaching music someplace . . . or whatever, you know, I felt like doing."

It seemed to me that Joe's aim in the interview was to persuade me that although his lifestyle, habits, and associations were primarily blue-collar, he had the potential, if given the opportunity, to be "more." In this way, Joe seemed in the interview to be deeply ambivalent about his working-class status: on the one hand, he wanted to project the image of a salt-of-the-earth, no-nonsense type; on the other, he wanted to make sure I knew that his career as a working man did not reflect his intellectual limitations. When I asked Joe questions about issues that are sometimes invoked to stigmatize the working classes (such as those regarding social class and literacy), his responses and posture became guarded: he obligingly answered these questions about his views on such matters, but his terse, defensive manner told me that he suspected whatever he said would somehow be used against him.

Arlen Olson

As one whose presence at the bar is a constant of Smokehouse life, Arlen Olsen could be said to be at the heart of Smokehouse society. Because Arly lives in a room right above the bar and spends both his work time and leisure time at the

Smokehouse, he is an essential component of the bar scene. Arlen has been a part of the Smokehouse ever since the business came into existence: he worked for Perry as a cook at Perry's first restaurant in South Chicago, began work at the new Smokehouse as soon as it opened in the late sixties, and has been a fixture at the Smokehouse ever since.

Because Arlen must spend so much time at work, the boundaries of his social territory extend as far as the walls of the Smokehouse: all of Arlen's friendships (many) and leisure activities (few) are a product of his association with the place. It would be fair to say that Arlen has at least as much of a hand in ensuring the smooth functioning of the business as Perry does: Arlen cooks, orders supplies for the restaurant and bar, prepares banks for the bartenders and for the waitresses and balances them again at the end of the night, fills in for bartenders unable to work their shifts, oversees what goes on at bar, locks it up at the end of the night, and even delivers pizzas on occasion. Even though many Smokehousers believe that Arlen must be "made of money" as a result of working so hard and so much, he has confessed to me that he draws only a small salary in addition to his room and board. It is hard to imagine how the Smokehouse would keep going without Arlen: when he goes away on vacation, disorder and confusion prevail. Whereas Perry is the clear patriarch of the Smokehouse family, Arlen's role might be compared to that of a stepfather who, though he does not have the authority enjoyed by the official head of the family, is nonetheless charged with its care.

Because he spends most of his time at the Bar, Arlen is privy to many of the arguments that take place there. But although he has a clearly defined set of views (mainly conservative, by my standards, though he himself is reluctant to categorize them in this way), he does not typically initiate arguments. He has been known, however, to raise potentially volatile topics when I am present at the bar—and then to step back, laughing, to admire his handiwork when a strenuous argument ensues.

Though he does not identify in any way with institutionalized education, Arlen is generally regarded as "smart" by other Smokehousers. He is a widely sought-after partner in *Trivial Pursuit* and can call up a wealth of information about events and figures in the history of entertainment and sports. In a sense, Arlen is my (or I am his) intellectual doppelgänger. I am thought to be what Smokehousers would call "book smart," but Arlen is perceived to have the knowledge that Smokehousers know as "street smarts," or "common sense": he has practical wisdom in the world of everyday affairs (he can manage money and run a business), has accumulated a great deal of information in many areas, and is old enough to have enough life experience to "teach him about life."

When I first began to work at the Smokehouse, others warned me that Arlen could sometimes seem to be "a real grouch." At the time, I *was* intimidated by his curt, abrasive manner. But I remember Roberta taking me aside and explaining that I shouldn't be put off by Arlen's gruff demeanor, because he had, as she put it, "a heart of gold." And that is how Arlen continues to be regarded by Smokehousers: he is seen as publicly cantankerous and difficult "on the outside," but ultimately as loyal and kind.

Of all the people at the Smokehouse, Arlen perhaps knows more about the specifics of my study than anyone else and, in that sense, could be said to be my primary "informant." Arlen and I have a friendly relationship that extends beyond the barroom: we share a love of movies and often get together to see the latest films. Arlen keeps me informed about goings-on at the bar and apprises me of the latest Smokehouse gossip. For this reason, Arlen was perhaps more aware than other interviewees of my motives in studying the Smokehouse group in particular (he knew, for instance, that I was interested in the culture of working-class whites as well as in the linguistic particulars of argument). He was quite alert to the possibility that I might be interested in his responses not only as an "individual" but as a member of the Smokehouse group. Arly seemed a bit more guarded than usual during the interview and often qualified his answers to my questions with such remarks as, "I'm not like so-and so," and "I can't speak for everybody on this, but. . . ." My impression during the interview was that Arlen wanted to resist broad categorization of his views; he did not want me to identify him as someone who "thinks the same" as everyone else at the Smokehouse.

Although Arlen is now in his late fifties, he has never been married. He grew up in a neighborhood on the south side of Chicago, where his father worked as a police officer. Since moving to Greendale 23 years ago when Perry opened the Smokehouse, Arlen has lived alone at the Smokehouse, in a tiny room directly over the bar, accessible only via a steep rickety flight of stairs. In the past year, since Perry has begun to threaten to make him pay rent for the room, Arlen has been considering moving out of the Smokehouse and into a trailer Roberta's son has been wanting to sell.

Before he began working for Perry, Arly had worked several different jobs. "I had all kinda different jobs here and there," he told me. He has worked as a truck driver for a soft-drink company, as a construction worker, as an orderly in a hospital, and even, during his youth, as a carny. "I wasn't real good at it," Arlen confessed about his job with the carnival. "You gotta lie and cheat the people." Recently, he has been working part-time during the day as a driver for a company that delivers meat to area restaurants.

Like Walter, Arlen considers himself to be "working class." Like Joe, Arlen does not have strong ties to a particular ethnic group. His parents were born in this country, and he claims not to know much about the ethnic history of his family. "I'm French and Swedish," Arly reported. "But I'm really just . . . I don't know, American."

Whereas Walt and Joe clearly wanted to use the interview as an opportunity to invent, affirm, and clarify their identities in relation to the Smokehouse "public," I was struck by the extent to which Arly did not seem to be motivated by any such concern. Although he did seemed to want to be sure *that* his point of view was distinguished from those of other Smokehousers, he did not go to any great length to indicate *how* it ought to be distinguished. Arlen attempted neither to assert a connection to the working class nor to distance himself from it. For him, the interview did not represent a place in which to define a rhetorical self, or as an opportunity to refine the public self or to reflect on the private. I suspect that this is primarily because of our close friendship: Arlen probably approached the interview believing that there is little he could tell me about his life or perspectives that I don't already know.

Maggie Sullivan

Of the five Smokehousers represented here, only one, Maggie Sullivan, is a woman. The gender disparity in my sample of interviewees reflects, I think, the discrepancy between the potentials of men and women at the Smokehouse to shape the conventional wisdom there: although the Smokehouse bar is never an exclusively male environment (there is always at least the one woman who is behind the bar), it tends to favor the needs and interests of its male customers. Nonetheless, Maggie, like fellow veteran waitress Roberta, represents a strong voice at the Smokehouse. She is not seen by the male regulars as one who can be easily manipulated: despite her gentle demeanor, Maggie isn't willing to "take any shit."

Like Arlen and Perry, Maggie is a figure of high visibility at the Smokehouse. Her frequent presence, as well as her close ties to other Smokehousers, puts her at the core of the Smokehouse network. Though she is only 34, Maggie has been a loyal employee of the Smokehouse for almost 13 years: "The only time I didn't work was when I was pregnant with my twins and couldn't work, and right after I had them . . . so I took, like, four months off." Like Arlen, Maggie fills many work roles at the Smokehouse: she can waitress on the floor or for banquets, work as hostess, and tend bar at the main, service, and banquet bars. Lately she has been working more often behind the downstairs (main) bar, but her versatility makes her a valuable asset to the business.

In arguments at the bar, Maggie often plays the role of mediator, although she is not necessarily unwilling to state her own point of view on an issue if one is solicited. She seems to be less apt than some of the men to treat argument as performance, though I have seen her take on a performative role under certain circumstances. Her reluctance to take on a character as rhetor, combined with her obvious experience as a worker in the "real world," ensures that her opinions will not be received with hostility by other Smokehousers. That this is true despite her tendency to speak for women's interests bespeaks, I think, the probability that other Smokehousers see her as a canonical figure in the group.

Once, Maggie and I enjoyed a friendship that extended beyond the walls of the bar: we attended a series of karate classes together, often met for coffee or lunch, and spent summer days at the beach or at the amusement park. Since that time 4 or 5 years ago, our schedules and priorities have diverged, so we tend not to see each other outside the bar. We continue to maintain a friendship inside the Smokehouse, however, and I am always glad to have the chance to talk with Maggie when I visit there.

I sought to interview Maggie not only because of her central role in the group but because I knew from our many conversations at the bar and elsewhere that she was concerned about social and political issues and that she tended to be philosophical about them. Because Maggie was aware of my academic interest in Smokehouse arguments, I told her when I approached her to ask for an interview that I was looking for a chance to hear her views "on the record," outside of any argumentative or performative context. Maggie was highly receptive to the idea, saying that she was looking forward to the interview and that she thought it would be fun. As the Smokehouse was then open for lunch (a phase that lasted for about 3 months, before Perry decided that being open for lunch didn't make financial sense and changed his mind), we set up the interview for a day when Maggie was working the lunch shift at the bar, because the bar would be "dead" at that time and we knew we would be likely to have some privacy.

During our 2½-hour interview, we were alone in the bar except for one early regular (who, apparently bored by lack of attention, quickly left after I turned on the tape recorder); Perry's partner, Maria, who came in to ask Maggie to stuff some envelopes; and Perry, who briefly came into the bar to see what I was doing there so uncharacteristically early. As we talked, we folded flyers advertising the Smokehouse's new lunch hours.

Like Walter and Perry, Maggie spoke for some length in response to the questions I posed and appeared to consider the questions carefully. At no time did she seem threatened by the issues raised in the interview or behave in a way that could be interpreted as suspicious or defensive. I had the sense, as with Walt and Perry, that Maggie saw the interview as an opportunity for reflection and self-invention. But it is important to point out that Maggie is strongly individualist—perhaps even more so than the other four—and would not, I suspect, want others to read her as only a unit of what I am calling "the Smokehouse group." One striking thing about the views Maggie expresses in the interview is that they reveal a tendency to resist compliance with any kind of theoretical social categorization, including classification by class, ethnic, or political affiliations. In her discussion of education, Maggie speaks of the dangers of broad or inaccurate categorization of students in terms of their educational needs. When I told Maggie that I hoped to publish my findings about argument someday, she was excited about the prospect of providing the substance of an actual book: "So then, like, if it ever gets published, and stuff, I can buy it, and say, There I am in there, and [Arly], and [Walter] and everybody that you talked to? That'll be way cool!"

Maggie grew up in the south suburbs and now lives in a sprawling little town a few miles south of Greendale with her husband and three daughters. She moved her family there from a more densely populated suburb because "we bought a house with a lot of property, and a barn, because I value my privacy and I wanted to have horses and stuff . . . and we were just lucky enough to find that."

Though she spends much of her leisure time riding and caring for her two horses, Maggie told me that she still finds time to read, something she loves to do. Maggie rhapsodizes about books, saying she likes to read "everything, everything, everything. . . . I read my Chemistry book when I have, you know, no other things to read . . . but I just—I just read everything I can get my hands on." Like Perry, she graduated from college with a bachelor's degree; also, she holds an associate's degree in recreational therapy. Some years after she completed her bachelor's, Maggie did return to a local junior college to take classes in nursing, though she eventually decided that she did not want to complete the nursing program. Maggie is not presently enrolled in any kind of college degree program but occasionally likes to take courses to explore her own interests: "I go take classes now at the junior college and stuff . . . but I take classes that interest me, for no credit."

Her college education prepared her to work as a recreational therapist in a rehabilitation center, but her other jobs have been mainly in the manufacturing and service industries: in addition to having worked tending bar and waiting tables, she has worked in a factory that manufactures surgical tape and one that produces aluminum cans.

Like Arlen and Joe, Maggie does not feel any kind of real ethnic affiliation. When I asked her what she says when people ask her about her ethnicity, she explained, "I say American, because I'm not really sure what I am. I know that there's German in my family, and I know that I have Indian in my family, but we're not, like, a—you know, a specific thing, like Polish or Italian, or whatever." She went on to mention that the *idea* of ethnicity was not important to her family, in general: "I wasn't raised that way, so if we are, I don't—I don't know the difference." Like Joe, Maggie defines social class as an economic category, and, like Joe, considers herself to be "middle class" by these standards: "I don't think that I'm poor, but I think I have to work for everything I've got," she said.

Maggie presented herself to me as one who is fiercely independent, despite her close network of friends. "I've never thought too much about what other people think about me," she told me. "I don't really care." And indeed, Maggie did seem to be a bit more irreverent than the others; she did not hesitate, for instance, to challenge established structures of authority (such as institutions of education). Maggie gave the impression that, as a rule, she regarded group ideologies as suspect and that she saw herself as one in the habit of calling into question conventional myths and moralities. And although Maggie's views on certain issues (her veneration of presidential candidate Ross Perot, for instance) seem to parallel the views of other Smokehousers, others—such as her refutation of the attitude that women should not "swear" as much as men ("I think that they should swear *more* than men, because they have more to be frustrated about")—represent a departure from the prevailing ideology.

Perry DeMarco

Perry DeMarco is the owner of the Smokehouse Inn. He and Maria have run the Smokehouse for 25 years. Though Perry is not present at the bar as often as Arlen, he usually comes in for a few hours every evening, when he stands at the head of the bar, sipping wine and chatting with the bartender and regulars. Even when he is away from the bar, Perry makes his presence felt in a myriad of tiny injunctions scrawled on cocktail napkins and taped to front of the cash register behind the bar: "Important!!!!!! All bartenders MUST record 'freebies' on the 'narc sheet' behind the bar!!!!! The BOSS."

These ubiquitous directives notwithstanding, Perry is generally liked by both employees and regulars at the Smokehouse. For the employees, many of whom have worked for other restaurateurs, Perry is exceptionally sympathetic. For the regulars, Perry is a welcome participant in discussions of the political events of the day. He is regarded by the regulars and employees alike as somewhat eccentric in his ideas about how to run a business, but also as much more humane than other tavern owners and restaurateurs. Bartenders and waitresses acknowledge his authority as "boss" but do not seem to fear his presence. Perry himself tries hard to avoid being perceived as a bully or a tyrant, as he is aware many other bosses in his position are. "Probably, I've had good rapport," he reflects. "Or I don't think Cheryl would be here 12 years, and Roberta would be here 16, and Lurene, 17, 18 years."

I interviewed Perry several months later than I spoke with the others, when it became clear to me after listening to the other four that their views perhaps diverged more than I had expected from the outset. It became more and more apparent to me as I went along that these individuals were not as like-minded as I had wanted to believe; and with this in mind, I sought out Perry, the owner of the Smokehouse, who had always tended to ally himself with "liberal" politics rather than with the conservative views expressed by the majority of Smokehousers.

As a member of the Smokehouse group, Perry is regarded as one who has liberal politics, though he is rarely taken to task for these views. It was apparent to me from early on in my association with the Smokehouse that Perry enjoyed debating issues at the bar and that he saw himself as thoughtful and rhetorically adept. His views, though they are often in opposition to the conventional wisdom of the bar, are received with less hostility, and with less drama, than my own. Perry probably enjoys a certain immunity from attack because he owns the bar and has the authority to dismiss anyone from it at any time. But, also, Perry, as a middle-aged man and success in the "real" world of affairs, might well be seen as a more authoritative figure for reasons I will more fully develop in the following chapter.

Clearly, Perry very much wants to distinguish himself from the rest of the Smokehouse group—he refers to himself several times as a "liberal" and often points to the similarities between his political views and my own. Perry spoke at great length in his interview of the differences between his own professed social philosophies and the policies he feels he must, in order to be a successful businessman, put into practice.

When I asked Perry for an interview, I told him that I was interested in speaking to him in particular because it had become clear to me, in my experiences of argument at the bar, that his views were often different from those of others at the bar. I told him I would be interested to know why, given that he moves in the same social circles as others at the bar, his opinions did not correspond with those of the others. Perry told me that he thought my question was interesting, assured me that he would think about the answer to it, and agreed to give me an interview.

When I approached Perry the following week, tape recorder and notes in hand, he declined, explaining that he'd had too much wine and preferred to "have a clear head" for the interview. We rescheduled the interview for the following week, and, though the bartender insisted when I arrived and explained the purpose of my visit that Perry had probably forgotten about the appointment, Perry soon entered the bar and wanted to know if I was "ready to go."

We found a quiet table in a section of the dining room that had been closed for the evening. Perry was clearly uncomfortable at first, and he avoided my gaze by looking around the dining room. But not long into the interview, he relaxed considerably and was soon leaning forward over the table and speaking with a focused intensity. Throughout the rest of the interview, Perry was reflective, and often philosophical. He spoke at great length on topics concerning his home life, ethnic and class identity, and the nature of his political views. I had the sense that Perry seemed to see the interview not only as a time to provide me with information but as an opportunity to think aloud on questions that had been concerning him for some time.

Perry has lived in a suburb just west of Greendale for over 20 years but grew up in an Italian enclave in South Chicago. Like Maggie, he holds a college degree; Perry's is in biological science. Unlike Arlen, Joe, Walt, or Maggie, he does not have a history of blue-collar work. Before opening his first restaurant on Chicago's south side, Perry worked as a representative for a pharmaceutical company for 12 years, but his original plan was to go into medicine: "I did what my parents. . . . [T]hey indoctrinated me with the idea that, You'll go to school, you'll go to college, and you're gonna be a doctor."

For Perry, as for Walt, ethnicity is clearly an issue, and he spoke at length about how his Italian ethnic background has shaped his attitudes and identity. He described the place he grew up as a "rough, tough neighborhood" and seemed to want to make sure I understood that the values and allegiances of his immigrant parents are different from his own. It also seemed important to Perry to convey to me that though he had always been ambivalent about his status as an ethnic Italian, he had, in recent years, made peace with his "native" culture. He made equally clear, however, that he does not wish to place his ethnic loyalties above his allegiance to the larger society: "I am a very good American, a very proud American, and I love my country, I've served my country, so . . . I've done my thing." And although the subject of ethnicity occupies much of Perry's discussion, he speaks very little—at least directly—on the issue of social class. Perry told me, when I asked him what class he thought he belonged to, that he was "lower middle," but he seemed much less comfortable speaking about class than about ethnicity or about education.

Although only a few of the questions I posed in the interview dealt directly with issues of education, Perry's interview consists mainly of his thoughts on this subject. He spoke at great length on the importance of education as a means by which to "better yourself," and the transcripts of the interview show Perry consistently finding his way back to the subject from other topics. He seemed to want me to know that he was not like other Smokehousers in that he saw formal education as an opportunity to "rise above" the conventional wisdom of the community and that he was one who was willing to seize that opportunity: "I loved my education, 'cause I had to work so hard . . .to get everything," Perry emphasized. "I wasn't a bright student, I had to work hard to get everything, I had to travel such distances. . . . I really wanted education, really wanted education. I wanted it badly."

At several points in the interview, I perceived that Perry wanted to distance himself from his neighborhood and his blue-collar background. Indeed, he is unambiguous about his efforts to make social contacts with "better" people: as he put it to me, "I've always liked to, ah, upgrade—it's like tennis. If you play tennis, don't play with someone that can't play as well as you. Play with someone who can beat you, someone who's a little better than yourself." Of all the Smokehousers, Perry is clearly the one who most values upward mobility. He sees himself as a part of the Smokehouse community and takes part in its social life and its talk, yet he appears to want to distance himself from the attitudes, values, and cultural patterns it represents.

5

A Place to Tell It

Smokehouse Themes and Topoi

If you hang around the bar with Smokehousers long enough, you begin to notice that what first appeared to be a dense and formless thicket of discourse is really a well-traveled and elaborately mapped rhetorical landscape, that topics emerge and resurface with predictable regularity. You might even conclude that this terrain has an architecture of sorts; that of all possible discursive territories to explore, some are in fact more habitable than others.

The narrative materials of sociability at the Smokehouse make up a cultural text of heuristic themes, or frames of narratizability that organize discursive productions.[1] As these themes not only suggest ideological structures but also control how ideologies can be activated as the narrative materials of arguments, they serve as topics for arguments. I should add that here I mean *topic* in the classical sense—*not* as a set of extracontextual prompts for generating composed discourse, but as a constitutive body of sociolinguistic resources for argument. For Aristotle and other classical rhetoricians, such topics, or *topoi*, describe both the ideological basis, and technical craft, of persuasive speech; they determine the terms of a given argument *and* the linguistic resources of the argument itself.[2] That is to say, *topoi* structure the "common sense" of a community and let speakers know "where to go" to find the resources for a given argument. A structure of topoi thus accounts for a community's theory and its practice, inasmuch as it encodes a system of knowledge *and* identifies socially viable "techniques" of persuasion. In the Aristotelian model, topoi work as resources for persuasion by encoding "assumptions held in common by people who subscribe to a given ideology" (Crowley and Hawhee 1999:79). As thematic resources for argument, topoi organize a logos, or *common logic*.

73

The following sections show what Walter, Joe, Arlen, Maggie, and Perry *wanted to me to know they knew* about themes of class, race and ethnicity, education, language and literacy, and politics. Yet this thematic structure is not analogous to a jigsaw puzzle in which the pieces fit together neatly, and along the same plane, to make up a coherent picture. Themes do not operate syntagmatically or paratactically; they are, rather, points of entry into the textured densities of ideology. *Class,* for example, is not structurally parallel to other themes represented here—it is both metatheme and anti-theme, given that at the Smokehouse, everything and nothing is said about class. Smokehousers narrate class metaphorically and metonymically through discussion of race, politics, education, language, and, above all, work. Ideologies of class are articulated not only through narratives elaborated in response to questions about class per se, but also between, through, and around the edges of other themes. To draw a geography of themes in this way is to see what commonplaces Smokehousers have available to them in argument, to map the rhetorical ground on which Smokehousers find places to stand.

My own questions or comments that appear in the following text are printed in italics. I have chosen to include occasional lengthy quotations here to illustrate the narrative quality of responses and to highlight the distinctive voices of individual speakers. These quotations attempt to show Smokehousers "in their own words," but the reader should keep in mind that all narratives are mediated, that conclusions about the "meaning" of the following data are inevitably directed by my position as one who participates in, but, in many ways stands apart from, Smokehouse culture.

No Class

At the Smokehouse, *class* is a state of being, not a state of mind. Smokehousers never, in everyday conversation, invoke "class" as an organizing metaphor for conversations about social phenomena. A person, place, or thing may be described as "classy," but this assessment includes no gesture of cultural critique. To say a thing "is classy" or "has class" means that it is expensive, elaborate, or decorous: though Smokehousers clearly disapprove of obvious displays of middle-class symbolic capital, nobody would name something regarded as supercilious or affected as "classy." One's car may be *classy,* but one's language never is.

Smokehouse ideologies of class are highly narratizable, yet stubbornly unnamable. Unlike other themes such as work, education, race, and politics, the subject of social class is rarely discussed *as such* at the Smokehouse. Class is a felt identity, a logic enacted phenomenologically. It is the implicit subject of talk of money, jobs, education, neighborhoods, and standards of living and pervades the conventional wisdom about social predicaments and economic trends, yet "class" has no metalanguage, no life as a heuristic. As Smokehousers' responses to questions about *work* will show, class identity is linked in a fundamental way to attitudes about individual relations to work and about the importance of work in general.[3] In addition, perceptions and definitions of social class can be seen in attitudes toward other social groups: that is, what "class" Smokehousers see themselves as constituting can be read in their accounts of who they are *not,* as in Walter's half-proud, half-disdainful characterization of his own son as a "yuppie." Because of the unnamability of class, there is considerable disagreement among Smokehousers about precisely what constitutes class, and, by extension, how permeable class boundaries are. Smokehousers will tell you that class is an economic state, but the implicit connection in their narratives between upward mobility and social displacement suggests that they *experience* it as a cultural phenomenon.

Smokehousers voice common political interests—lower taxes, less unemployment, more pay, better working conditions—yet they do not claim membership in a "working class" as a group defined by a common history of alienation from powerful institutions or discourses. When I asked them directly about where they placed themselves in the American social hierarchy, these Smokehousers—with the notable exception of Walter, who is self-educated but *not* upwardly mobile, and who offered lengthy speculations on the subject— seemed unsure of how to approach the topic, questioning its validity as a construct in terms of which to consider social and political issues. Worth noting here is the diversity of responses to my questions: this variation points to an absence of a coherent philosophy about class—or, perhaps more accurately, the absence of a way to talk about it. Disjunctures in perceptions of social class structures are partly a function of interviewees' proximity to others who are not members of the working class (Walt, for instance, has a son who is a professional in a corporate job) and partly a consequence of the tendency to see social structures as flexible enough to preclude rigidly deterministic views of class.

Though I did ask Smokehousers what class they belonged to, I felt as though I were transgressing against a tribal taboo. Asking people to commit to a class identification is, after all, to demand an acknowledgment of the viability of class as well to force a definition.[4] Of the five, two—Maggie and Joe—identified themselves as "middle class"; two, Arlen and Walter, said they were "working class"; and one, Perry, described himself as "lower middle." At some point, all claimed that they were not unhappy with their class status; and, though they admitted they would enjoy the economic benefits of upward mobility, these Smokehousers did not want to reposition themselves in another cultural milieu, one that might demand different habits and manners. Yet these declarations of class loyalty emerged within, or alongside, complex and apparently contradictory narratives about what class is, and how it operates, in American society.

The prevailing definition of social class among Smokehousers has to do with economic, rather than cultural, capital: according to Maggie, for instance, the classes—two—can be delineated in terms of "people who have money . . . and people who don't." Asked to describe the class structure in America, Joe connects class directly to economic status and speaks nostalgically about times past when people seemed to be less obsessed with pressures to achieve upward mobility. Perry, who has achieved some degree of economic mobility, also defines class in economic terms, though he qualifies this by citing the mediating effects of other identifications, such as ethnicity and religion.

With the exception of Walt, who describes class membership in terms of a more complex system of signs and resources, these Smokehousers maintain that class membership, as an economic designation, can be read mainly in patterns of consumption and residence.[5] Joe explains that you can tell what class a person belongs to "basically by the area they live in . . . their neighborhood."

Yet Smokehousers' recognition of significant differences in distribution of resources coexists alongside deep convictions about the *possibility* of economic mobility. As a group, they resist the idea that (although money is ultimately what determines class), one's class is one's economic destiny. In speaking of his membership in the "middle class," Joe assured me that "I'm happy where I am," but went on to assure me that he could change his situation if he really wanted to:

> I think . . . well, the only thing that's keeping me in my same class is me. Uh, you know, if I wanted to improve myself, I could, you know, if I wanted to go back to school and get a degree in, ah, electronic engineering, or something like that. There's nothing stopping me from doing that except for me, to where I could move up, you know, to a different wage bracket, or . . . to a different wage class, let's say.

Maggie, too, said that she didn't think it was "hard to move up, out of your class,"

> if that's what you desire. I think that a person . . . can get anything that they desire to have. So if their desire is to go from . . . you know, being a poor person up into having a huge amount of money—if that's what they want from their life, then I think anybody can do it. You can do whatever you want to do.

That Smokehousers say it's possible to change one's class and yet do not do so can be read as evidence of their investment in dominant American myths of unfettered upward mobility, that Smokehousers wrongheadedly attribute to individual agency that which is structural. Yet there is no indication that all Smokehousers actually *want* to be middle class—at least, they feel that there are cultural costs to upward mobility as well as economic benefits. At the same time that Maggie, Arlen, Joe, and Perry describe "class" in economic terms, they imply that membership in a class also implies participation in a culture. When Perry, on the one hand, believes he has successfully moved up and out of his class, and when Joe, Maggie, and Walt claim that they are perfectly happy in the class they are in, they are speaking of a cultural, not necessarily of an economic, situation. At the same time that one hears over and over from Smokehousers that it is possible for working people to ascend to a "higher" economic group, one finds a real wariness of the cultural displacement suspected to accompany upward mobility. Maggie says that she believes that though it is possible to move up in socioeconomic status through individual will and effort, economic success is by itself an empty victory if it is not won through the character-building experience of work:

> I think that I belong to the group of people, the middle—you know, the middle-class people. . . . I don't think I'm really poor, but I think I have to work for everything I've got. . . . And I would sooner have it that way, than be in the class of people that didn't—you know, that GOT everything.

Perry tells his own story as an example of socioeconomic mobility:

How difficult is it to move . . . out of your class?

It wasn't difficult for ME. . . . I mean, as I go back to my old neighborhood, as I
go into the bowling alley and so forth, and I see my old friends, people I went to
grammar school with and so forth . . . they're not in the same class I'm in. Because
it's . . . ah, money-structured; they're not in the same class I'm in, ah, they don't
drive the car, or cars, that I do . . . they can't live the lifestyle I live; they can't go on
vacations and so forth, that aren't in the car. They're my friends, and I love 'em
dearly for the fact that they represent to me . . . but they are not in my class.

Perry's comment appears to indicate a view of social class predicated on
more than location in a simple economic heirarchy: he cites his movement
away from local interests, as well his increased buying power, as evidence that
he has "made it" out of the class into which he was born and raised.

Walter had the most to say about how to define and interpret class differences. He offered a detailed analysis of class distinctions and, notably, exoner-
ates the social hierarchy as he describes it to exist in America. For Walt, class is
not a simple economic construct but a structure of cultural differences. In dis-
tinguishing "people with class" from those without, Walt cites himself—and
me—as examples of the latter. He launches into an elaborated tale of displacement and feudal order, one clearly constructed to persuade me that his life
experiences have given him anthropologist's-eye view of class signifiers, and
have led him to the inevitable conclusion that social divisions are happily intractable:

Do you think there's such a thing as class structure in America?

Absolutely. Abs—and I think there should be. I know you don't like that, but that's
okay.

No, I'd like to hear about it.

Because—I tell you why there should be. Well, first of all, let me say this. Uh, my
wife and I spent a couple of years in Puerto Rico, stayin' at a very, very swanky . . .
guest and resort-type hotel, which the pro was Chi Chi Rodriguez, which you see
him on TV, see? I seen Chi Chi every day, for weeks on end. Uh, I myself . . . felt a
little bit out of place, staying at this resort, because most of the people there . . .
had money, beyond my means, see? And, um, and these people—whether you
wanna admit it or not, Julie—they had ways about 'em that are different from
yours or mine. Now you're a fully educated person, you're a class item, but a woman
of . . . of CLASS, that has as much education as you do, and is as pretty as you are,
and as young as you are . . . put together in the same environment, people'd be able
to pick her out, as opposed to you. They'd say, This Julie is educated, and Julie is
indeed beautiful, but the other one SHE'S got CLASS. Now—and I'm not alone
in this thought, because here you take their—Hmp, let me digress a minute. My
sister-in-law one time went to Florida—and her husband had a chickenshit sales-
tech job, that was about a labor grade two, see? And she just thought that he was
super, because he wore a white shirt, and had an expense account. So the one—
they go to Florida, and they rent a compartment on a train . . . and they had all the

meals delivered to the compartment—they were really gonna go top-drawer, see?—
and she come home told us about "the nice places in Florida that we couldn't even
get into, they were so nice." Other words, she worked at places where, ah, a shirt
and tie was just not enough, you understand? There are . . . you take—there's hotels
in New York and Chicago . . . where you could call up and say, I want the best room
you got! And they'll give you a good room—but there's rooms that you just could
not get. They're reserved for Princess Di, or what—and it has to be that way. How
would you like, if you were the president of the United States, see . . . and now,
you're the ex-president of the United States . . . and now you go to a . . . to a resort,
and simply because . . . some hoodlum, who's peddled dope all his life, has got the
money to afford this place, is sittin' at the table next to you and your wife, and
he's talkin' about all the whores that used to work for him, using every word in
the book . . . you got to separate them people from the people with class. And I
believe that it should be done. I don't belong with them people, and they don't
want me around.

Walter's narrative is a remarkable performance; as a Bourdieuian observation of *habitus* marshaled in defense of an almost-feudal system of class segre-
gation, it itself speaks volumes about oppositions and tensions that structure
ideologies of class. For Walter, social class concerns culture as much as economics: Walt allows that economic standing is important in determining class
but insists that habit and manner are nonetheless significant in making people
higher in the social hierarchy "different" from others further down. Walter narrates class divisions as significant cultural incompatibilities and ends up identifying with the anguish of the elite at having to suffer the vulgarities of the riff-
raff. Yet Walt does not—unlike Perry—wish to elevate himself in terms of class
standing; indeed, he is unequivocal in his assertion that he does not "belong"
anywhere but the working class:

Do you want to belong among . . . people with class?

No! No, not at all. You know, I . . . [laughs] I get in such terrible arguments with
some of my friends, who insist that they're middle class. I says, YOU'RE middle
class? You're LOW class! They say, whaddaya—!? But I'm low-class, too!

That's the way you define yourself?

Oh, absolutely. In social structure? I'm low class.

Is that . . . "working class"?

"Working class" is a better term . . . it's a more polite term. Yeah, I like that better.
I'm a workin' man. You understand? . . . And I believe you SHOULD have it [class].
I have no right . . . to sit across the table from, ah, President Kennedy, and his kind.
They don't want me. And I don't want to be there. And I'm not envious of 'em!
That oughta tell you something—not envious of 'em at all.

So if you could just—suddenly, somehow—make the leap into the—you wouldn't—?

No—I wouldn't belong with them people. I wouldn't belong with them people.

The frustration Walt reports at being unable to convince his friends of their "true" class standing implicitly comments on the status of conversations about class among his cohorts ("I get in such terrible arguments with my friends, who insist they're middle class . . ."). Though Walter himself does not introduce the term, he welcomes the language of *working* class when I supply it as a possible way to name his social affiliations. Like Fox's "blue-collar philosopher" Tyler Foote,[6] Walter theorizes class when he is invited to do so. He gives a detailed account of the kinds of manners and habits that separate the classes and describes how certain behaviors mark one as belonging to one class or another. He goes on to tell a tale of an event that marked his own coming into class consciousness, a process that not only taught him the truth about his own class standing but also assured him that this difference should not be taken as a liability:

I think "class," Julie, and I know I'm not answerin' your question, but I think class is—well, one of the reasons—well, now, let me set the parameters. First of all, you gotta have money. Now, just because your father was a dope peddler . . . that doesn't qualify you from the rest of the—but it qualifies you from the money standpoint, see? Then there—then there's honor . . . you gotta have . . . come by your money legitimately . . . either by inheritance from your father who owned an automobile factory or an airplane factory; born of the right blood . . . proper education . . . uh, proper training, of course—you don't pick your nose, you don't fart at the table—you understand what I'm trying to say? And these people of class and culture, they don't want that—and I don't blame them.

When I got my commission—now, listen to this, Julie—now, I'm only twenty-two years old, a snot kid . . . from the Southside of Chicago . . . where on the four corners—there was a saloon on every corner, see? Born of a Polack and a Loogin, my father was a lowly carpenter, my mother was a . . . a dishwasher, if you wanna call it that . . . and I got a commission in the service, and by an act of Congress I'm an officer and a gentleman, see. So I get my first assignment. And, uh, n—I met all the guys, and we agreed that we'd meet in a certain hotel in San Diego on the day of our admission into the regiment. But when I had an opportunity, I said to one of the guys, I said, Hey, how 'bout this prick Scanlon? [aside] See, that's Stosh, see? "How about this prick Scanlon"—I said, he looks like a goddamned snob, I says, but under all, I think he's good guy. And, uh, I says, And that wife of his, I says, You know, I says, I'm just a Polack from South Chicago . . . and I've never been exposed . . . to a woman like that. I said, she's not good lookin', but she had CLASS. He said, Well, Walt, he says, I've known you all through class training at Fort Benning, Georgia—he was a student, like I was—he says, When it comes to combat, I'll take you on my right anytime—which is an honor. Cause when you're in combat, you wanna know who's on your right, and can he protect you from someone comin' from that way and then knockin' your ass off, see? He says, and on my paper, on my evaluation of you in class, I wrote it—I'll take Penske on my right anytime. See? And now, he says, Save that, he says, I wanted to tell you about these two people. He said, he . . . is a Boston blueblood . . . his father owns a whole publishing concern, Scanlon publishing—he owns the whole concern. His wife . . . is a multimillionaire . . . come from the best school, the best training, the best family. And, he says, That's where she developed her mannerisms and her manner of speech, and the way she conducted herself. And she was class. And you can tell 'em.

As Walter tells it, he learns that what he lacks in etiquette, he compensates for in real integrity. Class differences are significant, but, in the end, presuppose only a hierarchy of manners, not morals. Walt's loyalty to his class is driven by his conviction that working people are more authentic, more loyal than their more privileged counterparts: Scanlon's wife has classy manners, but Penske will save your life. Because of his emphasis on the symbolic bases of class, Walter insists—unlike the others—that social categories are difficult to transcend:

Okay. How hard is it to move up, out of your class?

You can't. You can't. They'll spot you every time.

So—let's say—let's think of somebody at the—what if we, you know, took somebody from the Smokehouse—

[Emphatically] Nobody!

Despite divergences in how Smokehousers narrate their experiences and interpretations of class, these divergences nonetheless stand to indicate points of consensus about the structure and significance of social class in America. Though the five disagree about the extent to which class structures allow for movement between categories, all agreed that class had much to do with economics. Smokehousers' responses to questions about their own class memberships strongly suggest that they experience class not only as an economic category but as a social affiliation. Even when Smokehousers admit to wanting to belong, as Arlen put it, to "the rich class," they worry that there are cultural costs to socioeconomic "success."

Notably, none of the five differentiated between my class status—even though they perceive me as one invested in my own upward mobility—and their own. Perry, who sees himself as upwardly mobile, speaks to me as one who shares his class membership; Walter, who loudly proclaims his "low-class" status, speaks to me as one who shares *his*. No doubt this is further evidence Smokehousers see me as "other" not because I *am* different, but because I'm making a point of trying to be. Walt's comment about his contact with "upper-class" people is telling both in what it reveals about his perceptions of my attitudes toward my own class status and about his perceptions about the division between the middle and working classes: "Whether you wanna admit it or not, Julie, they had ways about them, that were different from yours or mine."

The Colors of Whiteness

Much of what is implicit in discussions of class is made explicit in discussions of race. To hear Smokehousers speaking on race relations and ethnic ties—and they do speak on such matters, lengthily—is to find an aperture into class ideology. In conventional discourse, Smokehousers don't describe cultural differences they perceive to exist between themselves and others as differences in social class. Rather, they rely on categories of ethnicity and race implicitly to articulate their positions in social and cultural space. The attitudes that Smokehousers articulate about ethnicity and race reveal important assumptions not only about the nature of social hierarchies but also about how Smokehousers themselves, as working-class whites, fit into these hierarchies.

Individual members of the Smokehouse group define themselves differently in terms of ethnic alliances; nevertheless, Smokehousers generally recognize the power of ethnicity to identify individuals within the group. My view of the place of ethnicity at the Smokehouse parallels LeMasters's observation (1975) about the blue-collar workers who frequent the tavern featured in his own study: LeMasters noticed that at The Oasis, "ethnic background is a constant factor. . . . [Y]ou feel its presence almost every day" (122). Race serves as a way for Smokehousers to identify themselves as a political body (as whites, against the "special interests" of minorities); the idea of ethnicity is central to Smokehousers' efforts to articulate a common cultural history and experience.[7]

Only Perry and Walter—the oldest of the five, and second-generation European-Americans—express strong ties to their ethnic backgrounds. Perry and Walt had much to say about their ethnic origins and (consequent) cultural conflicts—questions about ethnic backgrounds and affiliations provoked the most copious narratives of all. Stories of economic hardship and social alienation can be rendered through narratives of ethnicity; thus, narratives of ethnicity carry subtexts of class identification. Consider, for example, the story Perry tells describing how conflicts that have been a part of the Italian-American experience have shaped his own ethnic identity:

> Dad was born in the old country. . . . Mom was born here, but . . . had to go back to the old country. Her dad owned a grocery store, and in those days . . . the Mafia, so to speak, did not—ah, their basic, ah, way of raising money was to intimidate their own people . . . and so . . . my grandfather owned a grocery store so he had to pay protection money or they said they would kill . . . his first daughter, and that was mother, and that's—so he got frightened, Grandpa, and he went back to the old country. Stayed there five years, and in the interim, he made some connections with some people that were big here, and they allowed him to come back. . . .
>
> I had an incident that occurred, and I've st—I've told this story a few times, and I think it's probably . . . because I've been there. I was in, ah, in the service, in the Korean war, and . . . my papers were cut. My papers—I was on my way to the Far East, to Korea. I had just gotten word that my cous—my first cousin Carlo had been killed in Korea; second cousin got a grenade that had just gone off a ravine and was totally . . . disfigured from it, and I was the third cousin . . . only three of us were in that, ah, that particular war. Many many relatives went to the Second World War—I missed that one, but three of us were involved in the Korean War. And I'll tell you—I was very frightened about what was gonna happen. I was home on furlough, for two weeks, and, um, I was dating my wife, and, um, I like dancing, you know that, and she was a good dancer, so she wanted to go dancing. At that particular time, there was a place on Halsted Street, around seventy-ninth and Halsted. . . . And I had been told that, that they didn't like Italians in the place. It was about a hundred percent exclusive Irish, ah clientele who would go there; if you were Italian, you couldn't get in. If you wore a haircut—they used to call 'em DAs, you what I'm talkin' about, DA? You know, Duck's Ass, they used to call 'em, that Elvis Presley used to wrap his hair like that. They had a cow then, if you were—

if you wore, like a lot of Italians wore collars, big collars, button-down collars with a big windsor knot, ah, peg pants, and so forth. So in the service, they had taken all my hair away; I didn't have any hair. And I know that—what the requirements were, and I made a sincere effort to play by the rules—I've always been a person who plays a game by the rules. So I borrowed one of my father's shirts, and he made a straight forehand knot, and I went very square to this dance. The way it worked, it was a converted theater, so you paid, if you remember, the way theaters—well, I paid, and she looked very much like you, her hair color was basically the same— my wife could be a sister with you, as a matter of fact—um, and she walked in, and everything was fine, she had walked in and passed the second doorman, who was like, the bouncer, or the person who was gonna accept the tickets that you had to pay for, and I got up through the door, and he said, Can I see your—do you have any I.D.? And I went through the thing, and showed him my Army identification, and he said, ah, I'm sorry, I can't let you in. She can come in, but you can't. In essence, I had my first taste of what it was like to be . . . discriminated against. And we didn't get in.

Were you pissed?

Ooohhh, I was furious. I was so angry—we almost got into something. I was in good shape, and I was . . . [laughs] In my neighborhood, you didn't take that kinda stuff from anybody! And I just couldn't deal with it . . . if you couple that with the fact that my orders were cut, it was like, I was going over to Korea, it looked like— I had lost a cousin, just heard about that, the other cousin was disfigured, and I was on my way—and it was like, I am going over to defend this country, for guys like you. And then you tell me, I can't get in there, only because my name is [DeMarco]. So I think I had an experience that . . . most people don't have. Discrimination went on at that time. I'm talking, many years ago—I'm sixty-five years old—I'm talking, when I was dating girls that were fourteen, I can recall things like, people saying, girls saying, Listen, I'll meet you someplace, my dad doesn't like Italians. But that never bothered me like—THIS was a real confrontation, I kind of understood that. And I—I guess that was one of the reasons I probably used to tell my mother and father, Speak English! Become American, so we don't have this discrimination. But we were wallowing, in Bridgeport, that was—at that particular time, everyone you knew was either hijacking, or doing something that was illegal, going on. And yet they were nice people! They were relatives, they were friends; that was part of their life. Those who get into that life of crime, also very nice people, concerned with their families by and large, they loved 'em, did their best for their families . . . it's just that . . . what they do for a living . . . is . . . *that.*

Did this act of discrimination make you think, Gee, I wish I weren't Italian? or, I'm gonna be Italian, goddamnit; I don't care whether YOU like it or not . . . ?

You know, that's a good question. Ah . . . I can tell you a story that kinda keys into what you said: I'm about eleven or twelve years old, and my father was a barber, so Dad didn't come home 'til about nine, nine-thirty, and in those days, you did not eat supper until your dad—the patriarch of the family—came home. So my mother would let us take a nap or something, but when Dad came home, we'd wake up, and Dad would sit down and we'd eat as a family. Uh . . . this particular day . . . I had read in the paper that day that, I don't know, so many syndicate people had shot—I don't recall story; either they shot somebody or they got shot—and it was a multiple murder-type thing . . . and I was very ashamed, of being Italian. So, I, ah, had already seen James Cagney in *The Oklahoma Kid,* I remember . . . and he was Irish, and that came up . . . so, ah, my dad always sat here—in an Italian family, you sat on the right, I was the oldest son, so I sat on the right of my father—my father sat here; my mother sat at the end of the table. And, um, I didn't have a good appetite that night, I was just . . . upset about the incident. And dad noticed that I wasn't eating, and he kept bringing up the subject, What's the matter? and, you know, I wasn't answering his questions, and so forth. Ultimately, I burst into tears, I guess, and I asked him—now, he's a barber, he reads every paper, all day long, six times over—I said, Did you see the paper today? And he said, Did I see the paper, I read them all, so what's the matter with you, what's that got to do with not eating? And then I told him, I said, You see all those Italian ones that did this, or did that— I forget what they did, whether they killed, or killed somebody—and he said, Yeah, I read it, so what? he said. And I said, I'm ashamed I'm Italian; I wish I was Irish! Well—! The "Irish" never got out of my mouth, he cracked me backhand, the chair went down, it cut the lip, Mom was on the floor, you know, trying to doctor me and crying, and so forth and so on. So I think that was . . . my first time of being ashamed of my ethnic background. In later years, I was to become . . . probably overly proud of it. I don't know why that happens to people.

Perry's narrative is a classic tale of hardship and assimilation: he begins by telling of the trouble his family members had in establishing themselves in the new country and recounts his own experience with discrimination in order to establish his authority to speak about what it means to be socially marginalized. In telling a story of his own childhood transgression against ethnic solidarity, Perry certifies the viability of ethnicity as a site of identification, even as he acknowledges its problematic role in his own life. Walter, too, expresses a distinct sense of ethnic history. Even though he characterizes himself as "kind of an independent bastard," he expresses a belief in the strength of cultural bonds. As a first-generation American, his own identity is closely linked to his ethnic background, and he sees ethnic alliances as potential sites of conflict between individual and group, between culture and society. Walter publicly defines himself in terms of his Eastern European heritage, and it seems important to him to be seen as one who is finely attuned to his ethnic history. Walt's story of the downfall of Lithuania illustrates his orientation to a cultural past, and his description of his ethnic composition places him as a player in an ongoing drama of cultural identity. A running joke at the bar has to do with the antagonism between Poles and Lithuanians; those who claim alliance with one or the other often invoke ritual displays of prideful anger in response to provocations of feigned ignorance about the real differences between the two. Here Walter asserts his claims to ownership of his Polish/Lithuanian ethnic heritage by narrating the history of nationalistic conflicts:

But, er, the origin of that is, that, um—and I get in a lot of arguments with people about this—was back in medieval times, Lithuania controlled, with their cavalry and their horsepower, about eighty percent of what is known Europe now . . . from Russia all the way down to the Black Sea . . . and they had this band of . . . cutthroats . . . that ruled all of known Europe. But what they didn't have was aristocracy. And the Polish people had aristocracy, and the blessings of the Pope, which Lithuania did not have—the Pope thought that the Lithuanians were nothing but a bunch of, uh, of heathens, you know, so, ah, the Lithuanian hierarchy said, We gotta have royalty! So they married a Polish princess . . . to one of their knights. And this knight was influenced by this ridiculous—you're gonna get this interview to go from here to—! But nevertheless—she encouraged this guy to go on to all kinds of conquests, and get more land, and rule more people . . . until the Lithuanian borders were so far-flung they were easy to chop apart. And little by little Lithuania, through double-crossing and double-dealing with the Polacks, ah, Lithuania got to be nothing [pauses, thinks]. But we got a terrific Olympic basketball team . . . they're gonna give the American black team a run for their money.

The Lithuanians?

Sure. We're gonna really—see, there, you notice I say, "we"? It's in me, and it's in you. You understand that—I say, "we," when I talk about the Lithuanian basketball team—the famous basketball team, you know, that everybody talks about's the Dream Team—when I say, "we," I meant the Lithuanian team . . . [here Walt addresses the tape recorder directly] Did you get that?

Do you consider yourself more Lithuanian than Polish? I mean, what's—who do you identify with m—?

Well, er, I'm not gonna lie to you . . . listen to me, tape recorder, I won't lie to ya honey . . . um, I consider myself more Lithuanian. But I gotta say, uh, if there's any measure of goodness in me, or if there's any measure of brightness in me, it comes from my mother's side. My father's side was . . . uh, a bunch of mudhut peasants, poachers, cattle-rustlers, and shit like that, whereas my mother's, ah, side of the family was what, uh, all what we would call semi-professional—priests, teachers, uh, private detectives . . . [laughs] You know what I mean?

As much as Perry and Walter want to be perceived as having maintained ties to their ethnic roots, they are no less eager to show that although ethnic identity is important to them, the appropriate status of this identity is secondary to a primary identification as "American." Both men qualify their expressions of ethnic loyalty by declaring themselves to be "American." Perry describes himself as "Italian," but immediately goes on to qualify this in saying, "I am a very good American, very proud American, and I love my country; I've served my country." Walt is unequivocal in describing how his Americanness should take precedence over his ethnic identity: "I'm an American. Born American, bred American, gonna die an American death" before quickly adding, "but I am duly proud of my heritage. Goddamn right I am!"

For all Perry's and Walt's assertions of ethnic affiliations, the role they ultimately ascribe to ethnicity is similar to that ascribed to it by Arlen, Maggie, and Joe, who have no such affiliations. The responses of these latter three to the question, "If somebody asks what ethnicity you are, what do you tell them?" show common alliances not to particular ethnic groups but to "America" in general:

MAGGIE: I say American, because I'm not really sure what I am. I know that there's German in my family, and I know that I have Indian in my family, but we're—we're not, like, a—you know, a specific thing, like Polish or Italian or whatever, you know. . . . I wasn't raised that way, so if we are, I don't—I don't know the difference.

ARLEN: Well, I'd just tell 'em, you know, French and Swedish, but . . . I'm really just . . . ah, American.

JOE: I can . . . I can be traced from, you know, of coming across the pond, and being here before they came across, to where it was just, you know, you talk about an American! I am not any generation, I am—I am the slag on the melting pot, I am the mixture, you know, a conglomerate . . . to where, I am an American.

These remarks imply that, in general, claims to "ethnicity" articulate not an ontological present or a political future but rather an originary tale, a kind of felt history. Not surprisingly, then, it is more present in the memories of Walter and Perry, who are the closest to their families' immigrant histories. Smokehousers assume that although ethnicity is an important way to locate oneself in *culture,* it should not be understood as a way to place oneself in *society,* to claim political rights. Ethnicity alludes to place, to originary tales and local commitments.

Whereas ethnicity locates class identity in an imagined past, race places it in an insecure future. Smokehousers speak of racial distinctions in terms of competition between races for social and economic resources. Of the issues likely to arise in barroom arguments, I find myself most at odds with others at the Smokehouse on the subject of race. Smokehousers in general refute racism as a structural system of dominance on grounds that they themselves—as working whites—enjoy no more authority and privilege than blacks do. The issue can be volatile, and arguments about race are more likely than most others to result in angry confrontations. But even though I have been implicated in many such confrontations, I am ultimately immune from ostracization from the group, despite my views. I am, after all, white. I may speak dissent, but I embody solidarity.

From my own point of view, conversation at the Smokehouse is often overtly racist. But whether or not racist language (e.g., references to "niggers") is actually part of the conversation at the Smokehouse, race is almost always at issue in discourse there, however covert. Narrating one's relation to race matters orients oneself in social space, naming an unnamable class identification.[8] I now understand that I was reluctant to ask Smokehousers direct questions about race for fear that these questions would be heard, given the antiracist feelings I have voiced at the Smokehouse, as motivated by a desire to "prove" Smokehousers' racism and thereby proclaim my own class superiority. The claiming or disclaiming of explicit racist discourse is iself a powerful class signifier and marks one way that discussions of race can be read as conversations about class operating incognito. That Smokehousers were nonetheless willing to talk to me about race relations, speaks, I think, to the pervasiveness of racial issues in narrating social dynamics in general. Yet it also indicates that people want to show their positions on questions of race as more reasoned, and more nuanced, than their expressions in the polarized dynamic of argument.

One of the most common ways Smokehousers narrate class as race is in relation to their fear of displacement in social, geographical, and economic space. Walt, for instance, explained to me that he moved from his Chicago neighborhood because his "neighborhood was turning black." He went on the tell of the economic dangers he read this fact as portending:

> I was forty years old—I lived in Chicago forty years—and, um, my neighborhood was turning black, and I had a very, very lovely home, and a very soundly built one . . . and, uh, property, well, the bottom was just falling out of it, and I figured, I better get out while I can still sell some of it. . . . I'm just too young to lose all that goddamn money and try to make a comeback. So, I got out. I got out very early. I was the third one on my block to go.

Though he does not himself admit to being threatened by the upward mobility of minority groups, Perry's comments on the reactions of others around him point to class insecurity—as anxieties about threats to one's economic status—as a motivator for racial tension:

> I live in Greendale Heights, and we just had, yesterday, a black move in on my block. And I don't know how to answer the questions of my neighbors that are just running around, you know, crazy . . . and they're running over to me, talking to me, and expecting me to sympathize with them, or understand their, ah, their basic nervous feelings at this point. And I do understand their feelings; in fact, this guy's one door away from me. But I—I—what are you gonna do? Where are you going to go? You came from Roseland, or you came from, you know, South Town, or something . . . now, you gonna run again? You'll create this same situation. I mean, these are nice people—they couldn't buy that one hundred and twenty five thousand dollar home they just bought, unless they . . . and what they want is the same thing as what you want. Well, when I say that, that isn't what they wanna hear.

Perry redresses racist motives as class anxieties by addressing the implicit fear that the arrival of blacks in one's working-class neighborhood predicts economic ruin. Yet Perry is the only one of the five who makes a point of insisting that he is not a racist. This illustrates, given Perry's desire to distance himself from working-class culture, the centrality of attitudes toward race in maintaining cultural identity and group solidarity: Perry clearly associates racist speech with working-class modes of identification. The stories Perry tells of racial violence in his original neighborhood narrate the historic confluence of economic desperation and territoriality (a black man is literally killed on the boundary between neighborhoods) and suggest that Perry believes racial hostility, even brutality, to be a characteristic feature of white working-class culture:

> [In Bridgeport] you could only go so far east, and then it was a case of—even in my youth, it was very bad, where when you crossed this boundary line, which happened to Wentworth, and you got into this area, which was a totally black area,

your life was in jeopardy. You literally—I remember running to save my life, as a young boy . . . because, here's Bridgeport, here's a black neighborhood, and here's Lake Michigan. On hot summer days, what we would do is, we would jump on a streetcar or a bicycle, and go to the lake. So . . . there were many, many times when I coulda gotten beaten up badly—and I probably should've. And I don't know why that never had an effect on me. I guess it was because conversely, when they came over here—they did that to us because we did it to them, or whatever. I mean, I don't know where it started. But when they came into our area, in Bridgeport—when the blacks came in, they were beat up as well. More so! I would say, they were the more li—and I think I knew them. When some of them would come here . . . they would *kill* them. I was a lifeguard at Armor Square Park; I remember coming—and I think it's incidents like this; it takes a lot of things, to ultimately form, you know, whatever liberalism I've got—I came to work that day, and that morning, the park was surrounded by policemen. And what had happened—this is a sad, sad story—er, in those days, all parks, you know, had those spears, you know, the park had a fence around it that consists of spears. I saw a black man whose body was dropped onto one of those spears. I think that was—and in hearing the story, this black man had worked with a group of whites, and he had knowledge of plumbing. He had come over into the white area to help a buddy of his—a white buddy—do some plumbing. And he was just walking home with his tools, going back into his neighborhood. And he met a bunch of crazy white guys . . . [who] beat him up and impaled him on those spears. Just for being in the neighborhood. And I've probably heard story after story like that . . . where—yeah, we would get beat up, and so forth, but I don't remember anybody of our group ever getting killed. But THEY killed—it was an Irishman that did it to him; it wasn't a Dago. Italians, Irish, and Croatians lived in that area, right next to this—this was Wentworth; the blacks lived here, and the whites lived on the other side. I mean, it was SO bad, that even to this day, that's an area that blacks don't go into. Blacks don't go into Bridgeport—it's still an isolated area.

That Smokehousers' orientation to race relations are driven largely by perceived economic interests is indicated by Perry's account of how his "liberal" attitudes toward race contend with his conservative business policies. In telling of his struggles between his own convictions and the prevailing racist ideology, Perry implicitly validates more directly expressed class anxieties about black empowerment:

I had a hostess come in—and God, she was great. She was a graduate student, extremely attractive, ah, very, very good background, hostess background—and I had to say no to this gal. I had to not hire this gal just for the fact that she was black. That was unfair, just unfair. I've had people see the blacks who were out digging the garden one time—and this fella, that came in every week, he lived over here at the Point, well, he ultimately lost his home at the Point, moved out, because the Point is all black—he saw my cook. He says, *You got blacks that cook in the kitchen?* Yeah, you know, all my cooks are black. I thought—somehow or another, I was under the impression that everybody knows, that in the back—but they don't; they *don't* know. They don't know what goes on in the kitchen, people don't know—well, when he saw my cook out there in the apron, he said, Is that your *head* chef? I said, *Yeah;* he says, *You know, you're makin' a big mistake.* And then it came out, one of my best friends, nice guy . . . he said, *You'll lose—this whole area is gonna go black, and you'll see, you're gonna lose your business here.* There's people with that strong kind of prejudice, that won't frequent a place because of it. So . . . I hate it, but I have to concede. And if *I'm* like that, and I'm forced to do it, for whatever reason—then this goes on, throughout the industry, I don't care WHAT business you're in; I don't care what you're doing—the mentality of the person doing the hiring is the same, and and therefore that poor black man, or black woman, is discriminated for no other reason, except that they're black. They could be extremely qualified, but it's . . . it's going on in every phase of the business, in some way or another. So that BULLSHIT, when they say that, ah, they're given every opportunity we are . . . well, they're NOT. In every hiring instance, I think it goes on. That's why they've got to have, the ah, quotas, the, ah—not quotas, the, ah, affirmative action thing. You know, they have no choice except to resort to that.

In much Smokehouse talk of race, Jesse Jackson seems to be a powerfully evocative metaphor for what many working-class whites perceive to be threatening about the emergent political power of blacks. As a symbolic figure, Jackson is a kind of palimpsest, one that bears the traces of white antagonism to black social mobility. Jesse Jackson speaks for the view held by many Smokehousers that black empowerment always happens at the expense of working whites. Joe holds that Jackson is a bigot because

his "Rainbow Color Coalition," he kept talking about that . . . and I'll never forget this: when he was, ah, running for president—it was one of the black, ah, newspeople on Channel Seven, and they had some kind of an interview with, ah, Jesse Jackson about his Rainbow Coalition, and Jesse Jackson came out with some racist remarks—and says, well—this black journalist, now—says, Well, I guess we just found out that Jesse Jackson's Rainbow Coalition is just several shades of brown.

And you agree with that?

Absolutely! Absolutely. He was dead ag—he was always, ah, trying to get the blacks to arise to be his political power—that was all he was ever interested in, was just the black vote. And he never tried to come across to get the whites. To where, he was too—well, his background doesn't help much, either—to where, you know, he's always been kind of a—an activist. And he's just a little . . . too . . . active for me [laughs]. To where, when he got in there, what's he gonna do, you know? I don't know what he expected to achieve, 'cause he'd still have, you know, the Congress and the Senate to work with. And I don't think it'd be any better for the blacks than it is now, even if he was in there. Ah, the social programs'd still have to go through the Congress and the Senate, and you know, it's just . . . there are no overnight cures, even if he did get in there; nothing would've happened overnight, it'd've taken years and years.

Joe's excoriation of Jackson amounts to a complaint that Jackson's focus on race signifies a betrayal of class interests. For people at the Smokehouse, ethnicity and race have different significance as social categories: if "ethnicity" could be said to be how Smokehousers construct identities at the micro level, then "race" can be defined as how they identify as a group at the macro level. To put it another way, Smokehousers see ethnicity as operating at the level of culture; and race, at the level of society.

At the bar, it is usually provocative to speak of one's ethnicity as if it were a body of social or political interests. Ethnicity operates as a way of identifying people in a group; that is, it explains in-group behaviors or cultural variations in taste and habit and suggests ties to the local. Smokehousers like to joke about individual ethnic differences, but these jokes establish, not threaten, group solidarity. Delivering and setting oneself up as target for jokes about one's ethnicity is to show oneself to be an insider, to be alike enough not to pose a threat by making an issue of difference. And because Smokehousers define themselves so strenuously against blacks, ambiguously racial or ethnic categories—such as Hispanic—tend, in most cases, to take on the status of ethnic, and not racial, groupings. In the end, what people are willing to say about race reveals much about Smokehousers' feelings about their own class status: that Smokehousers see themselves as entitled to resources by virtue of their membership in a racial category is linked to their perception that their class status offers them no such entitlements.

The Work Imperative

At the bar in the late afternoon, physical evidence of Smokehousers' working lives is everywhere. Impossibly heavy work boots rest under barstools; canvas work gloves rest in grubby piles on top of the bar; callused hands grasp icy mugs of beer. Though the bar is a place—for some, *the* place—for leisure, it is impossible to separate the culture of working people, and hence, Smokehouse society, from the material realities of work. Smokehousers' lives are attuned to the rhythm of the shift, to the cycle of the work week, to the regular allotment of wages. Most jobs that Smokehousers hold have to do with manufacturing goods or with providing services; in either case, Smokehousers—unlike most white-collar workers—are fairly close in space and time to the products of their labors. For Smokehousers, the importance of work as a life-sustaining activity is patent, and predictable attitudes toward the meaning of work do, I would argue, mark the "working class" as a cultural group, just as much as the jobs its members hold and the pay they collect define it as a socioeconomic one.

As Jack and Joe often lament, the job situation just ain't what it used to be, and many men have faced hard times as a consequence of plant closings, and so forth. Yet even as opportunities to *produce* fade, faith in the inherent value of, and intense identification with, *productive work* hold fast. LeMasters suggests that, though in a complex society work may no longer be central in the lives of most mainstream people, for the blue-collar worker, work "has retained its basic significance as a way to find a place in the social structure" (1975:19). My conversations with Smokehousers, together with time spent both participating in and observing what goes on in their everyday lives, lead me to claim that for Smokehousers, work—and in particular, attitudes toward work—have much to do with how Smokehousers view themselves as a coherent social group. When Smokehousers talk about their histories and everyday lives, the issue of work surfaces as a code for a set of assumptions about the nature of the socioeconomic landscape and their own place in it. Narratives about work and working lives encode values Smokehousers share regarding loyalty to employers and competence on the job and show connections between experiences in the working world and the expression of "work" as a rhetorical theme.

For the average Smokehouser, coming of age meant going to work. Smokehousers want you to know that they started working young and that they've been working ever since. They tell of having entered the world of work early in their lives, of having interrupted their working lives only to serve in the military or to have children. Joe, who started working as soon as he entered high school and then joined "the service" before taking a long-term job, narrates the experience of many at the Smokehouse. These five Smokehousers have held a variety of jobs, but as a group, their work histories include mainly labor, manufacturing, and service jobs. Joe describes his work as "strictly blue-collar"; Walter characterizes his working life as a series of jobs that demanded "all that grubby type of hard, dirty work." Between them, Walter, Arlen, Joe, and Maggie have worked in machine shops, foundries, aluminum can and tape factories; as carnies, hospital orderlies, and roofers. Only Maggie and Perry, who have college degrees, have held semiprofessional jobs (Maggie as a recreational therapist, Perry as a pharmaceutical salesman).

The idea that *work* must be separated from—and indeed, must be defined against, *play*— pervades narratives of work. As thematic categories, work and play show little overlap: work is what must be done to make play possible; work time is thus distinct from leisure time. Play happens after (and sometimes despite) work, not through or in it. The work/play opposition prefigures a distinction between doing and thinking, between producing and philosophizing. As LeMasters (1975) observes about the group of working-class men in his own study, "these blue-collar aristocrats actually feel that they are earning an 'honest living'—that working with your hands is more honorable than 'stuffing pages' or 'earning a living with your mouth' " (21). Or, as Walt explains in contrasting the "doers" with the "talkers" at the Smokehouse (and citing Joe as an honorable example of the former):

> You got people around there that—and I don't want to mention any names—but, uh, that are very quick, and very responsive, and, uh uh blah blah blah, they got the floor all the time, but they, uh, when it comes to the ability to do—I say DO, earn a living, and take care of yourself—Joe is head and shoulders above 'em.

The attitude Walter voices is no doubt amplified here by the Smokehouse commonplace that I am one who, as a student, spends too little time working, too little time producing anything of material value (and therefore too much time at leisure).[9] Smokehousers' narratives of their own and others' relationships to work link hard work, and the obligation to work , directly to individual integrity. In telling of his son, who has successfully entered the white-collar world and is now "disgustingly yuppie," Walt affirms the strong connection between class identity and loyalty to an ideal of productive work:

> The only thing I made him do—and I'm glad I did, goddamn it! I funded him fully all through school, high school and college . . . but I never discouraged him from

getting a job selling shoes at Kinney's—which he did [and] worked at the golf course rakin' sand traps and cuttin' greens—I never discouraged him from work— delivering pizzas . . . He done every goddamned thing, and I always encouraged him.

To Walt's way of thinking, one of the primary duties of a good father is to educate one's children about the moral duty, the character-building potential of work. Walt's idea that work builds character and increases the value of things earned is echoed by Maggie in describing her feelings about her role as a worker and about the standard of living she enjoys:

> I would rather have to work for everything I've got because I believe that gives you value. I think I'm the luckiest person in the world, because I have my horses and my three kids, and my husband, and my beautiful home, and I've worked hard for everything I've gotten.

Narratives about work experiences suggest a view of workers as commodities, or units of labor that fulfill a specific productive function in the industrial marketplace. This attitude is best expressed by Walt, who repeatedly stresses the importance of having a "marketable skill":

> [D]uring the depression I worked at whatever job I could get my hands on . . . uh, which was always labor, cause I had no education, I had nothin' to offer anybody. And I soon learned, that if you can't tell anybody who you are and what you are, you're nothin.' And I learned that years ago, that if you can't tell someone that you're a lathe operator, you know, er,—the biggest mistake that people make, they go to the employment manager, and they say, 'I'm capable of learning, I pick up quick.' They're not looking for people to teach . . . they're looking for people that can press a lever, and make something happen, so they can sell it. They're not in the business of training people.

Even though Smokehousers express a belief in being well-trained and performing well in the labor marketplace, this willingness to submit to the needs of productivity runs up against the desire to be free of such constraints: all describe the degree of autonomy a job allows as the thing that separates a good work experience from a bad one. Walt, who before his retirement worked as a product engineer for a major manufacturer of farm equipment, describes his job as one that offered him a great deal of satisfaction by encouraging responsibility and independence; Arlen, Joe, and Maggie agree that the "best thing" about their work is the opportunities for freedom and responsibility their jobs allow. Maggie, for instance, tells how working behind the bar presents the opportunities to enjoy what she most values in a job—independence and the authority to make decisions:

> The best things about my job are the people that I work with . . . and that . . . I feel that I do a good job, and that I'm able to do a good job, and that I'm able to make decisions to do a good job. . . . I like bartending a lot better than I like waitressing because it's not as frustrating, because I don't have to depend on anybody. I like to do a job, and do it to the best way that I can . . . and I don't have to depend on a cook, to make my job harder, or a buskid, or a hostess, or whatever. . . . When you

bartend, you're responsible for your own self, so if you screw up, then you screw up. If you do a good job, you do a good job. But you can't say, It was the cook's fault, or the hostess's fault, or the waitress's fault, or whatever. . . . [Y]ou're responsible for yourself.

Although Smokehousers' jobs differ in the skills they require, people share a common belief in the value of "doing a job well." If middle-class professionals identify themselves in terms of what they "are" as professionals, Smokehousers define themselves to a greater extent in terms of what they *do:* above all, Smokehousers want to see themselves (and to be seen by others) as *productive*.[10] Work is, above all, an essential enterprise that is meaningful primarily for its ability to sustain life. But whereas, on the one hand, work is seen as a discrete activity driven by economic necessity, it is regarded, on the other, as a "state of grace," an authenticating experience that gives value and meaning to the individual.[11] These coexisting views of work reveal attitudes about the place of working people in the socioeconomic hierarchy: if an individual gets worth by performing well in a particular job, and that job has worth as specialized activity, then a worker accrues value and achieves definition as an individual by his or her ability to perform a specialized task. Smokehousers want to be responsible for their own activities, their own decisions in work; at the same time, they believe in the importance of loyalty and performance on the job. Tensions between the values of conformity and independence in work notwithstanding, the conviction that work is a moral—as well as an economic—obligation is an enormously important theme in the common logic.

Street Smarts, School Smarts

If *work* is valued as a meaningfully productive activity, *school* is its thematic doppelgänger. At the bar, the topic of education—what it is and how it should proceed—frequently arises in everyday conversation, even though in general schools are not institutions with which Smokehousers identify.[12] Still, class ideologies surface in themes of education, for schools have the power to confer both economic mobility and class capital. Generally speaking, people strongly believe that they are set apart by their lack of formal education as well as by their resilience in the face of such a lack. Smokehousers are proud of their ability to find an education where they can get it and to learn selectively and efficiently, as befits those who have no time to waste. Those who have had the benefit of more schooling boast of being more "broad-minded" than the unschooled but are nonetheless unwilling to relinquish claims to "street smarts."

For parents, the issue of how to go about getting one's children a *good education* is of considerable concern. One hears frequent talk at the bar about what a "good school" should do and what things schools should and should not teach. Although what seems obvious in listening to people at the Smokehouse talk about education is the utilitarian orientation to learning in general and the tendency to value knowledge that translates directly into economic gain, Smokehousers' views on education are actually more expansive and diverse. In my conversations with them, Smokehousers expressed fairly strong feelings about how education suits the needs of working people, about the scope and limitations of formal education, and the connections of education to upward mobility.

The extent and nature of individual Smokehousers' ambitions for upward mobility have everything to do with how much they actually identify with institutions of formal education, in the way that they look to these structures for their relationships, values, or activities, or as a means by which to define themselves socially. But because identification with schools is not the norm and therefore represents dissociation from working-class interests, people read my strong identification with the university as a way to distance myself from, and thereby devalue, the concerns of people who "work for a living": I am perceived by many to be one who does not take seriously such aspects of working-class life as nonprofessional work and wisdom gained informally, through experience.

There is, of course, a danger in Smokehousers receiving my questions as an attempt to stigmatize them in a forum in which (unlike that of public debate) there is no established genre by which they can challenge such an attempt. In any case, being asked to speak about education by one who is so closely tied to the interests of the educational institution would have the effect of amplifying remarks about either the limitations of formal education (as with Walt and Joe) or the advantages of it (as with Perry). That is, I am both envied and disdained for my associations with higher education; these feelings reflect, I think, the ambivalence inherent in Smokehouse culture about the value—and the possibility—of allying oneself with educational institutions.

Yet all agree that there is an important distinction to be made between *education* (as formal education) and *knowledge*. Whatever else it might do, education should be practical and should teach applied, marketable skills—skills that refer to domains outside (what they see as) the autonomous marketplace of the school itself. Such orientations to education are narrated in conjunction with realities of work: as Smokehousers recognize the likelihood that their children will enter the workforce as crafts- or tradespeople, they value the education that will offer adequate preparation for this life. People complain about schools on the grounds that they are irrelevant to working-class experiences and prospects: there is a suspicion that schools don't prepare their children to be working-class any more than they teach them what they need to know to enter the middle class. In pointing out that the schools have "gotten worse," Walter speaks of some of the skills that schools fail to teach and expresses the dissatisfaction many Smokehousers feel at the failure of schools to equip youngsters with "basic" skills, complaining that "you could graduate high school now and not be able to draw a line. . . . [Y]ou could graduate high school now without being able to read . . . a goddamned menu!"

Just as schools are taken to task for a failure to teach skills, Smokehousers say that schools do not encourage productive relationships between students, teachers, and the institution in general. Smokehousers' complaints that schools are either too permissive or too authoritarian seem to indicate contradictory views on the appropriate disciplinary role of school, yet I think they point to a common concern among Smokehousers about how education socializes (or, more to the point, fails to socialize) children to function as adult members of society. Joe, who has two school-age children, bemoans declining order and discipline in the schools. He nostalgically invokes a time when schooling enforced clear disciplinary codes:

> They're more laid-back now. You used to have dress codes, ah, you know, you had to dress a certain way, ah, have your hair a certain length, ah, girls' skirts had to be a certain length, ah, it was just—they're too laid back now. You know, they got smoking lounges for students? I don't know! I think, you know, they're a little more progressive now, but I think it's—they're lacking discipline. They don't have the discipline that they had when we were there, um, they don't—they're not learning values, ah, all they're doing is just going there and learning subjects. . . . [T]hey don't have any kind of a value, or kind of, self-esteem. . . . I went to Lincoln, but they still had the dress code there. . . . [Y]ou had guidelines, you know, to what you could wear and what you couldn't wear. That's the things that are lacking now. . . . I think it's more of a self-image thing than anything else, I don't know, it gives you a little more self-respect, dressing well.

In contrast to Joe's and Walt's claims that schools have "gotten worse" because they no longer properly control or discipline students, Maggie contends that schools should be *less* authoritarian in order to communicate appropriate expectations about adult behavior and complains of the false division schools impose between childhood and adulthood.[13] She explains that

> they treat you like you're in jail, you know? You still have to have a note if you're five minutes late, and if you have, you know, ah, three tardies, you get suspended, and if you're in the hall without a pass—you have to ask to go to the bathroom, and all this—you know, all that stuff, I think is ridiculous—especially in high school. I don't think that—that teenagers, um are—you know what I never understand? You can get married when you're eighteen, you can join the service when you're eighteen; you can't vote until you're twenty-one, you can't drink alcohol until you're tw—I mean, they should decide. These kids are capable of making decisions for themselves, and if they involve them more in the decision-making process, then maybe there wouldn't be so much rebellion, and—and so much of the problems they have today in high schools. You know, you—you go to college right—you're a senior in high school when you're eighteen, and then—and after one summer you go to college—you can smoke a cigarette in the hallway if you want to; you can pee whenever you feel like it! What made you so different in three months? You know what I mean?

What Walt, Joe, and Maggie seem to agree on, though, is that schools do not adequately socialize children to conform to the demands of the larger society. Smokehousers will assure you that school is "important" and that they intend to see to it that their children will stay in school and work hard. Yet in keeping with the idea that labor should be productive and that education is not the same thing as knowledge, many express a strong belief in the primacy of experiential wisdom over knowledge associated with established scholarly traditions or institutions. Joe, for instance, contrasts "education" with "common sense":

[A]ll that school does is just—it teaches you how to learn. It gives you information . . . to where, your actual life experiences are what you learn from. You see—you see an awful lot of overeducated people that have absolutely no common sense! To where they—they have the intelligence, but they don't have, you know, the ability—the common s—the streetwiseness, the everyday experience to put into practice . . . to where they're not—either they were sheltered, or something, but they just, ah . . . but they just, are really intelligent, but no common sense when it comes to everyday things. Ah, I think that by sitting down and having a conversation with a person, you can find out, you know, if they're intelligent or not, and just because they didn't go to college doesn't mean that they're—that they're idiots. It's just that, you know, education and intelligence are two different things.

When I asked Walter if he thought it was true, as I'd often heard people say, that "you learn more outside of school than inside," he was passionate about the limitations of formal education:

Absolutely. Absolutely . . . even in your chosen field. Even if you—the first thing they almost always—everyone'll tell you: first thing you gotta do is forget what you learned in school! 'Cause you're out in the—the so-called real world . . . that's where it's at.

So it's possible for someone to have gone to years and years of school, and—

And still not be good at their work! . . . [T]hat's what I say, there—there's more to be learned in outside of college than there is inside of college . . . with the exception, now, of, ah, let's say, uh, engineering, ah, medical professions, uh, some disciplines like chemistry . . . you just can't do without college. . . . [T]here's where you learn, you learn the basics. Uh, the real test comes when you get out in the field . . . uh, I, um—here I go again—you're gonna think I'm really hung up on this subject—but I am! Ah, I judge an educated man by his ability to DO. You understand? That really says it all.

So . . . practical competence, something like that—?

Yes! If, uh, if he—two dentists both go to the same school, both graduate on the same day—one dentist is a skilled artist, he's successful, he's educated—the other guy botches everything that he touches—that man's not educated.

Even if he knows lots of the philosophy of—?

Yeah! Oh, no no no no NO—that don't mean shit. A man's ability to DO is what counts.

For Walter, work is the ultimate test of formal education's viability—the place where, as he might put it, "the rubber meets the road." One goes to school to learn "the basics" and to learn civic responsibility; one *lives* to know. Arlen speaks the essence of these attitudes about the importance of experiential knowledge to survival, holding that "you learn *life* more on the street than you learn at college." Whether school is valued for its ability to cultivate practical intelligence, or whether its benefits lie in opportunites for exposure to new belief systems, is largely a function of social aspirations. For Perry, arguably the most upwardly mobile of the five, formal education represents opportunities to reinvent oneself outside the parameters of working-class culture. Perry explains:

I think the friends I made, the, ah, black friends that I had in college that were my best friends, had something to do with shaping my life, and, ah, giving me the, ah, view—so yeah, I think in some respects you learn a tolerance, that you can't pick up if you don't get education, if you don't get into college, if you don't spend time with a variety of people, and around learned people. If you're just gonna be—you know, if your life is sitting around a bar . . . entirely, then that's all you're gonna know . . . is those people, it's those . . . rednecks out there, that you're gonna be doing most of your learning from. Unless you really are a person who can rise above it, still . . . to not get any kind of exposure—I don't know, I think you've got to have exposure to be more liberal, and I think that's part of the problem, is that they've just not had . . . that. I'm very different from my brother . . . and I think Carlo, my brother, he did all of his schooling in the city, he graduated from Chicago Teacher's College. . . . So he never went away; he stayed home and commuted, and so forth, and you know, and that kind of thing . . . and . . . you can see, he's very much like our friends, the people that share—their beliefs would be closer to his, than mine. I went away my first year, I went away to New Mexico, and then I spent a year in Chicago, tryin' to feel my way around. The last two years, I went—I graduated from a small school in Michigan. And those were probably very good years for learning—I was Catholic, in a Methodist school, ah, a very integrated school, ah, there were no, er, very few Italians, very few Catholics . . . so you were in the minority, as opposed to, in and around Chicago you were always in the majority, and always playin' big shot because you've got ten people to back up whatever you say. It wasn't that way in school.

Once again, Perry cites racist ideology as the defining feature of working-class identity. Maggie, who has "gone away" to college, also speaks of formal schooling in terms of its potential to expose one to alternate belief systems:

And a well-educated person is open-minded, and—to me, a well-educated person would not be a person that was bigoted, or close-minded, um, to such a degree that I think uneducated people are, and I—do you know what I mean? Because people that don't have an education, and aren't well-read, don't . . . have a chance to open their mind to new ideas. So if they're raised in a certain way, and they can never break out if it, and see new, then how can they think or accept new? So—they're more close-minded, I think, than educated people would be . . . the person would be more open-minded for new ideas—you know, alternate lifestyles, and things like that—than an uneducated person would be.

With the exception of Perry, these Smokehousers narrate their histories of struggle with and alienation from institutions of formal education; these narratives of alienation bespeak the suspicion that schools are really intended to represent middle-class, not working-class, needs and interests. In talking of their own experiences with schooling, Smokehousers recount stories of class barriers—both social and economic—that have been at issue in their educational histories. Joe, for instance, narrates his history of disenfranchisement as a story of information privation:

See, when I was goin' through high school, I knew my folks would never be able to put me through college—couldn't afford it—'cause they were both workin' two jobs, my dad as a janitor at the high school. And I knew—they asked me one time

if I wanted to go to college, and I said no, so I never took any of the entrance
exams, or . . . the placement test or anything, the SAT, or whatever, you know,
garbage that you. . . . And so, my senior year, I was awarded a scholarship to the
University of Illinois. Four years' tuition and the whole thing . . . for music. And
so . . . I couldn't take it, because I never planned on going to college, never took
any of the placement tests . . . and here it was handed to me, four years' tuition,
room, and board . . . and I never prepared for it, so I couldn't take it.

Walt speaks with considerable bitterness about his experiences with education.
In giving his reasons for dropping out of high school in his third year, he describes a prohibitive economic situation but ultimately blames himself for his
alienation from school:

> [M]y high school career was a disaster. I . . . screwed around, chased the girls,
> bummed school, went to the world's fair . . . you know.
>
> *But you got an education . . .*
>
> Yeah, but I got it after I got outta school, see. Then I realized what a terrible mistake
> I made, not paying attention in school.
>
> *Why were you not interested? I mean, were the classes boring, were you just—*
>
> No, I'll tell you why I wasn't interested. The high school I went to was strictly an
> academic school. By that . . . most of the kids that went there . . . were headed for
> college. My parents were so goddamn poor, that I didn't have enough money to
> buy pencil and paper and college was . . . the never-never land up there in the
> clouds, you know what I mean, with the spires sticking up above the clouds—and
> no road between me and the clouds. So I figured, I'm not going to college, so what
> good is this? All the kids around me were all rich. They had good, fancy clothes,
> and . . . they were certainly going to college. . . . [S]ome of the others had apart-
> ments already in high school. . . . Yeah! That's the kind of school I went to! And
> here I don't have enough money to buy mechanical drawing paper! What the
> shit—! My high school was a vacuum. . . . Well, hell, high school's preparation
> for college—and I wasn't goin' to college . . . so what the shit? Why go, then?
> Go look for girls.

Arlen did "go away" to college for one semester but quit because he felt socially
displaced. He explained that he left college because

> I don't know . . . didn't want—ah, I don't know . . . lonesome, I guess. I was kind
> of like a, what do they call them? A suitcase student . . . ah, I kept going home
> weekends . . . just about every weekend. A lot of my buddies didn't [go to col-
> lege] . . . and they were all—had jobs, and were drivin' nice cars, and I figured,
> who needs college?

Walt, Joe, and Arlen cite social and economic factors as responsible for their estrangement from the ways and means of formal education, yet none of these
men places the blame anywhere but on himself for his "failures," as Walt implies in his remark, "I realized what a stupid mistake I made, not paying attention in school." Even though Walt as much as says that college is a middle-class
luxury, he holds himself responsible for not gaining access to it.

Maggie suspects that schools, in seeking to accommodate the needs of the few, lose sight of the needs of the many who must prepare themselves for entry into the working world. In speaking of her experiences in jumping from one vocation to another, she admits, "I started a lot of things, and never really finished anything." When asked to account for this, she told me that it was really her own fault she never really stuck to anything but then went on to attribute her history of indecisiveness to lack of information about certain professions:

> I'll tell you why I think. And I really think—and I have given this a lot of thought.
> I think that when kids are growing up and when they're in high school, they have
> career days, and whatever—but nobody—high school doesn't prepare you for life,
> or school—you know, education-wise. And nobody tells you, or opens any doors
> for you, so that you can figure out what you wanna do. So then you get out of high
> school, and you go to college, and you think, oh well, maybe like *I* did—Oh, I'd like
> to help people—you go into a field, you find out that it's hard to get into, that it
> doesn't pay you any money . . . um, economics is a big, big motivator for what you're
> gonna do in your life, and then—you know, you go to school and do these things,
> and—and get accomplished in your education, and find out that you hate it! Or that
> it doesn't pay enough to . . . to . . . that you can live on. You know? And so I don't
> know what I would do to change it different, but I wish that when I was younger . . .
> someone—that my high school education had prepared me more for a career,
> um—not a career to actually do, but to open the door so that I would have had
> more choices for myself—because I was too naïve to know what it was I wanted.

In marked contrast to Maggie's, Arlen's, Joe's, and Walter's stories of disappointment with and alienation from high school and college, Perry narrates his experiences with formal education quite differently. His school history is a tale of discovery and redemption:

> Wonderful. Loved it! Yeah, I was a good student because I was a hard worker.
> I don't have a lot of, ah, I don't have a high IQ—so as a result, everything I've
> done, I've had to work hard for. I mean, ah, I can recall—not so much in high
> school, because it wasn't necessary, I was on the honor society many times in high
> school, but that's so easy in high school, all you have to do is basically CARE . . .
> and do your homework, and be an average student, and, ah, you made it many
> times. I've got all of my report cards. . . . [M]y mother was very—I've got all my
> grammar school. . . . Another thing—I never missed a day of high school, and I
> only missed two days of grammar school. I loved school. . . . I don't know, I'd have
> to say that the whole—the memory of the entire concept—I, ah, I am so enamored
> with school, that I ah, still—I have some great memories of teachers in school that
> I think were important and directed me in the right direction . . . but they didn't
> need to. I was always properly directed. I knew . . . I was motivated, and just—
> I just loved that part of my life.

Yet Perry sees himself as more upwardly mobile than Walt, Maggie, Joe, or Arlen and is therefore not unwilling to associate himself with middle-class institutions. But like Maggie, Perry says that he lacked information about how schooling translates into career preparation, about what options education offers: when I asked Perry if he wished he had gone on even further in his educational career, he told me he would have picked a different profession totally. I did what my parents—I was a very well-behaved child, who, ah—they indoctrinated me with the idea that, you'll go to school, you'll go to college, and you're going to be a doctor. And I said, Okay! And that was it. And it was like, there was nothing else BUT that—you know, I didn't know there were lawyers, um, and . . . not until I got into college and I realized I didn't LIKE that, that I didn't want to get into that, that it wasn't what I liked, that I took all the courses leading to that. You know, anatomy, and all of the sciences. That's how I wound up in a scientific field, you know . . . which was a mistake. No—if you're saying, in essence, If you had it all to do over again, how would you do it—without a doubt, I think I would have done exactly—well, not *exactly*, but something like you're doing. I mean, my . . . deepest wish is, in my next life, is that I'd have the opportunity to, ah, teach in a college.

The stories Walt, Joe, Arlen, Maggie, and Perry tell of their experiences with formal education and attitudes toward the relationship of schooling to knowledge and everyday life constitute the subtext of Smokehousers' socioeconomic circumstances and needs. Like the working-class whites in Heath's (1983) study comparing working- to middle-class language practices, people at the Smokehouse are generally alienated from what they perceive to be the methods and goals of formal education. The Smokehouse community, however, shows less consensus in definitions of and attitudes toward education and (no doubt because it shows a greater range of social mobility) is more heterogeneous than the Roadville community with respect to involvement with middle-class concerns.

Generally speaking, Smokehousers draw a sharp distinction between knowledge that pertains to "real life"—and specifically, to life in the world of work—and formal, theoretical knowledge that is not immediately applicable to work and to action. Schools in general—and colleges, in particular—are categorically perceived as middle-class institutions that do not suit the needs either of those who do not seek to enter the professional world or those who do seek entry but don't have the information they need about what it means to enter that world. The consensus is that the primary purpose of school should be to prepare one for "life" and work: all other purposes are secondary. Given that time and monetary resources are often limited, education should, Smokehousers believe, have an immediate economic payoff. Yet upwardly mobile Smokehousers like Perry (and, to some extent, Maggie) have faith in the ability of school to encourage "open-mindedness," or to offer the potential to challenge local belief systems. In the end, Smokehousers believe they must choose between competing commitments to a "formal" education that helps them look beyond local frames of reference and practical learning that answers to economic needs.

Speaking American

The bar at the Smokehouse is a place to be a *good talker*, to be clever, original, and quick on the uptake. Smokehousers cultivate wit and strive for eloquence. Yet even as they demonstrate their passion for language games and prove their rhetorical expertise, they express doubt—and in some cases, acute anxiety—about their ability to "speak good English."[14] Upon learning that I'm an English teacher, people inevitably react with some version of the following: "Well, I hope you're not gonna *correct* me or anything—I better watch what I say." Even though I always insist that I'm really not concerned with policing the language, telling people about my "other" job frequently has the effect of shutting conversations down entirely. So the unease people showed in speaking to me about their own language in interviews did not come as a surprise. Given what I knew of Smokehousers' often difficult experiences with formal education, I knew questions about language might be read as attempts to "prove" some kind of linguistic deficiency. Though I believe that I succeeded in reassuring everybody that I did not intend to call their language habits into question, for many Smokehousers, language is a source of social anxiety, so that the prospect of having one's language evaluated in some way can be unsettling. In such a scenario, the fact of my professed identifications with higher education is significant to Smokehousers' remarks in interviews about their attitudes toward language. They all knew that I taught writing at the university, so they were speaking not only to a fellow Smokehouser but also to an English teacher and representative of the academic world—a marketplace that explicitly devalues local forms of talk.

Talk of language often surfaces as a theme in arguments with me and points to a site of contested class allegiances. The responses people offered to my questions about language are no doubt motivated, at least to some extent, by each one's desire to narrate to me, the perceived guardian of language standards, stories about their own struggles with middle-class standards of linguistic propriety and correctness. Variations in responses about how language "should" be used reflect the extent to which a given person wishes to express solidarity with, or dissent from (and thereby define himself or herself against) my values. But, conversely, whether and how people *do* wish to show allegiance to the dominant linguistic values they expect me to speak for amounts to a declaration of class affiliations.

Beginning from the fundamental sociolinguistic assumption that language patterns, habits, and attitudes emerge from, and speak to, social identity (Labov 1972), I asked Smokehousers explicit questions about appropriate uses and applications of language and literacy in the hope of gleaning further insight into who Smokehousers think they are as a group (and in particular, how they experience themselves as a group positioned in the larger linguistic marketplace). Even though people were not entirely comfortable in characterizing the kind of language they themselves speak, they were more than willing to talk about the linguistic practices of other groups, to condemn inappropriate uses of language, and to affirm the idea that language should be used to assert solidarity and not to announce distinction. In fact, topics of bilingualism and illiteracy are frequent aspects of political discussions at the bar.

As one might expect from a group that, by and large, does not identify with institutions (such as schools or corporate structures) where prestige dialects are spoken and that tends to value pragmatic over theoretical knowledge, people see the ability to suit linguistic means to communicative ends (in contradistinction to the ability to use linguistic forms as displays of propriety) as a useful competency. When I asked Walt, for instance, whether he thought there was such a thing as "good English,"—a highly charged question, coming from an English teacher—he redefined the terms of my question before going on to explain what communicative skills he most values and to challenge middle-class fetishizations of the standard code:

> *Do you think there's such a thing as good English?"*
>
> Oh, that's kind of a vague one . . .
>
> *Okay, well, then, how do you define it?*
>
> Yeah, that would better—what do you CALL "good English?" [laughs] Let me say that if you could talk without swearing, that's good English. If you could be de-scriptive, and explain your thoughts. . . . [N]ow when we're talkin' about English, I'm not talkin' about elocution . . . and I'm not talkin', ah, the Harvard, eh accent . . . by "good English," I . . . to me, a guy that could speak English, uh, well, is the guy that could say something to me and I'll understand what he said . . . the man that has the language and the selection of words that . . . I can understand.

Other Smokehousers agreed that "good English" should be a pragmatic defini-tion, should have to do with situated appropriateness, a claim that departs from what Smokehousers indicate they believe English teachers like me think, that is, that "good English" has to do with an elite code of propriety and cor-rectness. Like Walt, Joe defines "good English" as the ability to assess commu-nicative imperatives and to effect an appropriate linguistic code:

> Um, good English . . . would be . . . the ability to, ah, make your thoughts clear . . . to be understood . . . ah, doesn't matter if you use, ah, slang, you don't have to use proper terminology, but if you have the capacity of getting your thoughts across . . . that's good English. . . . If you can get your thoughts across and be understood, that could be—that could determine good English.

Whereas Walt and Joe appear to reject as irrelevant mainstream institutional standards of language use—or, at least, to define "good" English in terms of communicative efficacy rather than as conformity to a standard dialect—Arlen, Maggie, and Perry *do* equate "good English" to some extent with "proper" or "school" English. These latter three have had more schooling than the others, although Arlen and Maggie tend to identify less with formal education than Perry does. Arlen defines "good" English as

> PROPER English. . . . Well, I mean, good English is speaking it the way it's SUPPOSED to be spoken. . . . I mean, you don't say, "dis" and "dose" and "dese" . . .
>
> *Why not?*
>
> Well, 'cause it's—that's—it's not the proper way!

Perry, who values formal education and the habits and values it imparts, equates "good" English with Standard English and laments his inability to speak it in his current environment. In response to my question about how he'd define good English, he was quick to say, "It's what I *don't* have!" He went on to account for his "deficiency" by explaining that

the environment that I'm in . . . doesn't lend itself to being around people th—
I think when I was in college, I spoke very good English; I don't think there were
many of those "dese, dose and dems" . . . and, um, English was always one of my
better courses; I always did well in English. . . . I liked English. I was very good at
English, very good at spelling; I was the last at most of my spelling bees in grammar
school, winner many times. No, education was always very important to me, and I
don't like hearing myself on tape, because I can hear the—I know how I would *like*
to speak, but I know it's too late now to try to correct the years of being—and I've
been in this business for thirty-five years, associating with people, most of them are
not—you don't run into very many college graduates at the bar . . . so my association has been with Jack, who didn't graduate college; I mean, these are very smart
people, Jack's got a high IQ; I know Arly's IQ is very high, that kind of thing;
Maria's IQ is very high; but Maria's English is worse than mine . . . because she
didn't have any—Maria didn't have any formal education, either.

Smokehousers show an acute sensitivity to the potential of language to
stigmatize, as shown in their commentary about how people are socially
defined by their speech. In discussing whether and how they "judge" others by
the way they talk, all five acknowledged that language conveys social information about a given speaker and indicated that they would be inclined to read
this information as a liability, depending on their attitudes toward the sociocultural affiliations that speaker's language conveys. Maggie admits that she
might "judge people" as being more or less educated by the kind of language
they use but hastens to add that these judgments do not reflect their moral
worth: "I don't judge them as, whether they're a good person or a bad person,
an honest or dishonest person, someone I would trust or not trust. . . . To me,
my judgment would lie more in the educational." Walt, too, uses himself as an
example of the tendency to use speech as a means by which to assess the intelligence of others and warns of the danger in making cavalier judgments of
people based on their linguistic habits:

I could take, uh, a very learned scholar, from any of the universities of Europe—
not England, now—Germany, or France; Russia—and have 'em come here to this
country, and, uh, the minute I hear 'em "talk like Polack" I say, Dummy guy, you
know . . . and the guy could be a brilliant brain surgeon. . . . [T]hat's stupidity on
my part. See, just by the way the man spoke, I'd say, This guy's a dummy, see? and
it's not true.

Perry speaks of the capacity to place one socially by admitting that his
judgment of someone speaking with "dese, dems, and doses" would "be nega-
tive" and goes on to imply that association with one who speaks well can confer middle-class capital:

I've always liked to, ah, upgrade—it's like tennis. If you play tennis, don't play with
someone who can't play as well as you. Play with someone who can beat you, someone who's a little better than yourself. . . . Usually, hand in hand goes, you know,
uh, with the dese, dems, and doses and the lack of education, comes the other
things, that, ah, generally, I know that person and I would disagree in many areas.

These five generally agree that language carries much information about social status and cultural affiliations; therefore, the judgments they tend to make about a given speech tend to derive from their attitudes toward the alliances that speech reveals. But, no doubt in part because they are aware of the possibility that they themselves might be judged as intellectually deficient by their speech, Smokehousers reject the notion, purveyed by institutions of formal education, that linguistic habits are good criteria by which to measure intelligence or moral integrity.

That Smokehousers are conscious—and wary—of the power of language as a socially exclusive code resurfaces in their remarks about their attitudes toward bilingualism in policy and practice. Talk is public, a vehicle for sociability, and to treat it otherwise is a clear violation of protocols of solidarity. I had always known that the subject evoked powerful feelings among many at the Smokehouse, but an incident at the bar one evening several months before the interviews represented here illustrated just how volatile the issue could be: I was sitting at the bar with a friend from out of town who had agreed to meet me at the Smokehouse, and we were, as we sometimes do for fun, speaking French. Although our conversation was clearly private, a couple of regulars—not, I should point out, any of the interviewees—overheard and expressed outrage that we should be speaking a foreign language "in America," in public. I had heard this sentiment voiced before, but never quite so strenuously. I wondered what it meant, culturally, that the public use of foreign languages was regarded as such a threat (especially as the speakers in this case were not, in fact, foreign). Since the admonitions of the two men at the bar were clearly performative, and were therefore intended to ratify a sentiment sanctioned by the group, I decided that getting Smokehousers to talk directly about bilingualism—how they felt about the use of languages other than English in the United States, what social predicaments such issues spoke to, and what policies they thought should obtain regarding such use—might help me to understand the connections Smokehousers assumed between linguistic behavior and social alliances in general.

Of the five, only Maggie expressed indifference to the presence of populations of non-English speakers in the United States, saying "it doesn't bother me at all." Yet Maggie's insistence that she has "no problem" with bilingualism "on a personal level" would seem to suggest, however, that she is aware that having such a "problem" is, in fact, the status quo at the Smokehouse. The problem is that language announces social alliances, and in speaking "other" languages, people are signaling inappropriate social loyalties. The responses of Joe, Walt, Perry, and Arlen bear this out. Joe, for example, told me that he gets "upset" when he hears people speaking a foreign language in public. He explained that

I just wonder if they're talking about me—What's this gringo doin' here? You know, or whatever, you know, just, ah . . . ah, it's kinda—what've they got to say that's so important that they can't say it in English—are they planning to overthrow the government, or what? You know, you kinda wonder about people, you know, what is it that they're saying that they don't want me to understand?

Whereas Joe's remarks about the practice of speaking a foreign language "in public" indicate his suspicion about the motives of the speakers, what he goes on to say about policies that accommodate nonnative speakers reveals something about his own:

> So we shouldn't accommodate [speakers of languages other than English] in any way?

> No, I wouldn't—I wouldn't think so, but you know, they could say, you n—well, you're discriminating against us, you know? It—so it's gettin' to the point to where, you know, it's almost reverse discrimination now. And it's . . . it's a real touchy subject.

Joe's remark about "reverse discrimination" suggests that in the larger narrative, there is a connection between the prevalence of a foreign language and the emergent political power of that linguistic group—at the cost, he seems to feel, of the interests of his own group. Arlen echoes Joe's concern that the presence of Spanish texts signifies "special treatment" of that group; Walt, too, voices clear opposition to the practice of bilingualism, saying that public use of foreign languages "pisses me off! The only consideration I would make, would be that if they don't know my native language. If they don't know my native tongue, then they got the privilege of usin' their own tongue." Walt, like Joe, believes in instituting public policy against bilingualism. He speaks passionately about the moral obligation to use English to show one's loyalty to "America."

> Should English be our official language?

> Ab-so-LUTE-ly!

> So . . . we shouldn't allow signs and ballots and things to be printed in another language?

> No, sir! Absolutely not! I'm really—I'm really pissed off about that—This is your country—your newly adopted country—you gotta support your country.

Walt goes on to explain that he believes that what often motivates people to speak foreign language is the desire to exclude others. He cites as examples of this phenomenon

> two languages in particular—Polish, and, um, Mexican. I use those because I been exposed to both of those. Ah, um—well, when I was a child, and my mother and father wanted to talk about something like—that we shouldn't know about, like there's gonna be a party, or what we're gonna get for Christmas—then right away they didn't talk . . . the Polish and the Lithuanian that we understood, but they were still using their language . . . but that's not as descriptive as, uh, when I was a child, there was a predominantly Polish group that I hung around with. And if they wanted to do something and not include you, they would discuss it right in front of you, in their language. . . . [I]f they were havin' a party, and you weren't invited, they'd talk amongst themselves, and . . . and, uh, like Mexicans do it. I say, "Mexicans," only because my daughter-in-law's Mexican. I could be in her company, and, uh, somebody else'll come along, and . . . [imitating Spanish phonology] *baranta baranta gallanta baramba,* see? right away . . . like, who is this guy?

You mean, you feel excluded from the—

Of COURSE you do! It's embarrassing.

Perry, though he says he has "no strong feelings on the subject," wants to assure me that he has "liberal" views on bilingualism, even though he goes on to express sentiments that echo the remarks of Joe and Walt. Perry holds that when it comes to matters of language policy

> I guess I'm rather liberal about it, I . . . I do think that, ah, I can find—when, well— bilingual, we're talking Spanish, right? What else do we have, here? Um, when I hear them get adamant, talking on talk shows and so forth, I get a little on my thing, too, like . . . the fact that they should have to learn English, like the rest of us. . . . [M]y mother, my father came here, had to learn English, didn't know it, ah, many of my relatives had to do the same thing, and . . . only when I hear, you know, somehow, they insist on that right, do I then get upset.

For these Smokehousers, language is the site of conflict between the interests of competing social groups; for this reason bilingualism has the power to provoke strong feelings of frustration and alienation among Smokehousers, as with Joe and Walter. There is a sense in which the speaking of foreign languages violates the cultural imperative to subordinate ethnic to larger social alliances and signifies the intent to show solidarity through exclusivity. The class implications of this are made explicit in Walter's description of his own son's speech. In complaining about the use of language to announce membership in exclusive groups, Walter speaks of his son's newly acquired "yuppie talk" as if it signified a betrayal. He cites the following examples of the use of speech—in this case, of a dialect—to signal exclusivity:

> Two cases in point! My son—who I love dearly—like I told you plenty of times, my whole heart went into his education, to make sure that he succeeded—and he pisses me off, because he's starting to acquire . . . this yuppie talk. You know, they do have a little twang to their, uh, words . . . I mean, the way he pronounces 'em! I have no objection to a guy bein' eloquent, and, ah, bein' descriptive, and havin' a good command of the language—that's great! But, like instead of sayin', "and," they say, "aahhnd"; they say, "this ahnd that," see? Now this lady across the street . . . who is ersatz, uh, oh, let's say, member of the intelligentsia, see—uh, she's above it all, see? She is, really. It's a crime if she gotta buy her groceries at the same store I buy mine, see?

While these Smokehousers express a general concern that speaking in foreign languages is motivated by the desire to show group solidarity and thereby exclude *them*, their narratives suggest the position that language should, above all, be assessed by its efficacy in face-to-face communication. Even though Perry, Maggie, and Arlen seem to be suggesting that "proper" English has value as a linguistic form, what is clearly more important is *function*, or the capacity of language to adapt itself to use in everyday situations. Smokehousers see an advantage in having the means by which to guard against exclusion by linguistic communities they may need to contact. This goes for foreign languages as well as for varieties of English: one should be motivated to learn a second language by communicative necessity, not necessarily by a desire to know a language for its own sake or for "fun." To hear Smokehousers tell it, language is a serious business, and it is significant that they express this attitude despite the frequency of language play—punning, teasing, joking, and the like—that goes on at the bar. It is as if it is well and good to play with language within the embrace of one's own social group, but the imperative "out there" in the "real world" is, above all, to be *understood*. Such an attitude points, it seems to me, to a belief in the instrumentality of language and suggests that it is an act of sheer will to make communication work (i.e., it is the responsibility of the individual to make himself or herself "clear"). This belief, as well as the prevailing conviction that they might not measure up when held against the yardstick of middle-class propriety and correctness, means that Smokehousers are more than marginally insecure about their ability to use language when confronted with the need to communicate with those outside their own community. I was surprised to hear Walt, who strikes me as quite rhetorically adept, say that he believes himself to be "really inadequate at times" when it comes to expressing himself to others.

Smokehousers keenly feel the power of language to work as an instrument of social exclusion. True to their convictions that alliances to the larger social body should precede alliances to smaller cultural groups, they believe that use of foreign languages represents unwillingness to show solidarity with, or assimilation into, "American" society. Because Smokehousers perceive their own primary allegiance to be to "America," even though they may feel alienated from mainstream social institutions, the general attitude at the Smokehousers seems to be that linguistic displays of cultural solidarity violate the "rules" of social affiliation that they themselves are careful to follow.[15] I would argue, finally, that Smokehousers' unwillingness to allow other groups to express group solidarity linguistically is yet another manifestation of Smokehousers' own ambivalence about how to represent themselves as a political group.

How Smokehousers narrate their views on literacy is important for what it suggests not only about uses of language but also about a general orientation to the production of knowledge and the relationship of intellectual currencies to class identity. Just as Smokehousers maintain that the most valuable oral language skills prove to be the most useful in everyday life, they express a similarly functionalist orientation to written language; as interviewees' views on the benefits of speaking a standard dialect vary with respect to their involvement with middle-class society and mainstream institutions, perspectives on standards and benefits of written language vary along the same lines. Smokehouse reading habits do not comport with research that suggests working people don't read as a leisure activity (e.g., Heath 1983): while Smokehousers do not typically hold jobs that require extensive contact with written texts, many do spend leisure time reading. And whereas they do not tend to use knowledge of books as means by which to claim social distinction, they often discuss the books they have read, recommend reading material to each other, and trade books (the horror fiction of Stephen King is a literary staple at the Smokehouse; his novels are circulated widely among regulars and employees). The choice of what book—usually, what novel—to read next is often determined by the recommendation of someone else in the group. At the time of our interview, Joe was reading a mystery novel recommended by a bartender at the Smokehouse, though he admitted he didn't care for the genre and would not have chosen it himself:

> I don't really care for—I like the action, I like Louis L'Amour . . . but I don't really care for mysteries, but I didn't have any books to read, so I just, ah, Little Debbie loaned me this one, says it's a real good book, so . . . I read it.

With the exception of Arlen, who says he "got too busy to be reading," those I interviewed claimed to be avid readers and to enjoy reading for recreation and information. Of the five, however, Maggie was the only one who claimed to be raised in a household in which books were a part of everyday life. Maggie expressed a real passion for books, saying that she liked to read "everything. Everything, everything! I'll sit and read my anatomy book, I read my chemistry book when I have n—you know, no other things to read." But although Maggie likes to read "everything," she says she most enjoys books that tell stories relevant to her own life. Perry, like Maggie, professes to enjoys reading stories that make sense of aspects of his own experience. Joe claims to prefer "fiction, mostly," and, like Maggie, says he is a fan of Stephen King. Walt, however, indicates that he reads to gain access to information that would otherwise be beyond the scope of his experience and to expose himself to "new" ideas, not for aesthetic pleasure or play:

Do you like to read?

LOVE to read!

What kinds of things do you like to read? Fiction, nonfiction; do you read—?

National Geographic! R. R. Tolkien! And, uh,uh, who the hell is this guy? I got his book up there . . . he's a . . . a Watergate guy [Walt later told me he had been referring to G. Gordon Liddy here]. . . . [N]o, but I like to read politics. . . . Editorials, oh, yeah! That's my—novels, I wouldn't give you a dime for any of 'em. Don't read 'em. You could mention the best novel writers in the country today and I wouldn't know their names—

But—th—drama—you s—you like Shakespeare—!

—Shakespeare I like, yeah! Yeah, but he's—yeah, well, wait a minute . . . hooooold the phone! I can—I can recite almost any like from Shakespeare without—and saying, "what is this guy saying?" He said something, and goddammit, I missed it! So you go back and read it again, and then you understand what he's talkin' about.

That Walter disparages novels though he claims to enjoy novels of Tolkien suggests that for Walt, the novel stands for an orientation to knowing that is inconsistent with the image he would like to project as participant in the world of ideas—or, perhaps more accurately, in the "real world" of ideas-in-action. It seems to be important to Walt to make it understood that the information he derives from the solitary practice of reading is applied to the active world, to the world of everyday life. Walter says he developed a passion for reading when he realized that

> every time you read something, you learn something . . . you learn something new, you understand? There's something new, see . . . and I used to like to read, uh, biographies, see? *That* I liked, see? Edison, Ford, ah, Tesla; uh, Westinghouse . . . all them people. I liked to read their life. . . . [T]hey were all good.

These Smokehousers' commentaries on their reading habits depict them, collectively, as a group that looks to written texts not only for parallels between the stories of their own lives and the stories of others' but for the means through which to access information not immediately available through everyday experience. In this respect, Smokehousers seem to read for the same reasons middle-class intellectuals do. I would argue that they differ from this latter group, however, in the way that they define the relationship between written texts and the acquisition of knowledge: that is, Smokehousers do not claim written texts as intellectual property. Knowledge of particular books, or books in general, does not function as cultural capital. When you talk about a book with a Smokehouser, you don't defend an interpretation or extrapolate a moral; you tell what it's about and whether it's worth taking the time to read. What a person "knows" is regarded as a function of his or her own everyday experiences, not as a state of apprenticeship to any kind of intellectual tradition as defined by a body of written texts.

Relationships to written texts further disclose beliefs about the nature of the connection between knowledge and social power. Whether a given person spoke of literacy as instrumental skill or a moral good had to do with his or her orientation to the goal of upward mobility more generally; Joe, for example defines "literacy" as a set of encoding-decoding skills necessary for success in the job market:

> God, you have to read in anything you do, you know? What kind of a job do you want to have? You know, if you can't even go in there and fill out the application . . . ah, you can't really get a very good job, if you just don't know what you—you know, if you can't read anything! That's—and it does matter. You can go in there and flip burgers and you don't have to read anything, but—if you want to get into, like, a more specialized trade or something, you gotta read.

Joe equates illiteracy with the inability to fill out forms, but Perry links illiteracy to a poorly developed critical capacity and political sensibility:

> I think that, um, the more educated—in my experience, it's been—the more educated people are, the more liberal they are in their views. So therefore, if you're not literate, and if you don't get educated, you're never going to be . . . you'll be lacking in—you won't be able to handle this big racist thing we've got.

With the exception of Joe, these Smokehousers accept the humanistic belief that literacy allows for, or is at least in some way linked to, critical thinking and political awareness. Their narratives show that they are quite aware that literacy is associated with an elite way of thinking associated with exposure to written traditions through formal education and, further, that talk of "literacy" might mark them as deficient: when I asked Arlen to explain what he saw as the connection between literacy and standard of living, he objected that he couldn't answer the question on the grounds that "maybe I'm a little too illiterate to understand you." But even though exposure to written texts is generally regarded as a virtue among these Smokehousers, I believe that they in fact hold books in high regard as sources of knowledge, but they simply do not use them as symbols of membership in a class culture that derives its identity from association with written traditions.[16]

Just as Smokehousers do not associate themselves with or define their knowledge in terms of established textual traditions, they do not "study" oral language as a way to claim knowledge and thereby achieve social distinction. That this is the case accounts, I think—at least in part—for Smokehousers' hostility toward speakers of foreign languages: that is, they reject the idea that exclusive linguistic behaviors should be a way to express cultural solidarity. As a group that can lay claim to no really exclusive oral or written code, Smokehousers, it seems, believe that they can identify with no oral or written tradition sanctioned by mainstream institutions. Nor, on the other hand, can the culture in which the Smokehouse group participates claim proprietorship of a truly "alternative" language that identifies it as a coherent political group with unitary needs and interests.[17]

Dirty Politics, Crooked Politicians

Although "rhetoric" is no more a feature of the cultural lexicon in Smokehouse society than "class" is, Smokehousers clearly take pleasure in talking about what public discourses mean and how they work and enjoy professing their own talents as critics of such discourses. Whenever I mention to someone at the bar that I study rhetoric, he or she is inevitably puzzled and wants to know what that means. Upon hearing me explain that I study "how people use language to persuade each other," however, most people express an immediate interest in the subject and hasten to offer their own observations of rhetoric at work. Most of the examples people volunteer of what they understand "rhetoric" to mean concern politicians and political discourses.

As a group, Smokehousers are "political" to the extent that they follow the progress of political campaigns and are interested in the outcome of local and national elections, have opinions about politicians and their issues, and discuss political events and philosophies with each other. They are concerned mainly with local and national politics and do not typically express an interest in international politics, except inasmuch as "foreign affairs" have a direct bearing on American interests. Talk about politics pervades every genre of Smokehouse discourse from joking to storytelling to conversation to debate; in this way, talk of political matters operates discursively much like any other topic that might be the focus of public dialogue. What distinguishes it from other kinds of talk, however, is that established members of Smokehouse society—Arlen, Joe, Maggie, Perry, Walter, and I, among others—take on individual identities, or argumentative personas, with respect to positions on political issues. This dynamic will be the substantive focus of the following chapter on the language of political arguments; I mention it here to show what is at stake in asking people, in interviews, about their political beliefs and affiliations.

In asking about politics, I wanted to find out as much as I could about how people at the Smokehouse positioned themselves as political subjects in a world of other such subjects, to understand how they defined the political relations that affected their lives. Because talk of politics is likely to be framed as performance—as metacommunication in which individual roles and group identities are established—at the Smokehouse, such talk no doubt carries the residues of these metameanings into other communicative situations. Although both interviewees and I may make a good-faith effort to leave our argumentative personae at the door before entering into dialogue with one another, no doubt these personae nonetheless shape the terms of the exchange during interviews. This is not to say that parties in the dialogue go right on speaking "in character" or in the roles in which they have been accustomed to performing in public debates at the bar: rather, it is the awareness each person holds of the connection between argument and performance that makes him or her wish to convince the other that conventional public roles do *not* prevail in this new communicative situation. It was quite clear to me in these interviews that each person to whom I spoke wanted to convince me that he or she was *not* the same as his or her argumentative persona (though this presentation of an "honest" private self could, arguably, be motivated by a desire to lend credibility to the public persona). In any event, I learned much about what Smokehousers wanted me to know of what they "really" believed when they were not compelled to take on performative roles. I had the impression that each interviewee, without exception wanted me to see him or her not as a one-dimensional representation of an established point of view but as a complex, evolving subject.

Even though my role in performative arguments at the bar has traditionally been to oppose viewpoints sanctioned by consensus, those I interviewed did not seem to expect me to take on this role outside the public space of the bar. Respondents referred only occasionally to my professed political views in explaining their own; in this context, nobody seemed to want to challenge my views one-on-one. Asking Smokehousers about their politics in interviews had the effect of carving out a space in which interviewees might elaborate freely on their own views without suspecting that I was motivated to "prove" them to be in error in some way. As "politics" is a subject that I can discuss with other Smokehousers on level ground—unlike "education" or "work," which throw into relief issues of class identity and social affiliations—interviewees were perhaps less likely to suspect hidden agendas in questions I put to them about "politics."

Though most of the people who frequent the bar at the Smokehouse enjoy theorizing about politics, they do not express confidence that they are empowered as agents of political action. When Arlen told me during the last presidential election that "it don't matter who wins; nothing ever changes, anyway," he voiced an oft-expressed conviction among Smokehouse people. Joe confided to me in our interview that he did not take part in the last national election and attributed his reluctance to vote to his belief that politicians in general do not represent his interests: "I just, ah, haven't had any people running that I really felt strong that I wanted to be in the Oval Office," he explained to me. Smokehousers believe that "nobody represents me," that no public, political voice speaks entirely for the needs of the white working-class—as evinced by the tremendous popularity of "independent" presidential candidate Ross Perot.

Yet despite this rampant skepticism, many Smokehousers insist that it is important, in any case, to *try* to make one's political voice heard.[18] Ironically, the pervasive "it doesn't matter what I do" attitude often expressed by Smokehousers parallels a conviction that it is one's obligation as a citizen to "get out there and vote." Arlen, on the one hand, laments the inefficacy of casting votes and the meaninglessness of political change, yet maintains, on the other, that it is important for people to vote because "if they're gonna bitch about something, they better get out if they wanna change it—it's the only way they can. Arguin' at the bar isn't gonna change anything." And Walter is adamant about the importance of voting:

Do you think it's important for people to vote?

Absolutely! Absolutely. I don't agree with the concept—you have some, ah, one of those hillbilly philosophers, says, he says, Yeah, I don't vote for the sombitches—the sombitches in politics because it only encourages 'em! See? In other words, you know, well, I voted for you—well, okay, you must think I'm a good guy. He says, I want them to know that I *don't* think they're good people . . . so I don't vote. And I think that's terrible. I think you should vote. . . . You make the best of the worst choices.

The ambivalence of Smokehousers' remarks about their political agency resurfaces again in their commentaries on the production and distribution of political information through the news media: that is, about public purveyors of information, as well as about the political process itself, there is a general belief that it is necessary, as Walter puts it, to "make the best of the worst choices." Smokehousers want to be regarded as individuals who are well-informed about politics and current events. They presented themselves as critical consumers of public information vigilant against rhetorical sleights-of-hand, and they wanted to be sure I understood that they were not taken in by everything presented to the public as truth. The suspicion that "they're not telling us the whole truth" was a theme that emerged time and again to express the conviction that the public (us) is always in danger of being duped by a power bloc or politicians and their media representatives (them). To a person, these five Smokehousers said that they did not trust news media to report "just the facts" and pointed out instances of deceptive rhetoric at work in the media. Joe, for one, complained to me that the media

try to color things, to—to bring you around to their point of view—they just try—they're—they're more into sensationalism than they are, into, um, the facts. Ah, to where they will, ah, kinda sensationalize things, just to make good news. . . . [A]h, if they gave you the real story, it's probably going to be boring as hell . . . but you know, they gotta make it sound better than it was. That's—that's—look at it, you gotta look at news as entertainment, right? It doesn't make it right, it doesn't make it good, but, um, it's like wrestling—it's entertainment; it's just there to—if they don't entertain ya, where they gonna be on the ratings? They're gonna be out of a job. . . . [T]hey just—they just feed you what they want you to know, they don't tell you the whole story, they just tell you the *best part* of the story!

Maggie holds that the news media are inevitably biased and explains that it is important to get information from different sources to make well-informed decisions:

I think that the direction that their [the media's] bias takes is, um, has a direct bearing on what's going on. You know? It's like—like, siding with the winner all the time. . . . [T]hey . . . like, when, um, when, um, Bush, with the economy, you know, during the election . . . then, I think that—especially in TV, you know, they portrayed him to be something other than what he was . . . and I think that's because that was the biggest issue, then. I think that—that, um, when the Gulf War was on, he was the big hero and the big savior of the day, because that was the issue then. So I think that they're biased according to the issues, and what is important to the public, because that gets ratings. . . . [Y]ou know, they can swing from one to the other. . . . [T]hat's what I believe.

Perry, who wishes to convey his reverence for knowledge, contrasts his own efforts to remain well-informed with the apathy and ignorance of those around him:

[I] used to read a lot of paper, but I don't anymore—I don't have time now . . . it's—it's TV. And I—and I am a person—ah, Sunday morning is mandatory that every, *every* talk show that's political is . . . ah, McLaughlin group, I listen to that, and the Koppel gang, I listen to that, and Brinkley on Sunday . . . every single political—you know, I'm glued to the—that's—that's very important to me. Just like, I like watching *Sixty Minutes,* which is interesting. But I think, as opposed to—I've had my brother sleep over, and so forth, and he wants to turn on the golf, or some other thing. . . . So his interests just aren't there, and yet he wants to argue those things, it's like, you don't read enough, you don't care enough, you don't listen enough to be knowledgeable enough. And that's, I think, a lot of the problem with people around here. They speak from emotion; they don't speak from really, ah, paying attention, from reading, and so forth.

Perry's references to the circumscribed logics of "the people around here" indicate that he perceives other Smokehousers to be characterized as a group by *lack* of information and critical awareness. No doubt Perry expresses this opinion in part because his views usually oppose those of the others in arguments at the bar and in part because he wishes, as indicated by his remarks throughout the interview, to distance himself from the values and beliefs of the group. Yet each of the five group members to whom I spoke seemed to indicate that it was important to them *to* be aware of "what's going on" and to know how to locate truth in a sea of conflicting bits of information. Even though individuals may wish to distinguish their own political knowledge from that of others at the Smokehouse, Smokehousers as a group seem to believe that, because their interests are not typically represented by political figures and institutions, they can't expect the media to convey disinterested information.

That there is a general feeling of dissatisfaction with the quality of information distributed by news media is grounded in (or linked to) a belief that politicians themselves lack any real integrity. Many political discussions at the bar include extended laments about the immorality or dishonesty of politicians: at the Smokehouse, it is fashionable to complain that when it comes to politicians, "they're all crooks." Arlen says that he does not trust "politicians or lawyers" because they both "make too many promises they don't keep." Joe asks, rhetorically, "Where ya gonna find an honest politician?" He goes on to provide an answer—"Maybe a dead one someplace, that'd be about it"—and explains that he has doubts about whether it is in fact possible for a politician to be honest:

> I don't know! I really don't know—because with all the, ah, special-interest groups
> going in there now, and everybody saying, Well, listen, you know, you do this for
> me and I'll put so much money into your campaign fund, and everything, it's
> just—I really think an honest politician'd be very rare, and I don't think he'd sur-
> vive very long. I think he'd get eaten by the sharks in Washington, D.C. . . . . [A
> politician] that'd win is not an ideal politician—he's just a guy that's gonna take
> care of the special interest groups . . . and, uh, cover, you know, the people that take
> care of *him,* these're the ones he's gonna worry about.

During the last presidential election, this belief that "every politician is tied to the interests of someone, and none of them is ours" manifested itself in a great reverence for Ross Perot, seen as someone who, because of his economic independence, was the only candidate not "in somebody's pocket." People expressed faith in Perot as an apolitical politician, who, as a rich man, could "afford to have his own ideas." At first I thought that Perot, a billioniare businessman, was an unlikely choice, but on further examination, maybe not. The rationale for Perot as a good candidate to represent the interests of working people might be expressed in the following syllogism: all politicians have vested interests. None of these interests is ours. Special-interest groups pay to maintain their interests. Perot doesn't need money, so special-interest groups have no power over him. Therefore, with Perot we stand a fighting chance to have our own interests represented.[19]

Although some Smokehousers, like Perry, claim to vote primarily with respect to "issues," most, such as Maggie and Walt, say that they tend to regard a politician's moral character as a matter of paramount importance when making political decisions. Maggie maintained that she votes with attention to "character, first," but went on to explain:

> That's how I would wish it to be, but I—how could anyone every really know what
> a politician's true character is, because of the way the—the press represents them,
> and whatever, you know? Ideally, it would be character first, and then issues . . . be-
> cause if you—if you're a person with a weak character, then you won't be able to—
> to take care of any issues, that, you know, the voters find important.

When I asked Walter what qualities he "looks for in a politician," he was un-equivocal:

> Character. Absolutely, character. We had a, a Democratic politician—uh, isn't it
> a crime, I don't remember his name—but how I loved that man! He, ah, he was
> a congressman from Illinois—and every time I heard him speak, I'd say, God-
> dammit, this guy's okay. And when he croaked, they didn't find shoeboxes full
> of money, they didn't find land trusts, and millions of dollars worth of stock. . . .
> [H]e died with a net worth of about sixty-five or seventy thousand dollars—which
> I had myself at that time! I figured, Jesus Christ, I got as much money as that bas-
> tard has! You know? And here he had all the opportunities in the world to make
> scads of money—which they all do, see? Uh, yes, he was an honest man and he had
> integrity. That's what I look for. . . . But you don't find it—you don't find that.
> Look at, ah, Rostenkowski, now, with the scandal he's involved in with the post
> office, he refused to testify, takin' the Fifth Amendment. . . . [S]ee, that's the kinda
> politics I don't care for.

Walt continues in a lengthy excoriation of politicians who, instead of serving as representatives of ideal moral principle, abuse the privileges that accrue to those who hold public office:

> [W]hich brings me to a subject. . . . Our country—and it's still the best system in
> the whole Goddamn world, as rotten as it is—we—we've accepted the fact that
> the president's gonna have a mistress, you know—well, even Eisenhower has his
> mistress! What more sterling character, warrior, or knight in shining armor—
> Dwight Eisenhower?! He had a mistress that went around with him. Roosevelt
> had a mistress. So—what's the logic? So therefore the new president must have a
> mistress! That's poor logic, and it's a sad commentary on the times . . . that we
> gotta say that the president of a corporation has a right to have a mistress, the
> president of the United States has a right to have a mistress. . . . I don't—uh, their
> morals—the congressmen are screwin' them little pages, fourteen and fifteen years
> old . . . like, oh, what the hell, he's a congressman, he should get a little nookie! You
> know? We make excuses for these people—and I think that's bad.

That Smokehousers perceive something of a crisis—or, at least, a lack of coherence—in political identity is suggested in their commentary on who they are as political subjects, as well. Though my perception of Smokehousers—in large part shaped by public performances—in general has always been that they are a monolithic conservative body (to call someone a "liberal" at the bar can be tantamount under certain circumstances to uttering "fighting words"), this turned out not to be the way those five to whom I spoke articulated them-selves and their politics to me in interviews. I would have expected all but Perry to define himself or herself unambiguously as conservative—but in fact, only Joe actually *called* himself "conservative," saying, "Well, I'm not a liberal. No, I'd have to be a conservative, I think. " But he nevertheless went on to qualify this definition of himself, adding, "I'm pretty flexible." Maggie says that she cannot categorize herself either as "liberal" or "conservative," saying that "some liberal issues I feel very strongly about, and there are some conservative issues that I feel very strongly about. So I can't say that I could be one or the other." She goes on to explain that her political identity is to some extent a function of (generally conservative) social contexts in which she finds herself and, in so doing, gives a succinct picture of the climate of public discourse at the Smokehouse:

> I've never—I've never really thought too much about what other people think about me—I don't really care. And, um, I guess if had to think about it, from discussions I've had, then . . . most of the times I get in arguments with people about things like that, it's over the liberal issues rather than the conservative ones. So if people were asked about me, I suppose they would say I was more on the liberal side. . . . Because those are the issues that invite discussion.

Just as Maggie does not wish to identify herself in terms of her political leanings, Arly says he "wouldn't categorize" himself as either liberal or conservative: "I'm conservative and I'm liberal—whatever *that* means." At the same time he suggests the particular nature of his political alienation, Walter makes a point of explaining how his politics are more subtle and complex than his role in barroom debate would have me believe. The following exchange narrates Walt's efforts to define himself against his public persona:

> *Do you consider yourself liberal or conservative? I mean, where on the political spectrum—*
>
> I tell you what Julie—I'm gonna shock the shit outta ya. I'm pretty much of a liberal.
>
> *You did shock me. Why do you say that?*
>
> Ah, I'll tell you why I said it. Um, this is complicated—uh, when I was very young—even younger than before your age, now—and during your age—I was *ultra*-liberal. Uh . . . and I argued with the Republicans, who were . . . mostly conservative . . . uh, according to the liberal view. . . . Now, why am I—why do I say I'm so liberal? Because I told my niece, I says, I gotta look back, and say, All the good things . . . that have happened to me in my lifetime . . . were as a result of social reform . . . fostered by Democrats. Unemployment compensation. . . . See, Julie, you don't remember a day . . . when you could come to work Monday . . . and the boss would say, No, no, go home now; don't punch in. And you sat there, without a penny income, until they called you back. Now, when they come out with compensation, and—er, the liberals, they're all pro-union. All the good things that ever happened in my life, like eye care, dental care, health insurance, vacation with pay . . . all come through the avenue of social reform. Social Security—I'd be in the poorhouse now, if it wasn't for Social Security—Democrat! See, all the good things come from the Democratic party.
>
> *And yet you—have voted Republican!*
>
> Yes! Now, you wanna know why?
>
> *Yeah!*
>
> Now—this is—mind you, at this time, I'm still a Democrat. My wife became ill, and, uh . . . she retired an early retirement with a disability, and . . . and, uh, she got her social security way before her time, which is . . . the Democrats. So now she's on Social Security. Next thing I know I get a letter in the mail, telling her that she should apply for food stamps. . . . [T]hey say if you have grandchildren who—

their parents don't work, or they're—can't find their mothers and fathers . . . apply for Social Security, see? In other words, they went way overboard. . . . Ah, just to use Reagan's words, he says, I didn't leave the Democratic party—he was a Democrat, you know—he says, The Democratic party left me. When it got so bad . . . that everything was "giveaway" . . . see, it went too far, Julie. I *believe* in social reform— I'm—I think the big thing we gotta have now is—is, ah, a subject very near and dear to my heart—care for the aged. It, ah—my father, ooh, he was adamant about it. He said, I helped build this country! Which he did. He said, [in Lithuanian dialect] *I helped make thees contry, ven I came here, notting but trees and voods— and now look! I do thees.* He had much to say about it—but he did do it. He says, *Now,* he says, *I get sick—go die!* You got no money in—oh, God Bless Medicare! Oh, God in Heaven, I could show you my files. . . . I got 'em that thick on Medicare . . . and the money that they saved me. Without that, I'd've been dead a long time ago. So . . . social reform? Uh, Democratic concepts? I believe 'em. But they go too far wid' em. That's the only thing.

Okay . . . do you think that other people see you . . . as a liberal, or as a conservative?

The smart ones see me for what I am. . . . I'm a phony, ah, a phony right-winger—

OH!

Yeah! See, 'cause my views ARE liberal—for the reasons I've just mentioned.

Clearly, those whose voices are represented here are invested in knowing about "politics." But they do not, I would argue, see this investment in political knowledge as a quality that defines them *as* a group, in the way, for instance, *work* does: indeed, the practice of argument is, in one way, about individuals seeking to show themselves to be more knowledgeable about public discourses than their peers. Knowledge of "politics," then, is a way for a Smokehouser to express solidarity with other Smokehousers, while positioning himself or herself—as an individual—in relation to their beliefs.

I learned much in speaking with Smokehousers about their struggles to define themselves as political subjects both in relation to one another and in the larger public sphere. Most of what I had previously experienced of people at the bar expressing their political views had been from a much different position, at the center of public debates. Until I spoke with these five people one-on-one, I had always perceived them to speak with one (to my mind, ultraconservative) voice. The reasons behind this perception are perhaps complex, but I think two points in particular are relevant here: one, that people arguing against me at the Smokehouse are generally motivated by a desire to define themselves as an alliance against whatever middle-class interests I might represent; and two, that the tyranny of my own identification with middle-class academic culture compels me to blur individual distinctions in my efforts to position myself rhetorically "outside" the group. So what had always seemed to me to be a group with a unified, coherent political orientation turned out to be, in a context removed from pressures to publicly perform opinions, a loose collection of individuals with a diversified—and, I am inclined to argue, fragmented—political subjectivity.

Much of what these five had to say about themselves as subjects in the world of political affairs indicated to me that, as a group, they were at something of a loss to define themselves and that this particular disorientation was linked to what generally seems to be perceived as a representational void: that is, people at the Smokehouse are struggling to know "who they are," given that they lack a voice in the public sphere to speak for their needs as working people. This much is indicated in their commentary on their distrust of the motives of the media and of the ethos of politicians in general. Given the social and economic needs of working people, mainstream institutions fail to persuade us of the legitimacy of their discourses; this failure of rhetoric means that Smokehousers tend to feel excluded from political debates going on "outside."

That people at the Smokehouse believe they have no voice in public political rhetorics means that they see themselves as removed from politics as a system that provides opportunities for parties to make and enforce *meaning* in a public sense, and therefore conceive of politics as social management: for Smokehousers, "politics" is what will happen in practice to manage resources (consider, in this light, Arlen's "it don't matter who wins" remark). Smokehousers do not see themselves as meaning-makers in the political sphere—they feel empowered only to approve or disapprove of agendas marketed by politicians.

Finally, I suggest that the representational void Smokehousers perceive has something to do with the value of (private) public debates to this group. Because people at the Smokehouse do not identify with a unified political orientation, Smokehousers can experience themselves as a group with common political interests is through the practice of argument, negotiating an emergent political voice.

Common Logics of Identity

In speaking with those whose views and voices appear here, I learned that even these five, who constitute but a small sample of the total arguing population of the Smokehouse, do not, in fact, "think alike." As their narratives illustrate, attitudes and opinions about most "issues" show a range of variation. But even though particular Smokehousers may express a range of beliefs about specific issues, the larger picture that emerges from data generated in interviews is one of a social group whose cultural identity is linked at one end to its means of making and gaining access to knowledge and at another to its political subjectivity.

As a social body, Smokehousers are, undeniably, a cohort of people with complicated motives, attitudes, and identifications. Yet certain features of Smokehouse common logic are important in understanding the terms of social identity. First, people share a sense of alienation from mainstream educational and linguistic institutions. Second, they believe that representation by political parties and their representatives is lacking, or, at the very least, ineffective. Third, they share a conviction that applied knowledge gained through experience ("street smarts") is more valuable than purely theoretical knowledge ("book learning"). And finally, their feelings of alienation and disenfranchisement from mainstream channels of knowledge and power exist alongside the assurance that, in the United States, opportunities for social mobility and economic empowerment are not significantly constrained by political structures.

These inconsistencies should not render meaningless a description of cultural practices; indeed, any culture is, as Lévi-Strauss (1979) and others have pointed out, fraught with contradictions. Lévi-Strauss has argued that it is the *mythology* of a culture that mediates (if not resolves) tensions produced by contradictions in its worldview. In the case of class culture, these "tensions" are in large part the product of what happens when structural determinants of culture contact local practices. What I have attempted to create, then, is a thematic map of the mythology that sustains the Smokehouse group as a social organism. This mythology, or common logic, is essentially normative but subject to challenge; thus, it determines not necessarily *how* issues are resolved but *that* something counts as an issue in the first place. Jerome Bruner (1990) has theorized that the role of narrative in a culture is to work against the grain of an ideology while maintaining its boundaries as a meaning system; I will show, in the chapter to follow, how argument participates in this process.

After participating in Smokehouse public life *and* speaking to individuals in interviews, I am further convinced that the Smokehouse cohort, which sees itself as belonging to a social group defined primarily by its orientation to the world of work, has an ideological structure organized by features of this identity. Smokehousers, who identify with the culture of working whites, see this cohort as both an established (white) and marginal (working-class) group, as simultaneously mainstream and "other." Unlike people who identify as members of a group in which marginality is a function of race or gender and who have a unified, historically established political consciousness as "other," members of the white working class are differentiated from the mainstream only by their class status and therefore hold a kind of schizophrenic image of themselves as empowered and powerless, as perennially both and neither. People at the Smokehouse seem to feel that they have no access either to established or newly emergent power; they can claim as a political trope neither injustice nor privilege. It is, above all, this perception of existing in a social space that is neither "mainstream" nor "marginal" that imbues the cultural practice of argument at the Smokehouse with its particular shape and meaning.

6

A Place to Stand

Argument as a Class Act

et's get somebody in that can run this country like a business!" exhorts
Jack, in preparation for an oration on the virtues of presidential candidate
Ross Perot. Jack's imperative is publicly directed but carries the expectation that
I, as public dissenter, will take up the challenge it implies. Jack knows what I
will say (always that something is more *complicated* than that) just as I know
his routine (to bait me with a provocative declaration and then to appear to invite dialogue while assuming an increasingly stentorian posture). Both of us
know that the object of this game is to deliver oratory, not to fashion the perfect syllogism. At Jack's exhortation, a newcomer to the scene looks alarmed,
apparently having mistaken this ritual fabrication of a cultural text for a rup-
ture in the social fabric. I know that before my shift ends, the virtues of the
candidates will have been vigorously debated, and each of us will have been
changed only in our renewed commitments to our original convictions.

Smokehousers know, when they enter into arguments, that persuasion—
as a publicly professed change in alignment, at least—isn't likely to happen.
That arguments continue even so suggests that such occasions of agonistic rhetoric are, nonetheless, an important part of discursive processes through which
belief is constructed publicly. The practice of argument not only allows one
person to persuade others of the legitimacy of his or her claim to speak "for"
the group about something (and thereby to assure his or her own status) but
also works to persuade participant-spectators that there is a common social
investment, an assurance of collective identity. Yet these kinds of *indirect* persuasions demand that arguers commit to the public belief that arguments
stand a chance of effecting real and immediate change in *individual* speakers,
that they maintain the social fiction that *direct* persuasion—as a change in the

"deep structure" of belief effected by dialogue in argument—is possible. If arguers didn't profess this belief—if they did not proceed "in good faith"—argument would be revealed as a staging, a framing for narrative and occasion for performance. The persuasive potential of a given argument depends not only on what counts as truth for Smokehousers and on who has the right to speak that truth but also on what kind of authority it carries as an established genre. In treating arguments as attempts at direct persuasion, I aim to locate mechanisms of indirect persuasion by giving interpretive priority to the public processes by which ideologies are produced and negotiated.

Argument as Genre and Event

Smokehousers may be hard-pressed to explain exactly the rhetorical features that characterize an argument, but they know one when they see one. People know, through formal features and contextual cues, the operative speech in a given speech situation: they know, that is, when someone is attempting to initiate an argument, what signals joking, and for what purposes stories are told. Sociolinguists would say that this intuitive knowledge of the social rules governing speech codes means that Smokehousers share a special *communicative competence*[1] (e.g., Hymes 1974). Yet even though—and no doubt because—I share this competence, the information it organizes is difficult to codify: such knowledge is tacit, and varieties of talk at the bar shift and flex as a matter of course.

A newcomer arriving at the bar on a busy night would find herself a spectator at a carnival of discourse and could discern only with great difficulty which rides were truly dangerous, which acts involve trickery. She would be struck by how quickly friendly converse becomes heated debate and would no doubt be equally impressed by the ease with which loud disputes resolve into laughter. These abrupt turns and resolutions are possible because of the aggressively conventional nature of argument, a fact Smokehousers know: playful commentary on the the highly routinized nature of argument is a common strategy for participants and spectators alike. In a typical scenario, I enter the bar to find Walter embroiled in argument with Jim, another Smokehouse regular. After a perfunctory greeting, I ask, "Any sort of political issues get resolved?" Jim's reply is a comment on the knowledge-making limitations of argument-as-ritual: "No, we haven't figured out world peace, yet." Language games are a vital part of everyday goings-on at the bar, where rhetorical aims and forms are often the very subject of language play: here Roberta, who has been participating in a sustained debate with Walt, Jack, and Maggie about whether or not evidence of philandering would render Bill Clinton unfit to "do the job" of a president, interrupts the dialogue to taunt Maggie, who has teasingly complained about not being given the floor:

1   JACK: I'm not stickin' up—Clinton—in—to me, he's
                      done a good job—in a lotta things he's done.
                      I'm not knockin' him. I'll give him more credit than a lotta
                         people.
                      I don't knock him—I don't knock him for what he did.

5	MAGGIE:	So you're saying, that you would not—
	JACK:	That's what I do not think—
		if you're gonna beat him—just what Perot said—
	MAGGIE:	—vote for him?
	JACK:	I don't care. I don't want a gay in there,
10		'cause it's gonna cause problems.
		I want someone to—do—the—JOB.
		That's all I'm sayin.'
		I want someone, twenty-four hours, to do the job,
		to get people this, this, THIS. I don't need—
15	ROBERTA:	Maggie—if we're in here workin'—
		and we got one waitress—
	MAGGIE	[laughing] I don't even get to talk! You guys shut up!
	ROBERTA:	[singsonging] Nya, nya naa, yooou don't get to ta-alk!
	MAGGIE:	That's not fa-irrr!
20	ROBERTA:	Time's up! Discussion's over. Let's talk about religion now.

Following Maggie and Roberta's playful exchange, there is a burst of laughter and the argument about Clinton's infidelities resumes. Roberta's teasing commentary about Maggie's unsuccessful attempt to secure a turn in the dialogue (18) bespeaks her knowledge of argument as a conventional form, one that has a recognizable participatory structure and proceeds in predictable ways. In "artificially" bringing the argument to a close and comparing argument about politics to talk about religion—a subject barroom lore characterizes as one in which alignments are utterly intractable (20)—Roberta is calling on her interlocutors' shared understanding of argument as a "mere" rhetorical exercise, as a discursive practice that is distinctive apart from its outcome or content.

To the extent that it is recognized by participants in the Smokehouse group as having a distinct thematic shape and formal boundaries, argument constitutes a *genre*. A genre, Bakhtin tells us, is a form of speech in which "[t]hematic content, style, and compositional structure are inseparably linked to the *whole* of the utterance and are equally determined by the specific nature of the particular sphere of communication. Each sphere in which language is used develops its own *relatively stable types* of these utterances. These we may call *speech genres*" (1986). As Maggie and Roberta's commentary on the appropriate negotiation of speaking rights suggests, Smokehousers understand that argument is a "relatively stable" kind of speech. Though arguments are competitive forms distinguished by contention, arguers work together to create a coherent "text." In imposing generic boundaries on a given topic, contenders in argument mark a space to narrate the common logic. In argument, thematic materials of this logos operate as topoi that can be invoked metonymically by certain conventional symbols, which function in much the same way literary symbols do— that is, that they invoke constellations of historicized meanings within the contexts of generic texts. Even though participants in arguments do not always agree on the "truth" a given symbol conveys in a particular case, they would nevertheless recognize that symbol as a canonical representation of an area of contested *logos*. To invoke Ross Perot or Jesse Jackson or welfare in an argument is, therefore, to call into play a whole set of philosophies, assumptions, and values.

An important generic feature of argument is reflexivity: arguments refer to *themselves* as much as anything else. Participants in an argument frequently step outside its ostensible frame to comment on the way the argument is being conducted. An argument is like a role-playing game in which players interrupt the proceedings to interpret or enforce the rules; in this way, arguments are always *about* the subject of argument, no matter what other topics they appear to engage. Early one bustling Friday evening, for example, Walter called me over to where he and Dan had been excitedly discussing the potential of presidential hopeful Ross Perot. Perot had just announced his candidacy, and my opposition to the candidate had not yet become public knowledge. Walt's drinking companion, Dan, is privy to the argument but does not speak until the very end, and then only to comment on Walt's commentary. Note that the conversation begins as a civil dialogue but threatens to escalate into argument when Walt suspects that my motives are to make him lose his footing by challenging him to explicate his own position:

1	WALT:	So what do you think of Mr. Perot?
	JULIE:	What do I think of him? I don't like him.
	WALT:	I'm afraid of him. I like him—but I'm afraid of him.
	JULIE:	What are you afraid of?
5	WALT:	Uh . . . [long pause] almost like a draconian type of . . . atmosphere
		that he would . . . impose upon our country.
		And we're not ready for a draconian type of . . . enforcement,
		you understand what I'm trying to—
	JULIE:	Yeah, I think I do . . .
10	WALT:	To put it in a few words . . . you know . . . I think, in—
		now, now to be, ah, way out on it—
		ah, in three months he'd have our country in total anarchy.
	JULIE:	You think so?
	WALT:	Oh, he's just too ABRUPT—
15		and our system doesn't tolerate abruptness,
		And, ah—
	JULIE:	You mean, he's—as opposed to kind of thorough and methodical, and . . . that kind of thing?
	WALT:	Oh yes. Oh yeah—
20		[as Perot]This is it! This is IT!
	JULIE:	Well, that's what appeals to people so much.
		That's what appealed to them about Reagan—
	WALT:	But I'll tell you what! Probably in the long term—
		I mean the loooong term, not a four-year term—
25		this is what our country needs desperately.
	JULIE:	What . . . does our country need?
	WALT:	This type of leadership!
	JULIE:	But I don't know what type that IS!
	WALT:	[skeptically, with contempt] C'mon Julie, yes you—
30	JULIE:	What Perot represents? No.
	WALT:	[impatiently] Yes! Sure you do!

JULIE:	No . . . I suspect it's what you're describing, but—
WALT:	Sure you do, sure you do. . . . [Y]ou're just being provocative.
	You know what he stands for!
	And you know the type of leadership he would provide . . . and it's not at all in keeping with your concepts.
JULIE:	No, you're right.
WALT:	Well, of course I am! [laughs] I'm always right!
DANIEL:	Oh! Oh! Mea culpa! Mea culpa! Mea culpa!

35

My exchange with Walter nicely illustrates the self-referential tendency (as well as the generic boundaries) of argument. Like Roberta's "let's talk about religion, now," Walter's accusation that I am somehow operating in bad faith by being "provocative" and asking (what he suspects to be) rhetorical questions (28–36) indicates that he has picked up on generic cues that signal my intention to frame the conversation as an argument by demanding that he make explicit knowledge that we already share. The comic bombast of his agreement with my admission that he's right (38) signals his intention to derail my plan to frame the discourse as an argument by making our disagreement the subject of a joke (38), one that implicitly comments on the shared assumption that arguers are heavily invested in their own oppositional, intractable positions: we both *know* that arguers do in fact believe that they're always right, or at least behave as if they do. As the self-referential nature of arguments show them to be *about* the possibility of reaching truth through dialogue with others, what is always *at issue* in argument is the conduct of the rhetorical process itself. In arguments, people are free to contest the proper methods, ethics, and applications of rhetoric in a "safe" generic space, that affirms their commitment to the solidarity of practice.[2]

As useful as the idea of speech genres may be in describing how Smokehousers know an argument when they see one, it can't fully account for how argument operates as behavior-in-context; that is, it can't help to explain what argument *does* for those who produce it. Apart from its status as a special *form* of talk, every argument is a cultural event and has a layer of meaning as such. To get at this layer of meaning, the fundamental sociolinguistic idea that utterances must be interpreted in situ as *speech acts* is useful. As Richard Bauman tells us, "speech acts and genres are, of course, analytically distinct, the former having to do with speech behavior, the latter with the verbal products of that behavior" (1977:27). That Smokehousers themselves regard argument as much as an *act* as a kind of speech is suggested in their frequent commentaries on the rules and meaning of argumentative behavior. When I asked people outside the public space of the bar why they liked to argue, they spoke of argument as if the practice itself *did* something for them. All had mixed feelings about participating in barroom debates and spoke of arguing at the Smokehouse as an ideally stimulating and edifying activity, yet, in practice, all too often a frustrating exercise in futility. Everyone agreed that at best, arguing could present opportunities for exposure to "other" points of view. Walt, for instance, told me that he enjoys arguing with others at the bar because you get smarter that way. When you're talkin' . . . all you're doin' is sayin' what you already know, and what you think. But when the other guy's talkin', he might say something that you don't know. So I enjoy arguin' sometimes just to get the other guy's position. . . . [I]t's good to know how the enemy thinks.

Maggie speaks as well of how public debates allow for access to new perspectives and provide opportunities for self-definition:

I like to argue, because I think—only, argue, but not fight; argue but not judge, you know, try and—it's very hard to do that, because it, you know—I—one of the things I can't stand is when people say, never judge anybody else—you go through your life judging and comparing other people, because you only know what you are . . . and if you can't learn by other people, you know, you—you have to judge them to—to take the good and the bad and the right and the wrong from each one . . . and so I think that, things like, religious discussions and political discussions, and arguments, and things like that, *are* a way to grow—because if you can't ever argue, and hear someone else's viewpoint, then how are you ever gonna . . . open your mind to new ideas? Without reading, and you know, things like that . . . but . . . it's a way to learn.

That Walter and Maggie voice clear expectations about what argument *should* do—and concerns about its potential for abuse in practice—suggests that for Smokehousers, argument is not merely a way of talking but a meaningful social *event*.[3] As event, argument is a speech genre that serves a specific function for Smokehousers as a group: to manage ideological tensions in a safe generic space.[4]

One way to understand how argument-as-event accomplishes this cultural work is to consider its relationship to other expressive practices at the Smokehouse, such as conversation, joking, and narration.[5] Of these, conversation is perhaps the most difficult to characterize as an event with generic rules and boundaries, because it is the ongoing stream of discourse in which other genres, like islands, stand exposed. Conversation is the default, the unmarked case; the ur-genre. It is the generic stream of nongeneric discourse. Smokehousers refer to this unmarked, nongeneric speech as "shooting the shit," or simply "bullshitting." It is the form of talk that is perhaps the closest to referential speech and as such is least likely to be framed as metacommunication. Other practices, such as joking ("giving shit") and telling stories ("telling it" or "telling it like it is"), are more likely to be marked as routinized events, to have a more pronounced performative component, and to happen in conjunction with argumentative events.[6] Giving shit, for instance, provides a means by which views that threaten the common logic can be relegated to a safe generic space and also a way for members to express the kind of solidarity that comes of being sufficiently committed to the common interest to be permitted to exploit the limits of acceptable speech.

On any given night, shooting the shit makes frequent detours into giving shit; you don't enjoy the right to "get shit" unless you hold an established place in Smokehouse society. To give someone shit is to engage in playful metacommentary on the viability of one's distinctive public persona; it is, in effect, to distinguish someone as an individual by attributing generic features to her persona. The seemingly paradoxical nature of this act bespeaks the nature of the relationship of individual to group: one enjoys status as an individual to the extent that one can successfully embody, without sublimating one's distinctive persona to, the public demands of the collective identity. With such proximity, however, comes danger, and one who as been given enough shit may finally, in exasperation, direct one's antoginist to "eat shit." Yet most of the time, giving shit works to defuse hostilities, not to engender them. Here, for instance, Maggie's spilling of a drink provides the opportunity for Arlen to give Maggie shit and for Roberta to give *me* shit. As each person adds a voice to the event, it takes the shape of a generic event:

[There is a crash as Maggie's glass tips over and falls onto her barstool]

1	ALL:	Whoa!
	RANDY:	Oh, very good!
	ARLEN:	Uh-oh!
	ROBERTA:	Oh, Maggie's cut off!
5	MAGGIE:	*I* have to sit there!
	ARLEN:	That's okay. [Maggie laughs]
	RANDY:	Yeah, don't clean it up. She has to sit there.
	ROBERTA:	Oh! [laughs]
	ARLEN:	Your butt is like a big sponge, anyway.
10	MAGGIE:	[to Roberta] How come you put an olive on my chair? [Roberta laughs] Ooo—did you hear what he said? I'll have you know that my butt is my business, and YOU just better shush.
	ARLEN:	*Roberta* said that!
15	JULIE:	An OLIVE?
	ROBERTA:	[laughing] I did not! *I* put an olive on her chair!
	MAGGIE:	She put an olive on my chair.
	ROBERTA:	Oh, God—you'd think somebody goosed her—
	JULIE:	What, is it like—
20	ROBERTA:	—I don't know, she just jumped up!
	MAGGIE:	It was NASTY.
	JULIE:	How could you feel it? Is this like— the princess and the pea, or something?
	MAGGIE AND ROBERTA:	[laugh]
25	JULIE:	Someone'd hafta put an onion on my chair before I'd feel it, you know?
	ROBERTA:	[slyly] More like, a watermelon!

By giving shit in this way, Smokehousers habitually strengthen the bonds between them by implicitly agreeing to stretch the limits of what it is appropriate to say. As metacommunication, the meaning of the above exchange is something like "We're all such good buddies here that we are willing to tolerate such transgressions."[7] The implication of the insult—that Maggie and I are bottom-heavy—(9, 27) is not quite true *enough* to press the limits of appropriateness; the joke has a metcommunicative, not a referential, function.[8] Joking creates a climate of nervy goodwill that both produces solidarity and indicates the contributions of individual personae to the distinctive constitution of the group. Such a climate of aggressive sociability yields fertile ground for the seeds of routinized agonistic discourse.

Giving shit is one rhetorical strategy Smokehousers use to manage the demands of intense public engagement. But it is upon narrative—*telling it*— that I now wish to focus, since the status of narrative as a particular kind of collaborative text is important in understanding the role of argument as another such text. In anthropology and folklore, there is a long tradition of reading oral narratives as repositories of cultural information, and studies of storytelling practices in a variety of cultures have yielded data that suggest, according to folklorist Robert Georges, that "stories can reflect cultural reality or distort it. . . . [T]hey can reinforce the social structure and threaten social cohesion. . . . [T]hey can function as conditioning mechanisms and instruments of social control or as escape mechanisms and instruments of social criticism" (1969: 315). Along these lines, Jerome Bruner theorizes that "stories, carried to completion, are explorations of the limits of legitimacy" (1990:50). At the Smokehouse, publicly recounted stories allow for collaborative evaluations of everyday events. One way that Smokehousers realize, confirm, and challenge the prevailing logos, in other words, is through the public construction of narrative. As event, telling it can be enacted in the terms of various subgenres—the race story, the revenge story, and so on. As "storyable" genres, these narratives realize topoi and are themselves persuasive events.[9]

One particularly storyable subject in Smokehouse talk is race relations.[10] Late one uncharacteristically indolent Monday evening after the dining room had closed, Roberta, Maggie, and Arlen were relaxing at the bar after finishing work in the kitchen: Maggie and Arlen with mugs of Lite beer, Roberta with her usual Tia Maria on the rocks. It had been an especially slow night, and of the regular crowd, Jack, who had been waiting for Roberta to finish her side work in the kitchen, was left behind as the sole survivor of the late crowd. I sat on the tiny stool Perry allows us to keep behind the bar for the slow times, enjoying a leisurely smoke. The mood was too congenially lazy for argument, and the topic of conversation found its way, as it so often will, to the quirks and entanglements of other Smokehousers. In this case, the subject was Trisha, a waitress who lived in Roberta's neighborhood and who had been embroiled in an ongoing feud with a neighbor. In what follows, Roberta has control of the floor as she narrates the story of Trisha's feud, but the narration frequently takes the shape of dialogue, with Jack and Maggie contributing testimony and exegesis to move the narrative along. The story is clearly meant for all to hear, but Roberta begins the narration by addressing Maggie as audience:

1	ROBERTA:	Oh, God, she [Trisha] is so funny. . . . [L]isten to her. . . .
		[D]id you hear about the fight? They had another fight,
		um, the black people that live next door to Trish.
		Now, you heard about the ongoing fight, right?
5	MAGGIE:	The lawnmower . . . ?
	ROBERTA:	Yeah. All right—now, Don [Trisha's husband]

was playing his tape—er, his, uh, stereo—
and Don doesn't play it REAL loud, but it's—
you can hear it in the house, you know—
10   and, uh, they called the police, and said,
Tell him to turn down his stereo,
and when the police got there, he had his stereo on, and
         they said,
Well, did you just have it blaring, or what? You know, he
         goes, *No, I said,*
I haven't touched it. . . . [Y]ou know, he says *I turned*
15   *it on, and it's set at a certain dial,* and you
know, a certain, you know, thing. . . . *[N]obody touches it.*
And they went, *Forget it, then,* you know.
Well, I guess Don and the guy got into it, okay?
And—now, Trisha already called the woman,
20   *You bitch, nigger bitch,* and everything else, and
I don't care if your monkey's sleeping. Okay?
Now, they're going to court for this one. Don went out
there, and the two men are now fighting, and . . .
Don called him an orangutan. . . . [H]e goes, *Why don't*
25   *you hop over the fence, and hit me?*

ARLEN: Didn't the guy call him a faggot?

ROBERTA: Yeah. And, well, anyway, they—back and forth, back
            and forth—

JACK: Yeah, and that's after he called him a faggot first, and said,
30   *C'mere and suck this!* and that's when Don said,
            You orangutan, come on over here. . . .
            I mean, you gotta make it—

ROBERTA: Well, anyway, they both wanted the other one to hit
            first, right? And neither of them would hit, because
35   both wives got on the phone, like, Whoever hits first gets
               the police button.

MAGGIE: Oh, God!

ROBERTA: It's to the point where—you know, this is getting weird.

ARLEN: Well! [greeting Sid, a newcomer] Hey, Sid!
            Lookit—you've got all the friends in tonight.

40 JACK: Sid!

ROBERTA: Well!

JULIE: Hey, Sid!

MAGGIE: Hi, Sid.

SID: Hi.! Hi, everybody.

45 ROBERTA: So anyway, one thing led to another, and, uh . . .
            now, I—we—we cannot WAIT for police to do any—
            we're going to court. We're going to court,
            we're all gonna wrap up little monkeys, uh, stuffed animals
               in blankets,
            and we're gonna be rockin' 'em in the back of the
               courtroom,
50   making Trisha laugh when she has to go to court . . .
               [laughs]

	JULIE:	Is this TRISHA?
	ROBERTA:	Yeah!
	JULIE:	Now how did this whole thing start? What—?
55	ROBERTA:	Trisha was . . . what the hell—? Oh! she let her dog out.
		Now when you have a dog,
		one of the first things it does when it goes outside is,
		it barks . . . no matter if there's a leaf moving,
		or whatever . . . maybe three or four times.
60		Trisha does not let her dog bark—I have been there.
		This woman . . . called the police, and said—
		instead of comin' over and sayin',
		Hey, I got a baby, would you have your dog . . . not bark—
		well, she called the police. Three times!
65		Trisha has never had the police at her door, okay?
		And . . . one thing led to another, and so
		Trish got mad because the police gave her a ticket—
	JACK:	No, no, no—
	ROBERTA:	—for her dog barking!
70	JACK:	—no, no, wait, no—
	ROBERTA:	Wait, wait—
	JACK:	[to me]—you have to understand, wait, wait, wait—
		now, this is—what I'm listenin' to Trisha—I've
		known her for twenty-three years—
75	MAGGIE:	And nothing ever happened . . .
	JACK:	[to me] Wait, Foop, I've been livin' here for twenty-three
		years—
	MAGGIE:	The dog's nine years old . . .
	JACK:	—I have never had a ticket, where a policeman come in,
		and ticketed me for anything my family, my whole thing—
80	ROBERTA:	She even buys her village stickers on time!
	JACK:	—and because they have—they have called you, you're
		comin' in to my house, and giving me a ticket
		for my dog barking . . . at eleven in the morning.
	ROBERTA:	Yeah.
85	JACK:	She . . . FRIED.
	ROBERTA:	So, she decided, *Okay fine, my dog can't bark,*
		well, by God, you're baby ain't gonna sleep, either.
		She got her lawn mower out—now, in between the
		houses—
	JACK:	NOW you pissed 'em off . . .
90	ROBERTA:	—here's Trish, NYRRRRRRRR!!! I mean,
		she has no grass in between the houses. . . .
		[T]his is how long Trisha was cutting grass.
	MAGGIE:	And she left it run, and went inside and
		was taking a shower. . . .
95		[T]he lawn mower's right outside these people's window!
	ROBERTA:	[laughs]
	MAGGIE:	And now, the—
	JACK:	Now, you have stirred up—oh, man—

	ROBERTA:	Now the police come back—
100	MAGGIE:	—and tell her to shut off the lawn mower—
		and she comes out of the shower!
		So she can't say—
	ROBERTA:	No, no, she come out of the shower,
		she said she was on the phone . . . with her daughter from—
105		the lawnmower was only runnin' for five minutes—
		the call—*I had a long a distance phone call from my daughter,*
		I didn't have time, I can't keep her on the line, I didn't have time,
		that lawnmower was only runnin' for five minutes,
		she's tellin' the cop. Cop gives her a ticket for a public nuisance! [laughs] And
110		it's just one thing after an—
		so that's when Trisha goes, *Hey, nigger, nigger bitch, c'mere!*
		You know, and it's like—Trisha is not one to mess with. I mean, she is—
	JULIE:	No—I—
	ROBERTA:	I wouldn't—I mean, I'll tease Trish, you know,
115		I call her up every once in a while and go,
		You know, you wanna shut your dog up, it's really givin' me a headache. . . . You know?
		And she just hangs up the phone now [laughs],
		This is very SENSITIVE. . . !
120	JULIE:	She might—she might start on ethnic slurs, or something—
	JACK:	Well, no—Trish'd go—Trish'd go in a second.
		But she has got that temper, but she also has—
		you know, she backs off. But I mean, I do not—and I've known her
		for a long time—I just gotta laugh at her.
125		She's—she can get . . . GRRRRRRR!
	JULIE:	Did she have any confrontations with this neighbor before?
		I mean, did they know each other?
	JACK:	No.
	ROBERTA:	Nothin.'
130	JULIE:	Did they say hello, did they know—?
	ROBERTA:	No.
	MAGGIE:	No, but the lady just had a bab—
	JACK:	No, you know what I told her, my advice to her was?
		No, I told her, ah, if—if—you know, what kinda people are they?
135		Go to the black preacher, where they go to church.
		And I told her, Nip it in the bud. And she didn't wanna hear it.
		And I said, Look: get it—I said, Get it—I said,
		There's no sense in your kids, your old man, their kids, their old man—

		I mean, no, you start something—
140	ROBERTA:	All right, no—give ME some advice!
		What about the ones that live next door to me?
	JACK:	Your boys . . . set it off. They told you to shut up—
		they did the same thing when they were kids—and to leave 'em alone!
		When—
145	ROBERTA:	Wait . . . wait, wait, WAIT. My kids . . .
		did not get picked up for carrying sawed-off shotguns down the middle of the street.
	JACK:	That ain't the point. When they were harassing you, they said,
		Shut up, and don't worry about it. Okay—
150	ROBERTA:	Oh, yeah—?
	JACK:	—all I can do is . . . you know what you're doin' here.
		They know what they're doin' there.
		So I'm not gonna jump in to what they're doin'—*I* don't know!
		I'd go out there—I would take ten guys . . . and beat 'em to death.
155		Are they gonna come in now and throw a—a thing in your window,
		and blow ya'll up? *I* don't know that! THEY know that!
		THEY got the barometer for it . . . ah, fine!
		I could get anyone killed, you know . . . that don't take nothin.'
		You can take a gun, or you can pay someone five hunnerd
160		and THEY can kill someone. That's bullshit!
		But the point is, what's gonna happen to you and your family?
		You—you have to THINK.
		My point was, get a happy medium, and let's just talk.
	ROBERTA:	I don't want a "happy medium" with them.
165		I just want them to go a-way!
	JACK:	That ain't the point. Ah—ah, it's—the point was—
	ROBERTA:	Well, they ARE gonna go away . . .
	JACK:	—well, with Trisha, it's—you're better off just to talk, all right?
	ROBERTA:	Yeah, well no—I told Trish, I says,
170		Go out there, say Hi to her, smile. . . . [K]ill her with kindness.
	JACK:	Y—You've got an Israeli; you've got a Muslim—you c—
		you know, this's what's wrong with the world—
	JULIE:	I agree—
	JACK:	—you got people that—you know—but I mean,
175		you gotta have a medium, to talk . . .
	ROBERTA:	Yeah. Well—but see, her—her neighbors aren't . . . violent.
		The only—the—the worst thing they've got is
		they yell at each other. . . . [aside, to me]
		No, and they're not blacks that live next to me—
180		it's whites. And they carry shotguns.

In addition to its storyable potential, this story is also highly tellable—that is, it not only expresses an important theme but also functions as a social event to identify individuals and to promote social cohesiveness. Although Roberta frames the story of Tricia's feud as a humorous anecdote, it is nonetheless a narrative encoding of the common logic of race relations. On the one hand, Roberta does not overtly sanction Trisha's behavior—in fact, the very extremity and irrationality of Trisha's actions are the source of the story's humor; Jack, who is interpreting Roberta's narrative to me as something other than a story that applauds racist behavior, comments on Trish's volatility (121–125). On the other hand, Roberta's construction of Trisha as a (hapless) comic character serves to exonerate her of any real responsibility for the incident—and, by extension, absolves herself of the racial implications of the narrative. She frames the story as a tale of one person's eccentricity, not as an exemplary account of race relations (1–2). At several points in the story, Roberta's testimonial is supported by others in the group: Jack, Arlen, and Maggie supply background information and explicate motives and events (26, 28–30, 70–79). The dispute between Trisha and her neighbor is presented as seriously funny; Roberta's account of it explains the absurdity as the result of two idiosyncratic actors in a dramatic farce. The deflection of the serious matter of race relations into comic anecdote bespeaks the heuristic power of narrative to impose meaning on an unstable situation, one in which social power is very much at issue: Trish's experience, thus recounted, serves as an example of the state and meaning of race relations. Narrative becomes one way for the group to explain itself to itself while foregrounding the importance of individual roles.

The rhetorical situation constituted by the story's audience dictates its meaning beyond its referential "content." My presence as part of the audience for Roberta's story, for example, affects the terms of its rendering. Although Roberta, Arlen, Maggie, and Jack collaborate to create the narrative text, both Jack and Roberta are aware that I represent an opposition to the common logic of race relations (the essence of which expresses itself here as "black people make bad neighbors"). Even though I never overtly challenge the terms in which the story is told, it is, finally, an attempt to persuade me of the truth of the logic it encodes—and by making me the putative audience, the tellers persuade themselves that the dispute that is the subject of the story is a buffoonish skirmish, rather than tragic confrontation. Jack, who knows I would disapprove of Trisha's behavior, attempts to justify Roberta's claims to me. He constructs an ethos of rational observer and defends Trisha's motives to me to create a more sympathetic character in order to make the narrative logos credible. In mentioning her shotgun-carrying neighbors (175–180), Roberta appeals to her own ethos as well to convince me that her motives for telling the story are not racist by implying that she knows that whites can make bad neighbors, too.

The referential connotation of "telling it" (like it is) notwithstanding, constructing narrative in the realm of public discourse not only reframes events and expresses authority over the social world but also works as a process whereby individuals can cultivate the social authority that will work as situated ethos. As the Tale of Trisha shows, people rely on narratives to help them manage the chaos of everyday life, to relegate the unmanageable to a bounded and contained social routine. Storytelling can be a way to run events through the interpretive mechanisms of the common logic without directly intervening in them or appearing to challenge the terms of the logic itself. On another occasion, Roberta and Maggie were chatting about Mark's reputation as a wife-beater. Mark is an important figure at the Smokehouse and runs a martial arts school where many of the women who work at the Smokehouse go to learn karate and kickboxing. Going to Mark's classes has become a weekly ritual, an important way women spend leisure time together outside the bar. Here, Roberta tells Maggie, Arlen, and me of Trisha's contempt for Mark:

1	ROBERTA:	You gotta hear this one! Trisha wanted to pull
		over—Mark Morelli has a billboard of himself—
		I mean, he has a biiig billboard, right by—
		you know where St. Thomas is?
5	ARLEN:	Yeah . . .
	ROBERTA:	Well, there's a billboard—it says,
		[in a deep, important voice] 'Bad Choppers, Kickboxing by Mark Morelli'
		it's got a picture of him there, and T—and Trisha goes,
		Let's get a can of spray paint one night, go up there, and put down,
10		"How To Kick"—the way it says, "Kicking," and all that; "Kickboxing"—
		"Kick Your Wife"—ah, I mean, just—all this stuff in spray paint . . . [laughs]
		and I go, with our luck, we'll be arrested, I says, I ain't doin' that!
	JULIE:	Oh, God . . .
	MAGGIE:	Oh, it's just—it's just . . . nature's justice,
15		you know, nature's justice—a bird shit right
		on his head. There's a great big bird doodie right
		on his head!

In telling this revenge story, Roberta and Maggie make their disapproval of Mark's behavior public by making him the butt of a joke. Just as Trisha expresses a desire to revise the story of himself Mark has made public via the billboard, Roberta and Maggie revise his story to challenge his authority as member of the group. Though Mark himself is not challenged—to do so would be threaten the structures of sociability that good relations with him organize—the narrative challenges his authority indirectly by divesting him of situated ethos. The Tale of Mark establishes the roles and relationships not only of the narrators but also of the narrated.

Although narrative, like argument, is a way for people to construct public commentaries vis-à-vis the common logics, argument differs from narrative in significant ways. First, it is an agonistic genre in which dissenting viewpoints are foregrounded. Second, and perhaps more important, it is, as a speech event, closely associated with verbal performance.[11] Events such as narrative and jokes are often rendered performatively, but incidents of argument are almost always expected to be occasions for performance: in fact, the decision *not* to perform can be read as a decision to make a "statement," the meaning of which, qua statement, is usually something like, "What I'm saying is not being said for the purposes of competition of gamesmanship; therefore, you know it's motivated by nothing but honesty" or "I'm not really one of *them;* therefore, I'm not trying to persuade you of anything *they* would be likely to think." As we will see, resisting the pressure to perform—*refusing to call attention to one's appeals to ethos*—is one way to invent a more effective persuasive ethos.

That Smokehousers themselves sometimes don't recognize the *extent* to which argument overlaps with performance might be taken as evidence that argument-as-performance could pass as an unmarked, "natural" phenomenon. When I began my fieldwork at the Smokehouse, for example, I didn't set out to study *performance.* I knew that arguments were dramatic, but I had not yet begun to realize that they may in fact *be* drama. In one especially telling entry in my field journal, I confidently asserted that there was "nothing much happening tonight"; now, looking over the data again, I see that what I was really remarking on was the absence of *performers.* What I had been calling "argument" is what I would now, after reinterpreting argumentative events in light of their structures of participation (and in light of other research on verbal art), call "performance." Yet from the start, I knew intuitively that what counted as "good data" was speech that had a distinctively performative component. My own attempts to *generate* such "good" data by provoking performances indicates, I think, my implicit knowledge of the status of the genre of argument as performance. Now, however, I would claim that the following relationship obtains: arguments make performances possible; performances frame narratives; narratives proclaim the relation of the group to the world.

Performance is not, therefore, a special *kind* of language at the Smokehouse. Rather, it is the act of calling attention to the very *performability* of special topics, and to the people whose social "job" it is to *enact* speech in which cultural values are encoded.[12] Arlen's reactions to my efforts to collect ethnographic data on argument underscores performance as a function of argument: Arlen, who was always aware of what I was "looking for" at the Smokehouse and who always knew when I turned the tape recorder on, was of all Smokehousers most alert to the dynamics of specific data-collecting episodes. He would not uncommonly make oblique references to my study when he knew I was taping an argument in progress and would chuckle, full of suppressed mirth, into his beer when he knew things were "happening." He would sometimes even make provocative statements that he thought might inspire "good data," as when, during an argument about Perot among Walt, Tom, and me, he opportunistically seized the occasion to "heat things up" by invoking a recent series of performances in defense of a local artist's having put (as part of a display) an American flag on the floor of Chicago's Art Institute:

1   TOM: Perot's very refreshing to a lot of people because
                          he's not afraid to stand up and say what people did wrong. . . .

		[H]e's not saying a lot of what he would DO about it, but he's refreshing for people to listen to.
5		But I agree with you, he scares a lot of people—
	WALT:	Oh, he frightens the shit out of me!
	TOM:	—because y—the way he would wanna run the office, the presidency's no longer a one-man job—
	WALT:	I think he's the kind of leadership we need, but—!
10	TOM:	—but Congress would never let it happen.
	WALT:	Oh, no! And the people wouldn't let it happen! Oh, they'd hit the streets, and they'd be burnin' the goddamn buildings, and . . . Julie and her friends'd be out there with the frickin' flags, and—
	ARLEN:	WALKING on 'em!

Arlen's sly attempt to trigger a performance from Walt indicates that he sees arguments as generic opportunities for performance and that he knows just what topic is likely to provide the thematic material for a potential performer. Arlen's mention of the flag is both a commentary on the dynamics of my relationship with Walt and a provocation of the kind of confrontation that typically leads to performance. It also bespeaks the tendency of particularly memorable performances to find their way into the canon of Smokehouse lore, where they themselves become resources for narrative.[13] Although Arlen attempts to urge Walt into a performative posture because he (Arlen) is "in on" what I'm up to in my study, he has been known, on other occasions, to raise volatile issues when the circumstances are ripe for confrontation, only to withdraw into spectatorship. As Arly's provocative behavior demonstrates, arguments can be much like boxing matches arranged for the entertainment of a public and are therefore "best" when they are highly stylized, dramatic, and (apparently) spontaneous. As his mention of the flag incident shows, performances can be signaled by the invocation of culturally significant symbols, which act as cues for players to get into character and perform a scripted role.

Though performances may appear to happen spontaneously, they are in fact anything but spontaneous. Whenever one launches into a performance, one is, inevitably, speaking in dialogue not only with one's history, sociopolitical position, cultural assumptions, and social alliances but also with the imperatives of a particular speech situation. Smokehouse performances are enacted in predictable ways and might appear to follow generic formulae; they are highly structured events that conform to complex orchestrations of rules and circumstances.[14] At the Smokehouse, they are marked not only by special codes and paralinguistic features but also by a discernable shift from speaking *to* or *at* or *with* an audience, to a speaking *for* them. It is almost as if the performer becomes a medium who channels the voice of a displaced collective consciousness and who earns notoriety by his convincingly poetic rendering of this consciousness. The audience is as much the source of the speech's logic as it is target of its effect; the performed speech becomes an appeal to pathos masquerading as logos, in the service of ethos.

Jack and Walter Tell It to Me Like It Is

Insofar as a performance entails a *speaking for,* it is an assertion both of a logic and of one's right to articulate it. Because a performer is, in effect, saving face as well as preserving a tradition, he or she must identify entirely with the view professed. An exemplary performance, starring Jack, happened as part of an argument that took place late one evening in the summer before the 1992 presidential election and illustrates some of the culturally specific ways a speech event is marked as performance by those who take part in it. Here the topic is (as was so often the case at that time) Ross Perot, who has just announced that he would reenter the presidential race after having dropped out of it some months before. I had just finished the early shift and was then seated at the bar with Roberta, Arlen, Randy, and Sid; Maggie had taken over behind the bar for the late shift. Jack, who speaks in support of Perot, here gives a series of dramatic monologues. Jack begins with an exposition on why Clinton's lack of military experience would make him a bad choice for president and ends with an exhortation in the voice of Perot himself:

1	JACK:	Most presidents get you in a war, just don't know what a war is all about—
	ME:	Aauugh, God—!
	JACK:	[in reference to the Gulf War]: At least we went in
5		and won!
	RANDY:	And Clinton doesn't have the credibility to—
	JACK:	But usually—like Kennedy, he just lost everything.
		Uh, you know—he didn't know what he was doing.
		I would rather have a military man in there now. . . .
10		I'd say . . . get somebody in that's gonna realize,
		the people in this country need WORK.
		And I don't think either candidate knows that.
		Clinton will—Clinton will ask people to give people that aren't working,
		and to /do/ something, but it's . . . I have a business,
15		Perry has a business—there's no more left!
		There's no more left, you understand?
		And so somebody . . . that is a businessman . . . has to take over this country
		—and the hell with the world! say, the HELL with the world!
		But we have to again . . . build up an army . . . with the Army. . . .
20		I think this man—ah, he owes nobody nothing.
		He don't have people who are . . . trying to elect him. . . .
		[Y]ou know, he got to be bought—he can't be bought—
	SID:	Right . . . you're talkin' about Perot . . . ?
	JACK:	Right. And I am for him, because he said—
25		and I listened to him say it a thousand times to people who are interviewin' him:

>   We're talkin' about jobs!
>   We're talkin' about jobs.
>   We're talkin' about—Clinton, what's HIS policy?
>   We are going to straighten out Medicare;
> 30   we're gonna have it so everyone's gonna have an insurance
>   policy . . . out of a business!
>   I can't afford it!
> ARLEN: [to me] Yeah, be FOR it—we'd close NOW!
> JACK: Yeah, we—what is he TALKING about?
>   There is no business knowledge there!
> 35   No, frick the world, frick the arms; FRICK all that—
>   I want a man that knows how to run a business. . . .
>   Get this country back working,
>   get those good jobs back!

During Jack's monologue the others are, like a well-behaved audience at a lecture, attentive and silent. Everybody here understands that Jack's speech is meant to display his oratorical style and to articulate the group's logic of practice by showing how an issue has real-life applications for Jack and others like him. His speech articulates a common theme: the emphasis on work and jobs (11–23, 26–28) endorses the work imperative and casts him as one who speaks, from his own practical experience, to the practice of Perot's political theory. Rhetorically, the speech is constituted by heavily stylized chunks of narrative—in this case, anecdote and testimony—which are themselves constructed from devices such as parallel constructions (35), repeated words and phrases (18, 26–28) and reported speech (26–28). My move to challenge the assumptions I see underlying Jack's assertions that the country can be "run like a business" is what cues the performance: that challenge to Jack's logic prompts him to move even more squarely into oratorical mode, a mode that amplifies, but does not explicate, the original premise:

> 1   JACK: Let's get somebody who understands . . . money!
>   JULIE: But he understands it from a point of view—
>   now, what is Perot's plan for welfare reform?
>   ROBERTA: The people would be WORKING!
>   JACK: The point is, hon, we're going like this—
> 5   JULIE: HOW? Is he going to—is he going to advocate child care for
>   women—
>   JACK: —Jul, we're going like this! [makes a masturbatory gesture]
>   People are bein' taxed, taxed, taxed!
>   JULIE: —who want to go back to work?
>   JACK: Do you understand what's happ'nin'?
> 10   ROBERTA: They already GET child care free!
>   JULIE: No, no, but I mean, if they want to get OFF welfare,
>   and go get a job at minimum wage—
>   how are they going to get ahead?
>   JACK: You didn't even understand what we just said.
> 15   He is the ONLY one talkin' about jobs,
>   and neither candidate talked about jobs,

		until Perot got in, and was thirty-six percent! He said,
		I don't wanna talk about nothin'—Jobs!
		They said, Well, what about the gay issue?
20		He said, *Bitch, I said, JOBS!*
		And they said, What about this issue? He said—
	ROBERTA:	If everybody in America pulls together and everybody was working, then MAYBE—
	JACK:	—the country needs jobs! Don't worry about the tax system, if we have jobs there'll be taxes,
25		all the programs'll stay intact.
		And they kept askin' him questions.
		I don't wanna know about that—JOBS!
		He's the ONLY man that talked,
		If you don't get this country working, then you're gonna have no money—
30	JULIE:	How's he gonna do that? How is he gonna do that?
		HOW is he gonna make it so that people have jobs—?
	JACK:	[more loudly] I would rather have him than Bush or Clinton,
		that don't know nothin' about a job,
		other than suckin' government money all their life,
35		they don't know a thing about a job,
		they don't know a thing about people in here, who are workin';
		they NEVER have.
		Here's some sonofabitch at LEAST had a company that PAID people!
	JULIE:	Well, you ac—
40	JACK:	[still more loudly] He knows something about jobs,
		what he was talkin' about.
		The other two know nothing!
		They been suckin' off the government,
		Bush and Clinton, Gore and Quayle,
45		they been suckin' off the government!
		They know nothin' about jobs.
		Perot has got a big company—you're right!
		And I—I don't know—I will STILL lean toward him,
		because he wants to get people—he understands—
50		I have a business, and I know there's kids come in every day,
		and there's one thing they lack, that I didn't have twenty years ago.
		Donny [Jack's friend and business partner] and I went— thirty years ago—
		we went in the mill, you had a JOB.
		I had a credit union,
55		I could buy a car,
		I could buy a house,
		there ain't a FUCKIN' kid today that could EVER buy a car and a house today—
		he got nothin'!

He—I mean, he's a SCAB!

60   He's makin' five bucks a—you know, an hour, or less—I got
        a daughter!

Ah, five BUCKS?! I was makin' seven, in frickin' 'sixty!

I was—you know—ah, forget it!

This man's at least talkin,' ah, *the one thing this country
        needs, is jobs!*

I don't care about Germany, Russia, nothin'!

65   And Perot is the only man that talked that shit—he's the
        ONLY one!

I don't care about insurance, I don't care about THIS,

I don't care about gays, I don't care about THIS; abortion,

I don't care about nothin'!

I wanna get the country JOBS.

70   I don't care about Europe, Mexico,

I don't care about nobody!

Get the kids in my country jobs! They can't buy nothin.'

And! The more they tax, for the system they're in, less and
        less people have business.

Here's a good example—right here.

75   There's less money, the man is makin' less money,

he's fuckin' over the employees—it's less, and it's less, and
        it's less.

I'm no different. For the first time in my life, I laid off two
        people! You know?

And I mean, I watch Tony's Pizza—no! it's less, they keep it
        up!

The real estate taxes went up, insurance is up forty-

80   seven percent, but—and—they keep it up! Whaddaya
        gonna do?

You need someone that got some frickin' sense!

NOT, oh, we're gonna make the government—

MAGGIE: People WANNA work—people don't wanna sit home.

They want—to—work!

85   JACK: That's bullshit. There's people that want to work, though—

MAGGIE: That's what I'm SAYIN'—they wanna work!

JACK: Yeah . . . but . . . there's gotta be someone who can direct,

that knows what jobs are all about.

It's—you can't have—Clinton, Gore, Quayle, Bush—

90   you know, huh, the government'll pay 'em! You know—you
        know—but,

do THEY have vacations? They have, you know, I mean,
        they're paid all the time!

If—if [Perry] don't have the money, he don't get a vacation,
        no one gets a vacation!

I don't get a vacation! This is BULLSHIT!

You should—the government should work . . . and balance
        their budget; if they don't,

95   they penalize them, where the government is trillions of
        dollars in debt!

Bullshit!
Get someone in there, that understands—the Japs don't do that,
the Germans don't do that. . . . [T]hey help their people.
And they have—you know—NO.
100   This is . . . the only guy, that—
I don't know anything about—talk for talk,
you can take your Clinton, he's gonna run you under;
Bush is gonna run you under;
I don't KNOW if the other guy's gonna run you under,
105   he's makin' sense to me. . . .
Get the people in this country jobs.
I don't wanna talk about gays,
I don't wanna talk about abortion,
I don't wanna talk about ANY of yer other bullshit. . . .
110   Once everybody has a job in the country,
it'll be right..
We—we'll be able to feel good about it—
Everything!

Jack's oratory is marked as fully performative in the rhetorical strategies it employs: there is, in fact, little new information delivered. Jack establishes his authority not by displaying his intellectual virtuosity but rather by constructing an ethos of experiential wisdom, or "common sense." By rendering the common logic in a style uniquely his own, Jack both showcases his own rhetorical expertise and articulates the group's conventional interpretation of its political predicament. His performance draws from topoi that articulate the common logic of the group: politics is a bunch of privileged types blowing smoke. The more talk there is, the less action. Work is the life experience that qualifies you to speak and to make decisions about the lives of others. The job situation is getting worse. Unemployment is the most pressing issue in national politics and is the economic base of—not just another example of—social identifications. Jack's authority as cultural spokesperson accrues exponentially and recursively: his role at the bar entitles him to speak these common logics and, in so doing, he qualifies himself further to do so.

Having assumed the force of this unitary voice, Jack protects his narrative from challenges from other logics by drawing his own ethos like a protective shield around the common logic. He resolutely resists any efforts at intervention in his speech: he cannot be induced to qualify what he says, nor is he willing to answer any of the questions I pose along the way, but instead escalates into a performance in which he amplifies his point as he dramatizes a familiar Smokehouse theme, declining opportunities for manufacturing jobs. He maintains his dominance of the floor by controlling the topical structure of the argument: Jack insists that the solution to all other social ills is "jobs," and though he doesn't explain how Perot will actually create them, he implies that I'm missing the point by complicating the Perot equals business sense equals jobs equals solutions to all social problems equation. Roberta attempts to intervene, but Jack will not allow an aperture into his oratory even for others to voice support.

Jack's technique of reporting Ross Perot's words gives his narrative added momentum. Far from removing layers of metacommunication to reveal another's speech in its most unmediated, referential form, the strategy of reporting (really, resituating) the words of another amounts to reinventing his or her words for one's own purposes. As Tannen (1989) explains, reported speech both reinterprets the utterance reported and produces a constructed dialogue that adds dramatic force and calls upon a fictive collaborator to authorize the utterance (109–112). In effect, Jack's own exhortations come together in a duet with Perot's yet more powerful ones; Jack's voice situates Perot's, and Perot's authorizes Jack's. Jack-as-Perot-as-Jack speaks powerfully of the interests of *those who must work,* if not the "working class."

It falls to me, then, to support the performance by dissenting from its terms. If the speech seems to be directed as a response to my challenge, it is actually aimed at, and stylized for the appreciation of, his larger audience. Although Jack's performance is attuned to the pathos of the group as a whole, it does so by attempting to discredit my ethos as Liberal Democrat Clinton Supporter. That the speech emerges in the context of the challenge allows Jack's performance to succeed as a dramatization of Smokehouse common logic—albeit disguised as an impassioned exhortation of an individual speaking, in the most immediate way, "from the heart." Though I become more and more peripheral to Jack's oratory, my presence as obvious dissenter makes the performance possible: without a contrasting background against which to set the common logic of the group, Jack's argument would by heard by his audience as "pure show," would be revealed as strategic discourse, and would undermine Jack's authority to speak cultural truths. By rendering these truths publicly and in a style uniquely his own, Jack manages to distinguish himself even as he proclaims solidarity with the group. And by speaking to persuade the others of what they already believe to be true, Jack constructs an ethos of practical wisdom, or "common sense."

Jack's audience facilitates his performance more than it would appear, given his dominance of the floor. As much as his speech looks like the composition of an individual orator, it is profoundly dependent on the complicity of others, whether or not these others actively endorse its logic. That this is in fact the case is indicated by Sid's reaction to Jack's polemic. After a reverent silence, Sid—a foreign-born portrait artist who makes short but frequent visits to the Smokehouse and enjoys congenial relationships with the regulars, though he shares neither work history and nor social ties to the larger community—speaks. He implicitly calls into question the motives for, and rhetorical purpose of, Jack's speech:

1	SID:	If Perot has approached you and proposed to pay you—
		to pay you to say all the things that you are saying
		on his behalf tonight, would you say them?
	JACK:	Would I WHAT?
	SID:	Would you say them the way you did? If Perot had
5		approached you before tonight, and paid you—
		proposed to pay you, you know, with a proposition

to pay you, would you tonight say all the things you said, or—?

[There is an uncomfortable pause. After a moment of consideration, Roberta speaks.]

10   ROBERTA: Noooo, because if he believes in something, no—

JACK: No . . . no. I said, I LIKE Bush. I'm gonna be honest with you.

I don't care if this kid [indicates me] don't like him—*I* like him! [laughs]

And I—I would—he's [Perot]an asshole.

He [Bush] don't know nothin'—no! He don't understand the need of the country.

15   I'm goin'—if I don't like Perot—this sonofobitch won't let an employee have a beer,

and you have to wear a frickin'—I mean, I don't—

I don't like nothin' about him, other than what he says is correct.

I wanna see kids. . . . [Y]ou know, I have kids come in the store; they need jobs!

Because it is raised by one who is not generally seen as a central member of the Smokehouse group—and who himself has no performative persona—Sid's question about the purposes of Jack's rhetoric throws its status as *event* into relief and effectively violates the tacit rule prohibiting public acknowledgment of performance *as* performance. In calling attention to the performative nature of Jack's speech, Sid raises the possibility that the speech does not succeed in making appeals to logos, that it actually relies on an interplay of appeals to ethos and pathos. Sid's implication that Jack's oratory has another metacommunicative purpose besides its ostensible purpose of allowing the speaker to "tell it like it is" causes both Jack and Roberta to hedge uncomfortably and prompts them to disclaim the very performativity of Jack's performance (10–15). Jack, who is aware that Sid has exposed him in his real capacity as performer and that this perception damages his ethos and thereby his right to narrate the logos—to tell it like it is—attempts to reestablish his ethos as nonperformer by announcing that for all his support of the independent candidate, he doesn't really *like* Perot: "he's an asshole!" (13) In this way, Jack reaffirms his own status not as a rhetor but as a truth teller by intimating that he, as one who deals in pure logos, is not in fact trying to construct an ethos. He is, after all, persuaded not by Perot's own political ethos, not by his own pathetic identification with him, but by the intrinsic logic of his views (11–18). Roberta, then, helps to restore Jack's credibility as one who tells it like it is by recasting Jack's ethos as situated, rather than invented (10). Paradoxically, Jack is fulfilling his responsibility in *speaking for* by disclaiming that very responsibility.

It is significant that the performance is delivered in response to my implicit critique of the conventional association of work and moral virtue. To disrupt the syllogism that *good presidents understand work, Perot understands work, therefore Perot will make a good president* is to encourage Jack to reassert the terms of the syllogism stylistically: what he can't prove through appeals to the common logos, he'll demonstrate through appeals to ethos. Because performances at the Smokehouse do tend to appeal to the thematic structure of the common logic, however, implicit challenges to that logic often trigger performances. It is for this reason, I would argue, that argument is the genre in which performance is most likely to happen—and why I, as one who in many ways *embodies* opposition to the common logic, tend to have the effect of cueing performances.[15]

Here Walter, who has been declaiming his admiration for Perot, clicks into a performative mode the moment I voice my opposition to Perot. Stephanie, who has overheard the conversation between Walt and me from her post behind the bar, comes over to ask Walter about his feelings about Perot:

1	STEPHANIE:	Did you like him before more than you do now? Perot? Is that what I heard you say?
	WALT:	Well, I still like him, but I'm afraid of the man . . . I'm afraid of him. He'd have our goddamn country in flames in three months.
	JULIE:	I feel very apprehensive about him. . . . I don't—
5		I'm not impressed with him.
	WALT:	I love him! Oh, I'm impressed with him!
	STEPHANIE:	As soon as he opens his mouth . . . you wanna know why I'm so disappointed when I hear him speak?
	JULIE:	Yeah! There's not much substance, it seems . . .
10		Arlen [aside, to me, speaking of Walt]: He loves him, but he'd have the country in flames in three months . . . ha, ha—shit!

In speaking to Stephanie (whose ultrafeminine, nonconfrontational presentation of self makes her neither a viable candidate for performance nor a potential antagonist), Walter expresses lukewarm enthusiasm for Perot. In response to what he perceives as a challenge to his logic, however (9–10), Walter is unequivocal in his loyalty to him. In commenting on Walt's immediate shift from "I like him, but—" to "I love him!" Arlen attributes Walt's inconsistency to his subordination of reasonable discourse to the demands of a persona, and so implies that it is motivated by something other than the intent to enter into productive dialogue. Arlen's dismissal of Walt's argument (15–16) serves as further commentary on the tendency of argument to fail as persuasion by inviting performance.

As Arlen's cynical commentary on Walt's rhetorical motives suggests, the who of a given speech situation determines its status as performance as much as the what and the how: Arlen has come to expect Walt to perform and is therefore alert to cues that signal his assumption of a performative persona. The context of arguments is not limited to the situational elements surrounding the speech event; rather, it is constituted by the entire interactive arena, itself subject to mediation and redefinition by participants (Briggs 1988:14). In this way performers not only operate within, but themselves make up, performative contexts. The first criterion to which a Smokehouser must conform in order to claim the right to perform is that he or she (usually he) must, at some level, embody the common logic of the group. As Bauman has noted, performers are typically individuals who have been entrusted with the responsibility for defining the communicative competence of the group, for performance "involves on the part of the performer an assumption of accountability to an audience for the way in which communication is carried out, above and beyond its referential content" (1986:5).

Jack's monologue in praise of Perot is a fair illustration of the tight relationship between the what, the how, and the who of performances at the Smokehouse. First, there is Smokehousers' belief in the status of work as moral virtue, as well as a more generalized belief in the value of the practical over the theoretical that is such a central theme in the common logic. As a politician who presents himself as apoliticial, Perot appeals to Smokehousers in part because he represents these values. Jack, himself symbolic of hard work and ascendancy to successful entrepreneurship (he worked in the steel mills most of his life until he had the means to obtain a small business of his own), has, as one whose own life illustrates the claims of the common logic, the performative ethos to speak in support of Perot. Jack's gender, age, and status as regular at the core of the group coalesce to give a him a role as representative of the group's political interests and social identity. (Sid, on the other hand, as an immigrant and independent portrait artist, is less equipped to speak the logos, however much other Smokehousers may like him and even "agree" with his views.) There is therefore a reciprocal cause-and-effect relationship that obtains in the matter of *who* can claim to perform: only those perceived as having the status and authority to speak as legitimate voices of the logos may act as performers; but, in turn, the act of performing imparts status and confers authority.

Walter, like Jack, often speaks in the role of performer in arguments. Like Jack, Walt is an older man, a son of Eastern European immigrants, who "made his own way" and who has earned his educational credentials mainly from the "school of hard knocks." Roberta and Maggie sometimes take on performative roles in argument—roles they can claim by virtue of theirs status as workers—but these are often supporting roles to performances by men. On the rare occasions when only women are present at the bar, performances of this kind are rare (Roberta's occasional attempts to take on the role of performer sometimes earns her the disapproval of other other Smokehouse women, who see in her behavior a dangerous display of masculine "toughness"). In general, the right to perform corresponds, on the one hand, to the status hierarchy of the Smokehouse group: that is, men are more likely to perform than women; regulars, than nonregulars; bartenders, than waitresses. On the other hand, however, as social roles are dynamic rather than static, the meaning and nature of this right to perform changes from one circumstance to the next and from one time to another: that is, one may provisionally invent an ethos. Of course, this *invented* ethos establishes one's role in the community, and one's prior role constrains the possibilities for invention. Also, that someone is entitled to perform in the "lead role" does not necessarily mean that he or she will accept the part. Some, like Arlen, rarely perform but nonetheless serve as instigators of or catalysts for performances.[16]

Even though individual Smokehousers may choose to perform or not, performances are ultimately enacted for, by, and within groups: as such, they express the collective limits of the logos. Bauman (1977) points out that, typically, verbal performances express a tension between tradition and innovation, between conservative and emergent forms and beliefs. It is not surprising that this tension should be enacted at the Smokehouse, where conflict between political orientations is precisely at issue in political arguments. In order for performed arguments to illustrate the scope and pull of the common logic to Smokehousers themselves, performance situations must include not only someone who speaks *for* the logos but someone who appears to speak against its terms. Whether or not both of these poles are made explicit (that is, are actually voiced) in performances, it is the implicit presence of an opposition that makes performances possible and links performances to argument-as-event. Each person who participates in a performance, whether or not he or she is playing the lead, is positioning himself or herself in relation to possible poles of argument and is speaking *in terms of* the logos.

When I began my research at the Smokehouse, I was convinced that I was the unwilling occasion for these performances. I had not yet begun to realize the extent to which I had always been, however much I disagreed with views professed in performed arguments, complicit. As much as Smokehousers construct me as a symbol of bourgeois interests, I implicitly endorse such a construction by subordinating the local experiences I do share to my alignments with educational institutions. I now know that performances—even when they happen in arguments—are consensually engineered and are not the property or creation of a sole actor (no matter how imperious he or she may be) hamming it up for a passive audience. As in any drama designed to impart a piece of wisdom about what happens when people with different ways of perceiving the world come into conflict, performances at the Smokehouse begin with a cast of characters, some playing supporting roles, some acting as foils, villains, narrators, and so forth. Jack may play the lead, but his rendering of the script depends on the staging work others do, whether or not they are entirely supportive of the rhetorical positions he professes. Each player may interpret the same script differently, but these interpretations actually complement each other to create a unified drama: in this way, people at the Smokehouse play individual roles in a given performance, but the story the drama tells is the story of the group as a whole. The nature of the contention in performed argument is, in a sense, analogous to the relationship between the soap opera heroine and villain who spit at each other while the cameras are rolling, but who walk off arm in arm when the day's work is done. When Jack or Walt or Arlen attempts to "push my buttons" (that is, to say provocative things to elicit a dramatic reaction), he is in effect prompting me to get into character and play my part in a spontaneous, but nonetheless scripted, performance.

To see how the responsibility for speaking *for* is assumed and called into play, I present another example that features what Bauman (1992) would call a more "negotiated" performance. In this case, there is no coherent performative text as in Jack's speech; the exchange looks as if responsibility for speaking is distributed rather more evenly among the participants. In the following argument, I am cast by Walter in the role of antihero and am challenged to defend a position I am never given the floor to speak. Yet, unlike the prior episode featuring Jack, the argument appears to be more balanced throughout and looks more like an actual dialogue in its sequencing. The argument involves Maggie, Roberta, Jack, Arlen, Walter, and me and grew out of an exposition by Jack on Bill Clinton's suitability for the office of president:

1	MAGGIE:	And-and I wouldn't vote for Clinton. You know, he—
	JACK:	Julie—
	MAGGIE:	—he dodges the draft, and that's an issue, at least for me . . . you know?
		How come it's okay that—you know, my dad went, and his friend went, and—
		and I mean, my dad's brother went, and he said—
5	ARLEN:	Maggie—
	MAGGIE:	—oh, I just really don't wanna go there, because it's icky—
	JULIE:	Yeah. Well, no—but I don't—
	ARLEN:	Julie, can I have another beer? What time did you get here?
	JULIE:	Yeah, I see your point, except that—would you say there's any sort of, um,
10		moral righteousness to being a conscientious objector, and not going for that reason—
		AAAK! [Roberta appears suddenly in the doorway of the bar with can of synthetic "string," which she playfully squirts over the bar at me. There is an intermission of horseplay; a burst of laughter.]
	ARLEN:	Julie, what time'd you get here?
	MAGGIE:	No, I wouldn't, because my—I don't think that—
	JULIE:	You mean you don't think that it there's—there's an
15		immoral or unethical war going on, that people should say, This is bullshit, we're not going to participate?
	ARLEN:	[frustrated] Mag-gie, will you ask Julie what time she got here?
	MAGGIE:	Julie, what time did you get here?
	RANDY:	One o'clock!
20	JULIE:	Six o'clock.
	MAGGIE:	[to Arly] Six o'clock.
	ARLEN:	[to me] Do you know what time you took over?
	JULIE:	Six-thirty.

[There is more play with the Silly String; Roberta is running around the bar squirting people.]

	JULIE:	Well, this argument has been all over the place.
25	WALT:	What?
	JULIE:	This argument . . . about Clinton and his moral . . . fortitude, or . . . ineptitude.
	WALT:	Ooooh! He's a whore!

MAGGIE: I don't think there's anything wrong with conscientious
    objecting, you know,
    objecting for moral reasons, saying, It's an immoral war,
    and I don't wanna go.

30   But I think . . . that if you're a person in—of a family, you
    know, wealthy enough to support
    and blah blah blah, and you . . . just write a letter and say, I
    really don't—

JULIE: But he wasn't.

WALT: Yeah, but you know—

JULIE: He wasn't—he didn't—

35 MAGGIE: I know he wasn't. I know he wasn't. I just—

JULIE: Not like Quayle!

ROBERTA: That's bullshit, Mag. I've got three boys—

WALT: You know—you—you—

ROBERTA: Why can he sit there, and say—if you had three sons,

40   and your sons were in Vietnam, and Clinton said—

MAGGIE: Oh, no, I—

ROBERTA: —*listen, I'm a conscientious objector, I don't really want to go*—

WALT: That—you're goddamn right, honey!

MAGGIE: That was my poi—

45 JULIE: But what if one of your sons was—

MAGGIE: —the whole point I was trying to make—
    now you can't argue with me; I'm on the same side!

WALT: [to me] Are you of the opinion—

JACK: [to Maggie] No, I understand, hon . . . no, I understand.

50   And it's just—I—I ain't arguin.'
    My only point *I* was tryin' to make was—

MAGGIE: It's not the same for anyone that would not wanna go. If
    they sent you a letter in the mail—

JACK: If my kids are there—

WALT: Yeah, but what kinda country are we gonna have, if—if—

55   if some guy says, I don't like this law, so I'm not gonna obey
    it! The next—

JULIE: Well . . .

WALT: Wait a minute—you people talk about this bullshit! Now—

JULIE: But you ASKED me! [misreading Walt's question as
    nonrhetorical)

WALT: —now the next—now we're gonna have a war—[in a voice

60   of extreme contempt] "Well, I disagree with the war, so I'M
    not GOING!" See?

JULIE: So EITHER—

WALT: So—I don't obey the law, I don't go to war—

MAGGIE: Julie . . .

ROBERTA: Julie!

65 WALT: —I don't like this tax, so I'm not gonna pay this tax—

ROBERTA: Walter—

WALT: —everybody doesn't belong here!

JULIE: Everybody has to make those kinds of judgments—you
    mean—

	WALT:	[with disgust] OOOOHHHH—
70	JULIE:	—there's nothing—
	WALT:	Bull-SHIT!
	JULIE:	There's nothing that—well, LISTEN!
	WALT:	[loudly, banging on the bar] You gotta have a country of LAWS!!
	JULIE:	[with forced calm] Listen—okay, listen—!
75	WALT:	[banging louder] and the laws gotta—everybody's gotta obey the goddamn law!
	JULIE:	Okay . . . now, Walter—what if it were—what if it were a law that was so—so—
	Jack:	[aside, to Arlen and others] Ha Ha, *I* never instigate—
	JULIE:	[imploring] LISTEN to meee—so unpopular, and so contested, and so unethical, whaddaya gonna—
80	Walt:	[roaring] Then you change the law!
	JULIE:	So what about the—so what about the, ah, the people that—
	WALT:	Now, none of that—what about NOTHIN'! Let's stay on the subject! If a—if—if—if there's a war, you GO! You don't say, "Oh, I don't LIKE this war so I'm not going!"
85		Well, who the hell DOES like war?
	JULIE:	So for instance, if you—if—if you lived in Palestine—
	WALT:	Not FOR INSTANCE! Do you—do you think that kids, like this young man here— [indicates Randy]
	JULIE:	[whining] I'm trying to tell you, but you won't LISTEN to me.
90	WALT:	You—you—you—you're gonna change the argument!
	JULIE:	No, I'm not.
	WALT:	I don't wanna change—! I wanna stay— I wanna talk about this young man, here. Next year we get involved in a war—and he's ripe—
95		do you think that he's got the prerogative to say, "I don't like this war, so I'm not going?"
	JULIE:	[smoothly, patronizingly]: It depends entirely on the circumstances. Now, why don't you ask him what HE thinks?
	WALT:	[slamming his open hand on the bar] There's no CIRCUMSTANCES!
100		The law says—the law says, We've declared war on Mesopotamia. . . .
	JULIE:	So what if we declared war, and it—it did not seem like a just cause—?
	WALT:	WE didn't declare war on anybody! Well, this is why I say, I can't ever discuss anything with you, because here you always say, *What if? What if?*
105		BULLSHIT on WHAT IF! When OUR country—when our country says we're at war, it's his [points to Randy] job to go!

A VOICE FROM ACROSS THE BAR:		That's what *I* say!
	JULIE:	So you should do WHATEVER your country says to do, regardless—
110		
	WALT:	That's RIGHT!
	THE VOICE:	It's your job to go!
	JULIE:	So what if you lived in Germany—
	WALT:	Same thing! I don't care WHERE it is! If your country says you go, YOU GO!
115	JULIE:	But who makes these decisions?
		Aren't—aren't you, the people—this is a democracy—aren't—
	WALT:	Oooooh, FUNGU on your GODDAMN BULLSHIT!
		Now you're changin' the argument—who makes the laws, who done this, who done that—I wanna ask you one—
120	JULIE:	YOU said—
	WALT:	[again pounding on the bar for emphasis] I wanna ask you
		ONE [bang!] QUESTION [bang!] And ONE QUESTION ONLY!
		Do you think that each man has an individual RIGHT to obey the law or disobey it?
125	JULIE:	Sure, but I ALSO think people—SINCE this is a DEMOCRACY—
	WALT:	I don't want to hear it! I want a yes or no answer.
	JULIE:	[with exasperation] Wal-ter . . . !
	ROBERTA:	Wait, wait—I gotta ask one question—
	JULIE:	You're imposing all these conditions—
130	ROBERTA:	Do you THINK—
	JULIE:	—and you won't let me impose my own!
	WALT:	Gimme one—ah, I only say one thing [again punctuating each word with a bang on the bar] When OUR [bang] COUNTRY [bang] DECLARES [bang] WAR—
135		does each kid have the right to say, "I'm NOT goin'" or "I AM going?"
	ROBERTA:	NO!
	THE VOICE:	If he's fit to go, he—
	ROBERTA:	[joking] I got a solution to this
		We empty out all of . . . our prisons—
140	WALT:	[groaning] Oooohhh!
	ROBERTA:	—send 'em over to another country—
	WALT:	Aaaahhhh . . . [with a vigorous masturbatory gesture] Polish karate!
	ROBERTA:	—we don't have to pay for their prison—
	WALT:	Polish k—
145	ROBERTA:	What was that? [with feigned shock] WHAT did you say?
	WALT:	Polish karate!
	JULIE:	Oh, God.
	ROBERTA:	[in a mock-scolding tone] Oh, WALTER. That wasn't a nice gesture AT ALL.

[There is a brief episode of joking converse and play between Jack and Maggie, who have been sporadically involved in a conversation of their own. In the meantime, Walt stands to leave.]

	WALT:	Goodnight, Julie.
150	JULIE:	[with exaggerated politeness] Goodnight, Walter. Thank you.
	WALT:	Nice shouting at ya.
	JULIE:	Yes. Thanks. Likewise, I'm sure.
	WALT:	[laughs] Bye-bye, dear.
	JULIE:	Bye. Take care.
155	WALT:	Good luck to ya.
	JULIE:	Thanks.
	WALT:	And try to straighten out your goddamn thinking, will ya?
	JULIE:	Yeah, I'll make an effort.
	ROBERTA:	[singsonging, with cloying cheerfulness] Good-night, Walter!
160	WALT:	[playfully] Oh, shut up.
	ROBERTA:	It's been so much fun arguin' with you again . . . I love ya!
	WALT:	Send all the prisoners to war . . . Jeeeesus Chrrrrist!

Though it does not feature a speaker in full performance, as in the previous example, this episode, like the last, shows performers speaking in dialectic with local standards of eloquence, with a perceived opposition (again represented by me), and with the common logic. As an orchestrated event, it relies on all players to express the dramatic structure of a unified thematic composition. As a cultural text, it narrates thematic tensions not only between political alignments but also between appeals to ethos and and appropriate uses of *what-if*. Let's look more closely at what happens, here. I invite the performance by opening the discussion to Walt's participation (24). Maggie, Roberta, and I are having a civil dialogue prior to Walt's joining the conversation. Walt begins by bombastically reframing Roberta's question to me (39–42) about the circumstances of Clinton's refusal to go to Vietnam: though the question was directed at me and solicits an answer, Walt reconstructs it as a rhetorical question that needs only affirmation: "You're goddamned right, honey!" (43). That reframing is the fulcrum of the argument—it shifts from a dialogue to an occasion for Walt to move from speaking *with* others, to speaking *for* them, a change in stance that signals his taking on a performative persona.

Walter explicitly sets me up to play the role of adversary by addressing me directly and challenging me to state a position overtly: "Are you of the opinion . . . ?" (48). Meanwhile, Jack moves to the background (50): in saying "I ain't arguing," he yields the floor to Walter, who continues to move into a performative posture. He poses a question (54), which is ostensibly directed at me, but which does not wait for a response (57). In redirecting his commentary to "you people," he implicates the whole audience.

In the lines to follow, Walter demands that I answer questions that he either dismisses (71) or uses as opportunities to reassert his position that laws are laws and that it's one's moral duty to obey them (74). As he does so, I unsuccessfully attempt to get Walt to clarify his position (61) or to complicate Walter's assertion (68, 81), all the while acknowledging that such attempts are not getting heard (72, 88). My efforts at begging clarification/complication succeed only in encouraging Walt to assert his position more forcefully (73). Walt's insistence that we "stay on the subject" (83), and his aggressive deflection of any of my attempts to redefine or reposition the subject (87, 99), works to situate the "subject" in a circumscribed domain, one over which Walt has ultimate control.

My contributions to the argument are minimal, at best. Walt will not yield the floor to allow me to elaborate my position, though he insists I answer for it. From Walt's point of view, no doubt I am trying to maneuver the discussion into a place where the logos is exposed as ideology and its adherents revealed as dupes. Possibly, he sees this as a strategy to make him lose footing and face and thereby debunk the logic for which he speaks. To foreclose this possibility, he blocks my attempts to invent an ethos as rational interlocutor and reconstructs me as one who shows off by asking questions, but who ultimately has no answers. I am constructed as one who works against the common logic, though I never really offer any terms in which to do so—except, perhaps, in implying that things are more complicated than they appear. Walter figures me as representative not only of a certain political position but of a particular style of inquiry, both oppositional to the ones for whom he speaks. I continually try to get Walter to articulate the logic of his assumptions, a move repeatedly rejected in dramatic expostulations. Though I try to open questions, the very act of questioning serves only to heighten, not defuse, Walter's performance.

Whereas Walt's performance dramatizes the common logic of public duty and loyalty to country, here again the event is shaped, even made possible, by my role as dissenter. Walter's rhetorical strategy is to show that while I'm merely theorizing about a situation in which I have no real stake, he is advancing a real-life perspective in which philosophical questions have little relevance. When Walt meets my qualifications of the premises on which I view the argument to rest with "Bullshit on what if!" he is resisting my attempts to redefine the conflict as a philosophical rather than a pragmatic one and is really declaring my "theorizing" to have no place as currency in the marketplace of the Smokehouse. Yet Walter himself poses a hypothetical question immediately following his aggressive excoriation of my own (105).

The event finally loses momentum when Roberta intervenes to derail Walt's performance, which has become a runaway train. At first the train thunders along (132–135), and Roberta has to shout for Walter to attend to her hypothetical "solution" to the problem of who should go to war (138–139, 141). Walt, unable to avert the trajectory of his histrionic skepticism, resorts to an expression and gesture of incredulous dismissal that finally releases the pressure of the performance's accumulated steam: "Polish karate!" (142). At that moment the steam is released, and tension is resolved into joking: no one has lost face, and the argument can be aborted without consequence. Our playful goodbyes, as well as the closing commentary on the argument itself, act to recontextualize what actually proved to be fairly heated argument as mere play, to frame it in such a way that has the effect of disarming oppositions and reaffirming group cohesion (149–163).

Walter dramatizes common logics of practice (doing) over theory (saying), even as the argument itself serves to theorize practice, to raise the question: what is the proper place of what-if? The argument opens space for what-if as an activity integrated into the practice of everyday life, yet my own participation in a marketplace where what-if is a commodity—where saying *is* doing—undermines my ability to invent an ethos with which to persuade him to take my inquiry seriously. Lacking a language in which to explicitly theorize class as class, what-if becomes an occasion for performance when it people suspect that I'm using it as symbolic capital, to claim the privilege of the dominant marketplace of forms and practices. My ethos as an academic derails my appeals to the logos I profess: as one with intellectual pretensions who is suggesting that there may be circumstances in which refusing the draft is appropriate, I am read as promoting the interests of those with privilege, specifically the privilege of not having to *work for a living*. On one level, this an argument about the implications of one's class position: recall that the discussion opened with Maggie and Roberta critiquing the idea that social elites should be exempt from civic responsibilities their own sons would be expected to fulfill. My defense of Clinton's actions are read as yet another tactic to invent an ethos of class superiority, to demonstrate my own upward mobility. Walter suspects— and no doubt he is right, at least in part—that my rhetoric is driven not by appeals to logic but by claims to class capital.

My argument with Walter demonstrates tensions in performance between individual and group identities, between endorsements of and challenges to the common logic, and between the dynamism and stability of the speech event itself. There is, finally, a paradox in the act of *performing* arguments, for performances require the assent of the group as a whole whereas arguments are expressions of individual dissent from a unitary perspective. It is, as I go on to argue in the following section, this contradiction that makes performed arguments so essential to the social life of the Smokehouse.

Telling Shit from Shinola: Logics of Persuasion

For players in an argument, the stakes can be high. Arguments at the Smokehouse can be playful and even celebratory, but they can also be grim, petty, and vitriolic. It is a game won at questionable gain and lost at great cost. I have witnessed, and even been a part of, arguments that began as friendly disputations but quickly grew hateful under the influence of too much liquor or the threat of losing face. Once, for instance, Dan called me a "stupid bitch" in an argument about the local politics of race before leaving in a fury. He pointedly ignored me for several days thereafter before Walt persuaded him to seek reconciliation. Such crises are the exception rather than the rule—Smokehousers are willing to work hard to preserve the flow of sociability—but they happen with some regularity.

That Smokehousers are willing to risk much in arguing means that there is also much to be gained in its practice, that the practice of argument at the Smokehouse gives people who are part of that group not only an assurance *that* they belong but also a sense of how, where, and why they belong. To engage in argument is to commit to a belief in the value of the genre as a cultural practice and, consequently, to carve out a space for challenges to received theories (or common logics). I am convinced that my friendships with Smokehousers like Jack, Walter, and Roberta developed in large part not in spite of, but because of, the practice of argument. I did not come to argue with them once I felt "comfortable" with them; rather, I came to feel more comfortable with them because of our collusion in argument. Because the quotidian details of my life as an academic set me apart, I have few viable "stories" to tell—none, in any case, that works as currency in the rhetorical marketplace of the Smokehouse—I find a place by participating in a conventional communicative genre in which the subject of a story itself is less important than a shared belief in the value of it. Just as argument serves to unite Smokehousers *in terms of* their differences, it provides people with a way of achieving provisional status. Arguments are, after all, competitions between individuals for control of the discourse and the "right" to define (or affirm or challenge) the logos. What argument finally "means" for Smokehousers is tied to the system of cultural values in which communicative practices operate as symbolic currency in the rhetorical marketplace of the Smokehouse. This is especially important because the dominant marketplace values communicative competencies predicated on abstraction from local experience. As a kind of cultural currency, arguments are a locally legitimate, covertly prestigious way to achieve distinction, as other, outside status markers have diminished symbolic power within the confines of the bar.

Inasmuch as arguments attempt to affirm, deny, or redefine cultural values, they work as occasions for persuasive discourse. Whereas taking part in performed argument is a way to show solidarity with the group by expressing a shared belief in the value of its *practice,* it is also a way to show differences in *theory.* As such, argument is finally a means by which to take part in constructing (or at least, negotiating) knowledge in the public sphere by persuading others of the legitimacy of certain claims to truth. Clearly, it is easier to judge whether acts of persuasion "work" when they have demonstrable consequences in the public sphere. In performed argument, the primary suasive act has to do with convincing others of one's social legitimacy as a speaker of truth; the success of such persuasive acts can be determined by assessing how others receive performances.

The effects of persuasion on the deep structures of private beliefs, are more difficult to apprehend empirically.[17] In the public arena of the bar, one almost never witnesses a "successful" act of persuasion in which an arguer acknowledges that the persuasive discourse of another has changed his or her *theory.* The very public nature of argument means that social identities are at stake and that it is unlikely that persuasion will be acknowledged in the presence of others at the Smokehouse. Defections from or to the common logic are never apparent; because arguments display what "we" have in common as a group of individuals, the tension between group and individual identity discourages people from stepping out of established performative roles. In spite of what Smokehousers say about the potential of argument as a heuristic strategy, the consensus among the five to whom I spoke in interviews was that persuasion—that is, a fundamental realignment of one's viewpoint on a controversial issue—rarely happens in public debates at the bar. Arlen, who frequently comments on the futility of barroom debates, rolled his eyes at my obtuseness in asking whether arguments actually *work* in persuading others and assured me that

> it's like I said: you're never gonna change anybody's mind. I . . . never seen an argument where the—where the one you're arguing with'll say, "Gee, you know, you're RIGHT! I'm sorry, I've been wrong all these times, and you're right, so now I'll change my mind, and I'll do it THAT way!"

Perry, who had fairly rhapsodized about how much he enjoyed "debating with people about controversial things," admitted that "ultimately, it doesn't seem to ever accomplish that much. I go away with my views, and they go away with theirs." Yet, as we have seen, Smokehousers' ultimate skepticism in the possibilities for direct persuasion does not diminish their enthusiasm for the practice. Whether or not attempts to change the deep structure of beliefs of private individuals actually work, participants in arguments at the Smokehouse stand by the premise that persuasion is in fact the desired outcome of arguments. That people sustain an abiding faith in the transformative *potential* of dialogue means, in turn, that people who participate in arguments build their argumentative strategies not only with available speech genres in mind but with a view to articulating the common logic in ways that Smokehouse audiences find effective. A look at what people do in argument—as well as at how their strategies fail—demonstrates the appeals people see as authoritative under what circumstances as well as the role arguments play in the public construction of knowledge at the Smokehouse.[18]

Bullshit on "What If"!

If we could sketch a map of the domain of persuasion, it would be bordered by the common logic at one end and performance at the other. The common logic about the primacy of practice over theory, in particular, has a direct bearing on what persuasive strategies Smokehousers call on to construct arguments. The logic to which arguers appeal in arguments is one in which theory-for-theory's-sake belongs strictly to the category of leisure activity or *play* and is set in opposition to the category of *work*. This opposition, a theme so essential to the organization of the logos, finds its way as topos into all kinds of rhetorical appeals. On one level, to speak as a "theorist" is to undercut one's ability to invent an effective ethos. Recall Walter's invocation and subsequent dismissal of my point of view in an argument on the morality of Clinton's refusal to participate in the Vietnam war: "Here you always say, 'what if, what if'—BULLSHIT on WHAT IF!" Recall as well that it is not so much my assertion of an unacceptable theory that is rejected; rather, it is my investment in the theory as a cultural commodity—in the importance of "what if"—over narrative that undermines my ethos and calls into question the logic of my argument. My opinions on a range of issues are often challenged because I profess views that privilege abstraction over local, lived experience, something other than practice. My job at the bar ties me to practice in a way that is irrefutable, yet my membership in a culture in which theory circulates as a commodity ultimately sabotages my authority to tell it like it is.

In arguments with others at the bar, the theory-practice relation is almost always at issue—is the contested logos—no matter what the putative subject of the debate. It is a theme that surfaces again and again in implicit discussions of workers' political interests as expressed in debates about which politicians are more likely to represent these interests. Here, in discussing whether Ross Perot or Bill Clinton would make a better president, Jack and Roberta discuss the characters of the candidates. I implicitly challenge Perot's motives for withdrawing from the race, a challenge deflected into a challenge to the ethics of the other candidates.

1	JULIE:	So Jack, you'd vote for him [Perot],
		even if he dropped out . . . with . . . just like, no sign at all?
	ROBERTA:	So would I.
	JULIE:	That didn't make you mad, at all?
5	ROBERTA:	Not at all!
	JACK:	What are the other two people sayin,' hon?
		They didn't say anything which you could prove . . . everything that
		the two candidates brought up—when he was 36 percent and they were 33–32. But—the point is—he's the only
10		one that had anything to say. . . . [T]hat was the truth.
	ROBERTA:	He's the only one that has got—to *me*—common sense.

[Later, after a long epideictic monologue by Jack in praise of Perot]

	ROBERTA:	Perot wants to—if you're going to be on welfare, you will work—
	JULIE:	I mean, if that's the—if that's the choice.
15	ROBERTA:	Um, people—everybody has to work to make a living, okay?
	JULIE:	Well, that's what Clinton says.
	ROBERTA:	Nnnoo. . . . Clinton is—to me—a Bobbsey twin with his running mate, ah . . .
	JACK:	Gore.
	ROBERTA:	Yeah. To me, that—they—they're college twins and preppies.
20		This country doesn't need *preppies*.
		Bush, I think, has done a good job, but not with the economy.
		If we were gonna go to war . . . I would vote for Bush because he'll ge—he's d—
		I've got three sons, I don't want my sons going in . . . infantry and getting blown away.
25		We have the—the technology—you send an airplane in and bomb 'em—
		do what you have to do—but do not send in kids.

In the logos that Roberta constructs, Clinton has become emblematic of theory removed from the practice of everyday life. He is seen, even though his roots are deeply working-class, as the archetypal middle-class professional. Following her characterization of Clinton as a "preppie," Roberta's depiction of Bush as one who is sympathetic to her class interests (implicit in Roberta's praise of Bush is the idea that she is of the group of people whose sons will be called on to do the "dirty work" in the event of a war) may seem particularly ironic (20–26). It reveals, perhaps, something about the logics of class identity: even though George Bush cannot be directly connected in any way to working-class experience, Clinton is perceived as a politician who has even less authority to speak for that experience because of his obvious rejection of working-class identity. Perot, on the other hand, is seen as one who—though he may not share the same economic status as working people—shares their logic, and in particular their logic of productivity. The terms in which Roberta renders Clinton and Perot—as privileged and as "real," respectively—mirror the opposition that runs through the logos between theory and practice.

As Roberta's assertion that "everybody has to work for a living" indicates, the topic of *work* itself encodes the theory-practice relation. In the common logic, work signifies integrity, productivity, and civic responsibility. As we saw in the previous chapter, Smokehousers identify themselves to a great extent in terms of their work—not necessarily by *what* they do, but rather in that they are *doers;* that is, they identify with, and would like to claim control over, the immediate products of their labors. During the 1992 presidential campaign, Smokehousers found most persuasive rhetorics in which work was thematically central and rejected as unconvincing those that were more explicitly ideological. From time to time, I would try to convince people that their own political alignments were not working in their best interests; predictably, these attempts failed on the grounds that I couldn't possibly know, given my self-serving faith in symbols and abstractions, what their best interests *were.* Where I meant to express solidarity with the interests of others in indicating that I took such interests seriously, these others sensed a tacit paternalism. In keeping with their conviction that theory comes—no, is *earned*—through practice, Smokehousers see my investment in the *idea* of ideology as a luxury.

Impassioned exhortations about the inviolability of the flag notwithstanding, political battles over symbolic claims to the legitimacy of various identities are dismissed as beside the point, as irresponsible applications of one's political energies. Here, in invoking the conservative "family values" ideology as an example to convince Roberta and Maggie that the Republican platform would not be beneficial to them as working mothers, my *intention* is to express empathy for Maggie's and Roberta's predicaments as single mothers:

| 1 | JULIE: | It infuriates me that someone would tell ME that the only family configuration possible is . . . a nuclear family. |
| 5 | MAGGIE: | People are in a recession right now, and their families are hurting, they're trying too . . . to— to put on a—to project a picture that will draw people together . . . and there's strength in families, and unity— |

10	ROBERTA:	[speaking of Perot]: And you don't think a businessman can do that? Because I—
	MAGGIE:	I will tell you something from experience. Married people with children can starve just as much as single people without . . . you know?
15	ROBERTA:	Oh, "family value" . . . that's a personal thing; that's like abortion.

My purpose in introducing this topic is to expose the symbolism and coded ideology of the political campaign, to show that this symbolic activity might reveal something about the motives of the parties or candidates. It is significant, I think, how roundly Robert rejects that move and shifts the topic of the argument from ideology to everyday life. When I raise the ideology issue (1–3), Roberta dismisses it as irrelevant to the problem of who should be president, calling it "a personal thing" (15–16).

In considering the failure of scientific psychology to account for the social and the interactive in explaining human psychology, Jerome Bruner (1990) describes the resistance of *any* common logic (for him, folk psychology) to the kind of theory that claims to study human behavior objectively:

> [F]olk psychology, though it changes, does not get displaced by scientific paradigms. For it deals with the nature, causes, and consequences of those intentional states—beliefs, desires, intentions, commitments—that most scientific psychology dismisses in its effort to explain human action that is outside human subjectivity, formulated in Thomas Nagel's deft phrase as a "view from nowhere."

Although Bruner refers specifically here to the discipline of cognitive psychology, his explanation of the general relationship between "folk" and "objective" ways of knowing—of why common logics are resistant to theoretical challenges from the "outside"—is applicable to the thematic materials of arguments at the Smokehouse and would seem to offer an explanation of why my investment in academic claims to metanarrative is at issue in so many arguments. The failure of theory as persuasive logos at the Smokehouse, however, stems in part from alienation (or at least, isolation) from institutions of education and, consequently, nonparticipation in marketplaces in which "pure theory" carries any power as symbolic capital. It is not the case, I should emphasize, that Smokehousers do not "theorize"—in one sense, to argue is to do just that—rather, it is just that, as a communicative genre, theory *as such* does not have much value as currency in the linguistic market that is the Smokehouse. Or, to put it another way, the failure of theory can be located in ethos as well as logos: theory can buy you nothing, not even authority to make knowledge.

The Narrative Imperative

The rhetorical marketplace of the barroom constrains not only what topics carry persuasive power but also which speech genres encode these topics: that is, it constrains what counts as evidence in arguments. That immediate, lived experience is valued among Smokehousers means that *as a genre,* narrative is authoritative. It enacts the common logic of productivity and immediacy and contains the densities and contradictions of moment-to-moment sociality. To tell stories in the contexts of arguments is to lay claim to an unchallengeable empirical reality, to appeal to the legitimacy of the link between life and story, world and word. When invoked as evidence in arguments, narratives affirm that participants exist on the same experiential plane (if not necessarily on the same philosophical one). In telling a story to "prove" a point, an arguer makes an ethical appeal that says, in effect, *Now, here's my unmediated, not strategized, point of view.* As we saw earlier in the episode in which Roberta tells of Trish's feud with her neighbors, narrative serves to make sense of the world, in effect, to theorize it without resorting to *theory.* In the following example, however, Roberta creates a narrative in the context of an argument on welfare to provide experiential proof for a theory already established as part of the logos:

> I have a family living across the street from me—The mother's on welfare; the daughter, and now HER daughter. Now, wait! They have two guys living there. They are all working, and they hide when the welfare people come. And I thought, I can't believe this! I mean, don't—we have no ride, I mean, nothing! They drive brand-new cars. . . . [W]here does this money *come* from?! Are the welfare people that fucking stupid?

The decision whether to offer narrative evidence in argument points to one of the ways my own style of argumentation differs most significantly from that of others. My tendency to avoid calling on narrative as a way to provide evidence for truth-claims means that I inevitably take on a special role in arguments at the Smokehouse. Whereas my unwillingness to offer anecdotal/experiential proof means that I subscribe to the terms of a different (and alienating) logic and de-limits my ability to make appeals to the logos in argument, such a difference in argumentative style does, in a way, provide a necessary context for many arguments at the bar. By theorizing truths rather than narrativizing them, I open a narrative "void" that allows other narratives to rush in and display themselves to all, thus displaying the individual differences in perspective among people who might otherwise find themselves speaking from the same position. Though *I* clearly "don't get it," I provide everybody else with the opportunity to see a range of ways *to* get it; that is, my presence as one who challenges the theories of the logos confirms a multiplicity of otherwise irreconcilable experiential truths as concurrently *true.* At the same time, I offer the possibility of an altogether different place for narrative to emerge; this realigning of generic boundaries shifts the logical paradigm just enough for new possibilities to emerge without threatening the ideological unity of the group as a whole. This conflict between ways of making knowledge—in theory, and in narrative—fuels the generic tensions that both affirm and reconfigure the common logic.

That argument makes a place for competing narratives to emerge at the Smokehouse means that the symbols (e.g., Perot) encoded in such narratives are foregrounded. In argument, symbols of rhetorical themes are thrown into relief, because arguers' alliance with them gives them added representative significance. Conversely, those who participate in arguments often—and in particular, those who perform—inevitably become identified with particular viewpoints. In this way, oppositions become ossified, logos is calcified into ethos. But—as the terms of my own rights of participation show again and again—the kind of *ethical* appeals a speaker may make is ultimately determined by that speaker's investment in the cultural marketplace in which the Smokehouse participates. A speaker who shares assumptions with his or her audience about which genres have what value as symbolic capital will be regarded as a more authoritative speaker than a speaker who does not share these assumptions. This relation of speaker, genre, and audience is further complicated by the tension between persuasion and performance.

Although performances appear to express cultural traditions and thereby support the ideological status quo, a look at the relationship of performance to persuasion presents a different, more complex picture. That theory-for-theory's-sake is suspect at the Smokehouse means that those arguers who become associated with certain theoretical positions lose credibility as persuaders: to theorize is to do rhetoric; to be a rhetorician is to subordinate truth to conjecture. Paradoxically, a Smokehouser who enjoys status and authority as a rhetorician—that is, whose association with predictable views and positions means that he or she will play a consistent role in performed arguments—is likely to undermine, by the virtue of that status, his or her persuasive ethos. Having a strong performative persona works to sabotage one's credibility as a truth teller, for an excess of invented ethos calls attention to the machinations of ethos itself—to the ultimate detriment of one's ability to make effective appeals to logos.

Speaking of this phenomenon, Bauman (1977) points out that in anthropological investigations of verbal art in other cultures and contexts, "the association between performance and disreputability has often been remarked" (29). And, in fact, Smokehousers themselves have remarked on this association: when I spoke to people in interviews, I was surprised to learn that those arguers who seemed to be the most masterful performers were held up as examples of *why* arguments at the bar were ultimately futile. Of Walter, Joe complained,

> he's got his own opinions, and no matter what you say to him, he just, uh, doesn't, ah . . . everything you say is wrong, you know, he's not flexible enough to—when you make a good point, ah, it—even acknowledge it, you know, it—[in a gruff imitation of Walter's voice] "Oh, you're fulla shit!" You know how Walter is! If he wasn't arguing, he wouldn't be happy at all.

Maggie voices a similar complaint about Jack, who is perhaps the Smokehouse's most notorious rhetorician. Asked if she could think of anyone at the bar with whom she found it "impossible to discuss politics with," Maggie immediately replied, "Jack!" She went on to explain that she didn't like arguing with Jack "because . . . because I think that when he argues, he'll say things that he doesn't even really believe, but just to try and get your goat, and get you all frustrated, and angry, and stuff. . . . And that's why. So that any—they're like, pointless arguments."

Even though performers like Jack carry a tremendous amount of authority and prestige as storytellers, they are ultimately regarded as talkers rather than doers, as manipulators rather than truth tellers. In performing in arguments, Jack chips away at the foundations of his own ethos even as he enacts the common logic of the community. Performances are most likely to happen in situations in which there is a challenge to the common logic; however, the conventional belief in the disreputability of the skilled orator serves as a check on the powers of persuasive rhetoric. This check is itself balanced by the power performers have to demonstrate common logics. The tension between conservative and emergent ideologies is ever present in performed arguments; my presence in such speech situations, as the voice of opposition to the status quo, serves to augment this tension. Jack needs me around to make his oratory persuasive, to disguise his performance as dialogue. As one who speaks for an opposing point of view but who has little ethical appeal, my presence in an argument serves, on the one hand, to authorize Jack's claims. On the other hand, however, I must be afforded the authority to create the kind of logic that warrants opposition and am therefore granted provisional ethos. Ironically, the only way Jack can use my presence to advance the claims of the logos is to acknowledge my viewpoint as one with which it is worthwhile to contend. Even though I am often called on to provide the voice of opposition in argument, however, the authority I do have to assert truth claims is conferred by the group, for its own purposes. As a young(ish) woman who is also an "intellectual," the particular role I play in performances demonstrates the obvious ways in which I depart from the logos. To urge me into an established role in order to challenge me in argument is to stage a dramatic challenge to the values of the marketplace I "represent."

Tex the Loser

The parameters of the common logic have a certain predictable flexibility, however, and in this way work much like the ropes mooring a canvas tent to the ground maintain the integrity of that structure: when the ropes that anchor one side of the tent tighten in response to a breeze, the ropes fixing the other sides slacken accordingly. This dynamic of ideological equilibrium is illustrated by the special circumstances under which I am *not* impelled to take a performative role. That I seem not to be called into performance when disjunctures in the logos are not at issue reveals something about how argument works to establish social roles: when the group feels a sense of unity with respect to its common logic, the need to affirm solidarity through practice of performed argument becomes less germane. For people who have socially established roles as opponents in arguments to voice assent is rare, but it does happen on special occasions when there is a stronger challenge to local practice from without. In one such case, for example, Jack, Roberta, and Maggie expressed solidarity with my views when a man who was clearly regarded as an outsider to the group attempted to insinuate himself into Smokehouse society—and worse, tried to claim the right to perform. This outsider (whom I'll call "Tex" in deference to his professed love of all things Texan) is generally regarded as a tiresome boor by others at the Smokehouse. When he shows up at the bar, there is a display of sighing and eyeball rolling as everyone registers Tex's presence. In the words of Arlen, Tex is a "loser."

In the episode to follow, Tex's plays for acceptance are met with a peculiar kind of resistance: that is, other Smokehousers who would have otherwise taken on opposing roles ally themselves as a united front against the insurgent theories of the unwelcome outsider. At the time of this exchange on a Saturday night, I have just come from working the "Pit" (dining room service bar), which closes on Saturday at 11:00 when the kitchen does. I sit near Jack, who is suffering Tex's company with only a thin pretense of goodwill. Tex is now working hard to persuade a skeptical Jack and an incredulous me that there is no such thing as rape within marriage. Maggie, working the bar, and Roberta, standing in the waitress station cashing in her night's tips, have been listening with increasing disgust. What follows takes place immediately after Tex's eagerly anticipated departure and opens with Jack's review of Tex's unsuccessful performance. Here he takes on the fictive voice of Tex's wife as a way to comment on the inappropriateness of forcing sex on a woman:

1	JACK:	—*if you touch me tonight, you'll pull back a bloody stump!*
		But no, what I told him is, you know [sarcastically, with reference to Tex's large size]
		—*all right, let's go—you are a lot smaller than your wife, who is a lot—she's tougher than you.*
5		Now she comes home and just—boom! and *I want it!*
		Is that fair? I said, you think—? Oh, well, THEN it wasn't fair, remember?
	JULIE:	I know, THEN it wasn't fair—
	MAGGIE:	No way!
	JACK:	And he [Tex] didn't—he didn't like what I said. . . .
10		Yeah, you're smaller than her, and he comes home, and she says, *You're gonna do it!*
		Boy, he didn't like that, at all!
		Well, then it was a different thing, to him!
		He didn't even—he hasn't even THOUGHT about THAT one yet.
15	ROBERTA:	[seating herself at the bar] Well, don't start THIS again, because you know what?
		[slyly] Maggie agrees with him totally!
	MAGGIE:	[making a wry face] EEEeeuuuw, GOD—
	ROBERTA:	I mean, you know?
	MAGGIE:	You know, no court, no police, that's okay—
20	JACK:	A man's right!
	MAGGIE:	—judge, trial, and jury, what do you need—
	JULIE:	It's really amazing that he [Tex] believes that . . .
	ROBERTA:	No, it doesn't amaze ME—
	JULIE:	He truly, sincerely, believes that!
25	ROBERTA:	He DID! He was very—
	JULIE:	He's a LaRouchie.
	Randy:	[who has been listening from the far side of the bar] No way!
	JULIE:	Yeah!

30	RANDY:	I've never met one before—
	MAGGIE:	What is it?
	JACK:	A WHAT?
	RANDY:	He's a real live Lyndon LaRouchie?
	JULIE:	Yeah, he's a—
35	RANDY:	Wow!
	JULIE:	—Libertarian.
	ROBERTA:	What the hell is that?
	RANDY:	He [La Rouche]'s gonna run for president from prison!
40	JULIE:	It's a real, kind of, strange sort of set of beliefs. . . .
		Actually, you know—they appeal both to
		really . . . liberal people and really . . . conservative
		people. . . .
		They believe that government should not . . . do *anything*,
		in effect. . . .
		I mean, the government should not intervene in anything—
45	ROBERTA:	Ahaa . . .
	JULIE:	—including—
	JACK:	Well, this guy was just talking about, uh—
	JULIE:	—cases of rape.
	JACK:	—havin' the government do something [so] that they
50		couldn't . . . nail you away—
	JULIE:	No taxes, no nothing . . .
	JACK:	—so how can he be one of them?
	RANDY:	He actually votes for their candidates, and everything?
	JULIE:	Oh, yeah . . . yeah.
55	RANDY:	Wooooowww!
	JACK:	Yeah, but in the meantime, he's talkin' about the
		government . . . oughta crucify a woman . . . that doesn't
		. . . put out for her husband whenever . . .
		he wants it. So I mean, now, h—now, this
60		is—how can you vote for—what you just said, and then . . .
		think like you're thinking?
		Ah . . . you—you know, I mean, he is just—
	MAGGIE:	Is he married himself, Julie?
	JACK:	—ass-backwards!
	JULIE:	Not anymore . . .
65	MAGGIE:	I WONDER why!
	JULIE:	Yeah. [quoting Tex] "Oh, I was married to a nun—
		my wife wouldn't put out!" God!
		I mean, I don't know *why*, I mean—
	JACK:	[as if to Tex] Why'd you marry her?
	JULIE:	—with such a tremendously attractive husband as that . . .
70		I mean, how could you resist?
	ROBERTA:	Yeah . . .
	RANDY:	Such a conversation, last week . . .
	MAGGIE:	I'd make him meatloaf every night! [laughs]
	ROBERTA:	No! I'll give you MY meatloaf recipe!
75	MAGGIE:	[laughs]
	JULIE:	[as if to Tex] You can DO IT with the meatloaf!

At first glance, it appears that Jack, Mary, and Roberta are simply assessing the reasons for Tex's failure to persuade them of the truth of his views regarding relations between men and women. What is significant, however, is the process by which Tex's lack of ethos compels an unequivocal expression of unity in an audience whose members would otherwise be divided against each other with respect to the common logic. Jack, who cultivates a dramatic persona as a "male chauvinist," and who often attempts to draw me into arguments about gender issues, here voices assent with me in disapproving of Tex's obviously sexist stance. At the same time, Roberta articulates the collective opinion that Tex is not a credible voice in her joking comment that "Maggie agrees with him totally" (16). Maggie's critique of Tex's assertion that there should be no legal intervention in "private" affairs, as well as the assent of the others to her critique, stands in sharp contrast to the claims I am entitled to make in speaking about such issues. Jack's excoriation of Tex for his libertarian views—at one point, Jack pronounces Tex "ass-backwards"—is a surprising reversal of his (Jack's) own characteristic antigovernment stance (63). Finally, the discussion is brought to closure in a congenial exchange of jokes among the women about how a wife might exact revenge via bad cooking on a husband who acted like Tex (73–76).

Because Tex is regarded as a "loser" among Smokehousers, he has no persuasive authority; this in turn means that he cannot establish a role in the group and can therefore build no viable performative persona. Those who constitute Tex's audience assume that what Tex says is what he "really" believes, because as an outsider he has no authority to play with the argumentative genre. Tex's antigovernment position, if advanced by someone with a powerful performative ethos like Jack, would incite an argument in which performance would likely be a part. But because Tex has no authority to engage in the kind of generic play that metanarrative speech requires, he has no authority to perform. Though Tex appears to be "conservative" while I am perceived to be "liberal," the difference between Tex's challenge to group norms and my own has less to do with our differing political orientations, finally, than with what it means to be a member of the Smokehouse cohort. As one who is competent in conventional discourses, I am authorized to present challenges to Smokehouse ideologies without threatening my status as group member. On the other hand, Tex's failure to comply with the rules governing conventional communicative practices—his boasting, hyperbole, and predictable repetition of the same tired stories featuring himself as hero—constitute "narrative abuse," mark him as outsider, and discredit his appeals to the logos. Tex, a bad rhetorician, succeeds only in convincing his audience that the logic he professes must not in fact be the common logic, but some other. The right to *speak for* comes in part from sharing a belief in the value of narrative, in part from speaking well, and in part from showing solidarity with everyday practice. Tex may indeed believe in the power of narrative, but he can't demonstrate it. If Tex is unable to *invent* a provisionally viable ethos through performance, he is equally unable to earn the right to perform by calling on on a *situated* ethos conferred by his prior position in the community (he is not part of social networks that extend beyond the bar). To persuade others that his logic is viable, Tex would first have to persuade them that he is entitled to speak for others.

That Jack (and to a lesser extent, Maggie and Roberta) is willing to argue against a more extreme version of their own logic suggests that willingness to publicly shift one's position on an issue happens not from listening to a well-articulated opposition on a given issue, but rather as a result of social circumstances that allow one to temporarily abandon one's conventional performative role (as Jack does here). As performances generally rely on the collaboration of all present, the refusal of an arguer to participate in a performance can sometimes have the effect of deconstructing conventional scripts.

Tom the Winner

This dynamic is especially apparent in arguments in which Tom, a peripheral member of the Smokehouse network, takes part. Tom's rights of participation come from the special status he enjoys in the group: even though he cannot claim a position as a core member of the Smokehouse cohort, he has a powerful situated ethos because he is the son of an established regular who works for the Greendale police department. Even though Tom often participates in public debates, he does not have a conventional performative persona. Though he is politically liberal by Smokehouse standards, he is never the target of attacks (as I am); nor does he play the part of foil for performers like Walter and Jack (as I do). Unlike Tex, who is a willing performer but an unsuccessful rhetorician, Tom is an *unwilling* performer and a *successful* rhetorician.

In what follows, Tom and Walter discuss the jury's verdict in the trial of the police officers accused of beating Rodney King, one of many discussions of the politics of race relations occasioned by news coverage of the event. There was general incredulity at the enraged response of the black community in Los Angeles, and many at the bar expressed amazement at the "riots," wondering aloud why *they would destroy their own neighborhood*. One evening after the ten o'clock news, Tom challenged Walter, who had loudly wondered that very thing, to elaborate his knowledge of the circumstances of the beating and subsequent verdict. Here Tom skillfully controls the floor by taking on the role of Socratic dialectitian, asking Walt a series of questions that are apparently intended to point up contradictions in Walt's argument:

1	TOM:	Do you think the verdict was racist? Because, admittedly, the people were mad because of the verdict, right? They didn't agree with the verdict.
	JULIE:	The Rodney King trial.
5	TOM:	Do you agree with the verdict? 'Cause that's what caused the riots.
	WALT:	I agree with the verdict one hundred percent!
	TOM:	And all you saw was the videotape— you weren't in the courtroom, and neither was I.

10		All you saw was the videotape, right?
	WALT:	And I reserve—now, wait, will you listen to me for a moment?
		Let me qualify my statement—
	TOM:	Okay.
	WALT:	Uh, in the many discussions we had at this bar—
15	TOM:	I'm sure there were many.
	WALT:	—and you might have heard me screamin' like I am tonight—
	TOM:	Nnnooo, I haven't been here for a while.
	JULIE:	[aside, to Tom] You probably didn't HAVE to be here in order to hear it—!
20	TOM:	[aside, to me] I coulda heard it anyway, huh? [laughs]
	WALT:	Well, all right . . . I've always said . . .
		that I will reserve my judgment until after the court—
	TOM:	Okay . . .
	WALT:	Now, wait a minute! I've been on jury duty twice in my life,
25		where we pass verdicts . . . and I gotta say that in our country,
		you will be tried by a jury of your peers, and the—and their—
		and their word is the law! You're guilty!
	TOM:	Okay . . . okay, did the fact that they took—
	WALT:	If the jury said they're guilty—and for that reason I—
30	TOM:	Did the fact that they took this out of the city, and
		out of the *county* where this occurred . . . and took it to
		a one-hundred-percent all-white county and community—
		do you think that had any bearing on the case?
	WALT:	I'm sure!
35	TOM:	Okay. And did you also hear the comments of the jurors
		when they said why they ruled the way they did?
	WALT:	Well . . . I—I heard a lot of it in passing, but I pay no
		attention to it, because as far as I'm concerned,
		what the jury said was final.
40	TOM:	Okay. So you—so there might be more facts in the case—
		besides the videotape—that you're not aware of?
	WALT:	Oh, absolutely . . . ab-so-lute-ly!
	TOM:	'Kay. SO . . . it's quite possible that this man did nothing
		to provoke it . . . ?
45	WALT:	Bullshit.
	TOM:	Okay, what'd he do to provoke it?
	JULIE:	But you don't KNOW that! You just said you didn't know—!
	WALT:	Bull-SHIT!
	TOM:	What did he do to provoke it?
50	WALT:	I don't know—and neither does anybody else!
		But I DO know, that the two people that he was with,
		they were arrested; they sat quietly in the back of the squad car,
		and they did not get beat, they did not get a knuckle laid on 'em—but THIS guy, he—

55	TOM:	He resisted arrest. He did.
	WALT:	He resisted arrest! And as I understand it—

WALT: He resisted arrest! And as I understand it—
now please correct me if I'm wrong—my understanding is that
the police . . . the police of various states—when they say,
you're down, you gotta be down, in a certain position,
in other words your head's gotta be down, your elbows gotta be down,
your knees gotta be down—you're not half up and half down—
and he would not assume that position!

TOM: So he would not do what they asked him to do.

WALT: So they had a right, as far as I'm concerned,
to beat on him, because—how many times has one of these sonofabitches,
whether white, black, or Hispanic—
would not assume the position, and out comes the goddamn gun,
and the law enforcement officer's dead.

TOM: Okay, police are given the right to subdue a subject,
to where they feel that they're . . . no longer in any jeopardy for their safety.
So they are allowed to do what it takes
to get this guy to submit to being arrested.
How may times did they hit him . . .
after he stopped moving, on the ground?

WALT: Wait, wait—he never did go completely down.
He was always either on his hands, or on his knees—

TOM: —no, he d—

WALT: I never seen him completely prostate, see?

TOM: No, he was rolling on the ground—

WALT: Rolling and moving!

TOM: And I never did see, on the videotape, one officer
trying to handcuff him, to where . . . he would have been . . . totally immobilized.

WALT: That's a good point. That's a good point. I think—
like professional football players, if they jumped on him,
and each one grabbed and arm, and put cuffs on him,
there'd'a been no problem.
But too many police officers—they got a rough-ass job.
Lose their goddamn life, 'cause some guy's got a piece hidden in his boot!

TOM: They go down when they get careless.

WALT: Aaahh . . . if I were a copper I'd do the same goddamn thing—
I'd get that son of a bitch down and *keep* him down. For my own protection!

JULIE: So every time you thought somebody might be a threat, you'd beat them senseless?

WALT: You're goddamn right I would! If I thought that he'd threaten me, I'd knock the livin' shi—

TOM: Would you be any more—would you be any more afraid of this guy if he'd've been white—er, any *less* afraid?

WALT: Same thing! Same thing! I'm afraid of people that carry guns! And—and if—now, please correct me—I'm sure you know more about this than I do

100   —as I understand it—now, I'm askin' for information—it was a lady officer,

a lady patrol person, that made the initial arrest.

And when she confronted him with—whatever the routine is—

as I understand it, he shook down his zipper and indecently exposed himself, and made somebody else take

105   his pictures, or some goddamn thing. Now is that true?

TOM: I don't know. . . . I don't know. I don't know.

WALT: Well, that's what I heard. That's what I heard.

He turned around, and pulled down his zipper, Take this! And that's when she—and that's when she called for help.

110   When she called for help, the other two squad cars showed up. And, ah—

TOM: I don't think you'd argue that racism is alive and well in America, right?

WALT: Pardon?

TOM: Racism *is* alive and well—would you agree with that?

WALT: Oh, God, it's alive . . . oh, God!

115   TOM: Okay. Now, given that—when our judicial system says that you're bein' judged by a jury of your peers—since racism IS so strong . . .

isn't it odd that there were no blacks on the jury?

WALT: Well, here again . . . he was represented—he was represented by his own attorney—

and attorneys have a right to select a jury—

120   and if his attorneys weren't that smart enough, to—

TOM: They're only allowed to disallow so many jurors, though. And if they use up all their disallowances, they can't' keep somebody off, after that. And—if they're only taking people

that are registered in that county to be able to serve on a jury—

125   they might not have had any black people to choose from.

WALT: Oh, I'm not—I'm not gonna sit here and say that I'm so goddamn naive,

that I know there wasn't some skullduggery involved there, which I'm sure there was, you know—

they were gonna be sure that this son of a bitch was gonna break his legs,

130   and the police were not gonna be confronted with a problem.

Now I gotta ask YOU a question! Are we—now, Julie, listen—

Are we now in a position . . . that every time we have a
  similar case,

which we have comin' up right now—a case,

ah, where this truck driver was dragged from his truck—

135   JIM: Um-hm . . .

       WALT: —and literally, they beat the SHIT outta him, and we've
                seen that—

               now, are we held prisoner—are we held prisoner by the
                concept that if we vote—

               rather, not "we," but if the jury votes that the black guys that
                did this go to jail for their

               crime, are we . . . a—a—are we allowed to expect another
                riot?

140   TOM: I don't in any way, shape, or form condone the violence that
                broke out because of it,

               because that doesn't make anything better.

               That—that's not the way to change things, okay? BUT—

       WALT: (to me) You didn't answer my question—

       TOM: —BUT—

145   WALT: We're held captive, right now—

       TOM: Do you know what that truck driver was doing,

               right before he got pulled out of his truck?

       WALT: I've got no idea.

       TOM: There's a videotape of him driving up and down the street
                no less than six times!

150   Now, if you're in that neighborhood, and you see there's
                trouble

               and you wanna save yourself, you leave—

       WALT: You get the hell out!

       TOM: You leave. Now, he drove down that street six times, blowin'
                the horn,

               and givin' the finger to all the blacks standing on the side of
                the road.

155   WALT: If what you say is true—if what you say is true—

       JULIE: Did he? I had no idea!

       TOM: Yeah, I just heard this the other day. I was very surprised at
                that.

       WALT: —he got what was comin.' He got what he had comin.'

       TOM: I lost a lotta compassion for this guy when I heard that.

160   JULIE: Yeah! And why are these things—why is this stuff not . . .
                common knowledge?

       TOM: 'Cause the white man doesn't want it to be common
                knowledge.

       JULIE: That's amazing. . . . I mean, that was my first inclination,
               to say, Yeah, of course—

       TOM: No, why is it this guy's fault, that . . . the judicial system was
                allowed to stack the jury,

165   and get done what they wanted to get done—it's not HIS
                fault.

WALT: Well, aside from that—let's assume that this guy got what
he had comin' to him—
but let's say from NOW ON—are we to assume that they're
gonna have a riot,
every time we vote that-that—
TOM: I don't think . . . the court system can judge—
170   JULIE: There have been instances of similar unfairnesses—
TOM: What?
JULIE: There have been instances of similar unfairnesses,
and there haven't been riots.
It's all because that community's felt so powerless to do
anything at ALL about
175   the situation, that the riots happened.
TOM: It's just so heinous that—yeah. No, a judge or a jury
should not worry about what are the implications of their
verdict,
once the verdict is announced. No, they have to take the
case on its merits.
I don't like to see jurors quoted in the press, and I don't like
to see jurors after
180   they're released . . . on the news.
WALT: Yeah! I agree with you.
TOM: They're exposing themselves to trouble they don't need.
WALT: There I agree with ya.
JULIE: In THIS case, it was pretty enlightening, though.
185   WALT: I've been on the jury twice, on some real heavy cases—
one was a shot right in the head—and I'll tell ya, it's tough.
It's hard to say, well, look, this man shot that man in the
head,
and he deserves to be punished.
Hard, hard, decision to make, you know what I mean?
190   What do *I* know about people that stab each other, and cut
each other up?
But when you gotta vote, and say, Yes, this guy shot that guy
in the head,
it's not easy to do.

What is most striking about this episode is the *absence* of performance.
Though Walt and Tom express opposing views on the topic, neither man ever
launches into the repetitious, highly stylized oratory that signals the advent of
a performed narrative. In the course of this exchange, Walter eventually moves
from his original hard-line position on the validity of the outcome of the trial
to a stance that acknowledges the complexity of the issue. In effect, Tom's unwillingness to "play" derails Walt's efforts to render the common logic dramatically. On those occasions during the argument when I issue challenges that
could be read by Walter as cues to perform (e.g., "So every time . . . senseless?"),
Tom's strategy of deliberately maintaining a series of dialectic "turns" with
Walter curtails the latter's opportunities to launch into performative monologue. Tom not only declines to perform; he also refuses to frame or facilitate

performance. His refusal to participate gives him persuasive ethos, which in turn gives him the kind of authority he needs to refuse to take on a performative role. Even though Tom is not himself a dominant presence at the Smokehouse, his congeniality to the thematic organization of work and leisure in the common logic (his maleness, his love of sports, and his status as working man) demonstrates his commitment to local practice. Still, his refusal to perform ensures that he will continue to occupy a position of low visibility in the group.

But let's look more closely at how Tom refuses to set Walt up to perform (and even defuses cues for performance I make available). Tom attempts to challenge the assumptions on which Walt's response is based: specifically, that the acquittal of the officers was fair and that the black community therefore had no right to its rage. He (twice) poses a question to Walt that is not contentious but appears to be a simple request for an opinion: "Do you think the verdict was racist?" (1,5). At this point Walt is unequivocal: "I agree with the verdict 100%!" (7). Tom then treats Walter's response not as an announcement of identity but as a matter of reason, a question of available evidence. He suggests that some evidence is simply unavailable, allowing Walt to save face for having come to the wrong conclusion: "You weren't in the courtroom, and neither was I" shifts the culpability for having come to the wrong conclusion to the state of the available evidence, not to Walter's own logic (8). Tom's tone is uncontentious; he himself is not signaling performance; he is not appealing to an audience beyond. He does not change his posture, or otherwise communicate change in rhetorical aim.

In 11–12, Walter moves to qualify his original assertion, a move to which Tom assents without further challenge (13). Walter offers an experiential anecdote (24) to support the reasonableness of his conclusions about the verdict, though he doesn't press the implications of his experience and moves instead to an assertion of the the authority of the legal system (25–27). But Tom refuses to engage the issue of how the legal system works; he asks another question, a strategy that keeps the dialogue on *his* terms and allows him to retain control of the floor. Walt launches into performance (as before) about duty and authority to law, because now he must respond to Tom's question if he is to show that he himself is motivated by the willingness to engage in dialogue, not the desire to perform (30–34). The question ("Did the fact that . . . had any bearing on the case?" is framed as a request for information but is so heavily qualified by evidence about the validity of the proposition it encodes that Walt has no choice but to concede, which in fact he does: "I'm sure!" (34). Tom continually suggests that Walt may have arrived at the wrong conclusions because of evidence that was either unavailable or misleading: (35–36, 40–41); these suggestions are framed as questions, so that Walt is forced to answer along the lines that Tom has established rather than deliver an oratory in reponse to a proposition that challenges the common logic. When Tom finally does assert a proposition that runs counter to Walt's logic "SO . . . it's quite possible that this man did nothing to provoke it?" (43–44), Walter moves to defend his position, even after conceding to Tom's suggestions that there is no way to reasonably decide about about the validity of the verdict: "Bullshit!" (45). But Tom continues to play Socrates, asking, "Okay, what'd he do to provoke it?"

My intervention at this point is in the form of a strident exposure of a contradiction in Walt's logic (47), a move that implies that because Walt's reasoning is flawed, he must have some other motive to reject Tom's proposition. At that point Walt stops elaborating or qualifying his position; rather, he loudly and defensively repeats his prior assessment of the possibility of King's innocence raised by Tom: "BullSHIT!" (48). But Tom, rather than defending his own proposition, challenges Walter to defend *his* by repeating the question: "What did he do to provoke it?" (49). When Walt admits that he really doesn't know, Tom offers a concession to Walt's assertion that King had in some way been responsible for his fate: "He did. He resisted arrest" (55).

The dialogue continues in a civil manner, with Tom keeping Walt off balance by posing questions, demonstrating his detachment from his position by conceding Walter's points, and paraphrasing Walt's own statements to him to show that they have been given a fair hearing (56–94). This continues *until,* that is, I interject an inflammatory turn that paraphrases Walter's declaration that he identifies with police who are threatened by the public: "if I were a copper I'd do the same goddamn thing—I'd get that son of a bitch down and KEEP him down! For my own protection!" (92–93): "So every time you thought somebody might be a threat, you'd beat them senseless?" (94). My own remark is antagonistic and deliberately reframes Walter's statement of identification as evidence of his own irrationality. Predictably, Walter responds with a combative return of his own: "You're goddamn right I would. . . !" Under normal circumstances, this would have triggered a performance by Walter about criminal behavior, but Tom is there to deflect the speeding bullet by posing yet another question that appears to take seriously Walt's prior assertion that he would be threatened by the public if *he* were a cop (96–97).

Tom presents his argument not as a challenge to the system of logic Walt participates in but rather to Walt's reading of the event given the peculiar circumstances of the trail and verdict, and the questionable status of the evidence. He is not saying "you're wrong and anyone who thinks like you is wrong," but rather, "you, personally, are wrong, because anyone stands to be wrong in a case like this." He thus inverts the usual order of representation and culpability: it's not that Walt is in error because the logic to which he refers—the common logic, that is—is faulty. It's only that individuals trying to reach a conclusion about this case are confronted with so much obscure evidence, so many impediments to reason. In other words, he responds to Walter as if he were *not* speaking for the common logic—not rehearsing topics—but rather, operating independently of an ideology. At no time does Tom appear to *identify with* the position he presents; the issue is not treated as a symbolic site of contending ideologies. For these reasons, Walt does not have to interpret Tom's challenges to him as challenges to the *common* logic and to move into performance to defend not only the logic itself but his own investments in it. Neither does he stand to lose face by *refusing* to defend it, the implication of such a refusal in other circumstances being (simultaneously) that Walt can't speak f or himself *and* that he isn't qualified to speak for others. Ultimately, Walt can't perform without obviously appearing to do so because Tom doesn't offer anything that appears to challenge the common logic, or his claims to it, directly. For Walt to launch into performance would be read as an attack on someone who implicitly endorses the common logic and would reveal Walt's motives as self-promotion rather than articulation of the collective interest. For Walt to perform under these circumstances would in this case make him lose, rather than further establish, his rights to speak for others.

Walt's argument with Tom and subsequent change in public stance is a remarkable event, made possible by Tom's dual status as skilled rhetorician and nonperformer. As a rule, Smokehousers are reluctant to participate publicly in rhetorical practices that might entail the kind of radical reinterpretation of the common logic that would threaten solidarity; in that sense, the group resists any persuasive discourse that might result in such change. Those members of the group who do attempt to challenge or critique the logos are quickly assigned a part in dramatic performance; to take part in performance means, finally, that one's role in the group is defined by the position one takes with respect to the logos. As long as everyone has a part in an ongoing drama, the group can function smoothly as a collection of different, even dissenting, individuals. The cultural practice of performed argument is a way for Smokehousers to make a place for and tolerate individual difference that might otherwise threaten the solidarity of the group. As such, it is a communication strategy designed to manufacture *and* manage dissent.

Argument and the Work of Identity

We have seen that arguments not only express social identities (both within the group and with respect to the group as a whole) but also play a role in the public construction of knowledge. In general, what the practice of argument "means"—how and of what it persuades—has to do both with what social roles and identities are at stake in the immediate context of the bar and with how communicative acts take on value as symbolic behavior in the cultural marketplace in which the social network at the bar participates. On one level, to take part in argument is to distinguish oneself from the person on the next barstool; on another, to argue is to do one's part to help the group establish its identity as a social organism. Encoded in arguments at the Smokehouse is information about everything from who's who at the bar to rules governing how belief is negotiated publicly.

The functional contradiction implied in the practice of *performing* arguments points to tensions and instabilities in Smokehouse culture and suggests how these tensions produce its status as a *class* culture. These tensions might be expressed in terms of the following relations, which have been useful in describing conflicts in various places in the course of my discussion: public and private, assent and dissent, solidarity and difference, theory and practice, working class and middle class, stasis and change. These terms should be read not as structural oppositions but rather as axes of instabilty. Specifically, they work in the following ways:

Public and Private. Because the bar houses a tightly knit social network even though it is open to the public, the status of individuals as "insiders" is necessarily ambiguous. Through the practice of argument, the social boundaries that cannot be enforced by brick and mortar are established with the help of generic speech codes.

Assent and Dissent. To participate in argument is to assent to the social rules governing the genre—that is, to agree that arguments are opportunities for performance and that individuals will take on predictable roles—while maintaining one's ability to dissent from aspects of the prevailing common logic. That arguments help to resolve this contradiction is related to the presence of cultural tensions.

Solidarity and Difference. Though the common logic of the Smokehouse is tied to the maintenance of a public identity, those who claim membership in the group do not necessarily "think alike." The practice of argument allows people to express their solidarity *in terms of* their differences; in this way, Smokehousers rely on knowledge of what is collective, conventional, and generic to show that they are individual, original, and unique. In argument, Jack can persuade others (and himself) that he's not a supercilious egghead, like me; I can demonstrate that I'm not a small-minded reactionary, like him.

Working Class and Middle Class. Argument plays an important role in the negotiation of Smokehousers' class indentity, for the common logic at issue in argument is both product and function of the collective ethos of the group. Tensions between class affiliations are especially apparent in arguments in which I participate: even though my status as worker associates me with working-class concerns, my association with the ways of making knowledge associated with the (middle-class) academic community—my tendency to "theorize"—ensures that I will "speak for" that community in argument. By engaging in arguments, other Smokehousers can affirm the value of belonging to a class that values work; I can assert an oppositional (upwardly mobile) identity as one who moves in the marketplace of "ideas."

Theory and Practice. This relation plays out in two ways. One, by participating in arguments Smokehousers can, by showing unity in practice, allow divergences in theory. Two, the cultural tendency to value practice over theory is affirmed in argument, for argument makes a place for *narrative*—as a genre that expresses the immediacy of everyday life—to emerge. Because I, by contrast, *do* participate in a marketplace that values theory-for-theory's-sake, I play an important role as dissenter. By opposing and collectively "defeating" me, Smokehousers can claim symbolic victory over values I represent and assert the primacy of the local marketplace.

Stasis and Change. Inasmuch as arguments proceed according to generic rules and engage performances with established scripts and roles, they are profoundly conservative. However—to the extent that the very common logic affirmed in acts of performance dictates that performers have little authority as persuaders—arguments have a built-in structural check against allowing the logos to stagnate. In that way, they have a dynamic, progressive component; even as those performers who do speak for the established logic gain social status, they lose in terms of individual integrity, or power to speak the truth.

That the practice of argument exists at the center of this matrix of tensions suggests that as a group on the margins of marginality, the Smokehouse cohort is fraught with ambivalence about the sociopolitical status of working-class whites in general. Most of the performed arguments that happen at the Smokehouse are, after all, about politics.

7

A Place for What If

Politics and Persuasion at the Smokehouse Inn

Speaking of his failure to comprehend the cultural meaning of Ilongot head-hunting rituals, anthropologist Renato Rosaldo concludes that what makes the meaning of such rituals so difficult for him to apprehend is the possibility that for the Ilongot, "the problem of meaning resides in practice, not theory" (1989:6). Meaning can be understood only in terms of its origins in everyday life for Smokehouse arguers as well as for Ilongot headhunters. Smokehouse theories of the everyday—that is, Smokehouse logos, or common logics—are tethered securely to the practice of everyday life: the socioeconomic reality for the mass of the population at the Smokehouse is such that Smokehousers' lives tend to be divided into episodes of work and leisure. The apparent inclination to value the practical over the theoretical—to say, with Walter, "Bullshit on 'what if'"—is, in no small part, linked to Smokehousers' profound orientation to practice in everyday life. The quotidian reality of working life sketches the shape of knowledge at the level of cultural practice and translates into thematic divisions between work and leisure.

The centrality of "work" as a metaphor in Smokehouse rhetoric suggests that the common logic of Smokehousers is, by and large, a cultural product manufactured to accommodate the material conditions of work. But though the discursive practices of Smokehousers emerge from material conditions, the practice of argument shows Smokehousers *as a group* to be engaged in a process of cultural invention. Because the common logic at the Smokehouse derives largely from socioeconomic circumstance but works at the level of cultural practice, it might be said to mediate between the two levels of social production Marxist social theorists have called "superstructure" and "base." If the working class can be viewed etically as social body defined by structural imperatives, on the one hand, and cultural resources, on the other, the common logic might be said to be that which translates one from the other. Each Smoke-houser who enacts (in any act of communication, but in performed argument in particular) this public process of translation plays a role in the negotiation of belief—indeed, in the construction of knowledge—in the public sphere.

Smokehouse common logic, then, is neither the sum total of idiosyncratic beliefs nor a stable corpus of mythologies shared equally by the Smokehouse co-hort. It is, rather, public belief-in-language, or, to put it another way, knowledge-as-resource. The common logic is thus what emerges when conventional speech genres are activated as symbolic capital. The forces that shape it, then, really ex-tend beyond the circumscribed "public" of the bar itself, because linguistic re-sources available to Smokehousers ultimately take on value from larger spheres of exchange in which the local marketplace of the Smokehouse participates—or, perhaps just as importantly, cannot participate.

As Smokehousers' investment in the practice of argument shows, the in-habitants of the Smokehouse do participate in theory making—for, as I have suggested, the very act of engaging in argument is theorizing. Smokehousers' rejection of my claims of theoretical knowledge notwithstanding, those at the Smokehouse certainly practice, and do in fact value, *what-if*. Recall, for ex-ample, Walter's unwillingness to take the video of the beating of Rodney King by the LAPD at face value—he wanted to know what had happened before and after the tape was shot. What if, Walter asked, Rodney King had acted as provo-cateur? Granted, this is not the sort of question that would, to progressive intel-lectuals, count as a "critique" of media rhetorics. But—given that for Smoke-housers what-if is permissible in some domains but not in others—the issue in understanding Smokehouse (and working-class) rhetoric becomes one of dis-covering when what-if is appropriate and when it counts as "bullshit." Under what circumstances what-if operates as symbolic capital, and under what cir-cumstances it is taken to be counterfeit currency, has everything to do with how rhetoric participates in processes of identification and knowledge making—indeed, with how these social and epistemic functions of rhetoric intersect.

In a sense, the common logic deployed in arguments at the Smokehouse is the group's own theory of practice. It is this theory that allows the group to identify and sustain itself as a social body: individual members of the group may subscribe to the common logic or not—indeed, may go so far as to pub-licly argue against it—but all challenges are issued at the level of theory. Be-cause theory (as such) does not confer authority in the cultural economy in which the Smokehouse participates, it is negotiable in public discourse. Chal-lenges leveled at practice, however, disrupt the social order of the group and mark the issuer of such a challenge unmistakably as an outsider. This explains why, for instance, gender cannot be a subject for real debate in the same way, say, that race can: challenges to the common logic about race may, in this racially homogeneous group, remain at the level of theory, whereas challenges to the common logic about gender (always and directly) threaten to call the norms of everyday social practice into question. As the theoretical base that unites Smokehousers, the common logic is essentially tacit, adaptive, and practical. It is devoted to the cause of interpreting the practice of everyday life.

To observe a set of communicative practices in its cultural context is not only to see "what's happening now" but to isolate a moment in an ongoing social process. Raymond Williams (1980) has argued that within the superstructure of capitalist society, many cultural forms exist with differing relations to economic structures, history, and social change; however, Williams finally expresses the culture-society dynamic in terms of oppositional (conservative versus progressive) cultural forces. *Residual* cultures are those practices that, though they "cannot be verified or cannot be expressed in the terms of the dominant culture, are nonetheless lived and practiced on the basis of the residue—cultural as well as social—of some previous social formation." By contrast, *emergent* cultures include "new meanings and values, new practices, new significances and experiences," which are "continually being created" (11). Although it is impossible to design an ethnographic study broad enough in design and scope to trace the movement of meaning through the larger social structure, looking at local practices—barroom arguments, for instance—helps us to understand how belief is created and arbitrated in social networks at a given moment in history and to see how political identities are formed and transformed in public spaces as part of an ongoing historical process. Though it happens under circumscribed, predictable conditions, argument is nonetheless an important process in the cultural production of knowledge. In observing an argument at the Smokehouse, one is watching but a single act in a long-running drama of cultural invention.

Political Persuasions

As we have seen, the ways in which arguments about "politics" serve as occasions for performance at the Smokehouse announce the strategies by which Smokehousers position themselves rhetorically as individuals within the group, as well as *as* a group (of working-class Americans) against the larger social landscape. And as I have suggested, what is important to an understanding of this process of rhetorical construction is the degree of dissent that seems to be permitted—and even required. Speaking of the highly consensual and orchestrated nature of cultural performance, Erving Goffman has observed that "within the walls of a social establishment we find a team of performers who co-operate to present to an audience a given definition of the situation. . . . A tacit agreement is maintained between performers and audiences to act as if a given degree of opposition and of accord existed between them. Typically, but not always, agreement is stressed and opposition is underplayed" (1981:238).

At the Smokehouse, the scales weighing agreement against opposition appear to be tipped the other way: participants in performed argument agree to "play," but players, once having consented to the rules of game, foreground dissent. Smokehousers see themselves as participants in a unified "working-class" culture, even though—and especially since—they seem, as a whole, to be reluctant to define it as such. In this way, the linguistic resources that operate as capital in the rhetorical marketplace of the Smokehouse derive value from Smokehousers' perceived position in the larger social economy. It seems hardly accidental that, given the ambivalent class identity of those who inhabit the barroom at the Smokehouse, argument—as a discourse of conflict—seems to be the genre of speech that consistently invites performance. Ritualized agonistic rhetoric clears a safe space for individuals to express their class solidarity in expressions of difference: even if individuals do not agree on the validity of particular arguments, they nonetheless assent to their value. Only by actively manufacturing dissent in this way can Smokehousers resolve tensions between solidarity and difference, between the specificity of lived experience and mainstream rhetorics of unfettered upward mobility. As working-class Americans, Smokehousers are particularly subject to the push and pull of these forces because they are unable to name themselves as a sociopolitical entity—for, as Smokehousers' varied and often contradictory responses to questions about their class memberships illustrate, Smokehousers have no conventional language in which to articulate a shared political predicament. For Smokehousers, every statement of dissent against the common logic must also contain the assurance of assent, a declared investment in the interests of the group as a whole. Performed argument is one way the group manages this tension without perceiving it as a strategic contradiction. That an investment in *practice* is a value shared by Smokehousers (and, I would argue, by the larger community of working-class Americans) alongside an equally powerful reluctance to form alliances with other disempowered social groups means that Smokehousers feel a powerful commitment to the common interest. However, this very solidarity is not without cost to the individual identities of group members: consider, for instance, the efforts of individuals, during the interviews I held with them, to distinguish their own views from those of other Smokehousers. Arguing with others according to conventional cultural rules offers people opportunities to assert their own identities without undermining processes of group identification.[1]

There is a substantial (and growing) body of scholarship generated by social theorists in response to the question of how people behave in institutional contexts within complex societies to simultaneously challenge and affirm their social realities through cultural practice—how, as Levinson, Foley, and Holland put it, " 'reproduction' could be both contested and accelerated through actions by the same people" (1996:9).[2] The function of political argument at the Smokehouse—that is, in the barroom as local institution—offers a glimpse into the dynamics of this apparently paradoxical process. Argument at the Smokehouse is a social strategy insofar as it establishes social roles and relationships, but it also has an epistemic function linked to the shifting rhetorical situations that emerge from these strategies. In performed arguments, the group is both speaker and audience; any attempt at persuasion is an attempt by and for the collective to enforce a particular structure of belief. Acting as both subject and agent, the Smokehouse cohort draws on available topoi to invent an argument about its own subject position via the scripted performances of individuals. This process does not, of course, describe persuasion in the traditional sense, as the outcome of a bounded discursive event in which one individual, acting as rhetor, convinces another, acting as audience, to shift position. It is in this sense that Smokehouse arguments are least likely to end in persuasion, because, as we have seen, argument at the Smokehouse works as a process of identification, the point of which is to locate individuals in social space.

This does not mean, however, that it would be accurate to conclude that persuasion—as a process of change in belief—does not happen at the Smokehouse. If we conceive of persuasion not as a way of inducing change in individuals (as a process of psychological adjustment) but rather as a means by which public belief structures change over time (as a process of social adjustment), then argument does participate in persuasion, even as it is marked as performance. Performed arguments allow Smokehousers to reinscribe topoi in which common logics are encoded, while simultaneously inventing ways to challenge and reconfigure them. Once the collective ethos has been established in the practice of performed argument, individual rhetors can redraw its limits: once a participant in an argument has dramatized his or her solidarity, he or she may then exercise the ethical authority to challenge the logos. Though it may seem that the performance of argument serves only to work against changes in the common logic, public performances help Smokehousers demonstrate the solidarity that then gives them permission to revise the social script in other contexts. In this way, and perhaps only in this way, might the cultural logos have the potential to be gradually transformed. To describe persuasion at the Smokehouse, then, one must speak of a gradual reconfiguration of the topoi available for cultural invention.[3]

Even as the social adjustments that result in such a reconfiguration must work against the gravitational pull of conservative forces (such as the forces exerted by established social roles and conventional speech genres), the process of manufacturing dissent may clear spaces (albeit small ones) for individual Smokehousers to shift positions. Inasmuch as arguments test the integrity of public belief structures even as they affirm their social value, argument may in fact open spaces to reconfigure topoi even as they are ritually reinscribed. Though these changes in belief structures—in Smokehouse common logic— are at the mercy of social imperatives, they are, finally, contingent on changes in the stances of individuals. As the social narratives inhabited by individuals change, so the cultural text changes. As we have seen, whether an individual is willing to publicly change position with respect to the common logic has everything to do with what is at stake, socially, in doing so.[4] Though persuasion can be viewed as the process by which incremental changes in public belief structures happen over time, it can be viewed as a means to social action only in the sense that the society inside the bar is so affected. The identity crisis that working-class whites feel as a result of claiming neither established nor emergent power manifests itself in a "rhetorical vacuum" in which representative voice is forever the subject of negotiation, as Smokehousers' expressions of political alienation and disenfranchisement demonstrate. What can be read in argument at the Smokehouse, finally, is the story of a particular group of working people trying to create a marketplace for its theory, to construct a safe place where it can explain itself to itself, and to say finally "what if."

Notes

1. Rhetorical Practice and the Ethnography of Class Culture

1. "The Smokehouse Inn" is a pseudonym. But I think it invokes the spirit of the place, because its restaurant is famous for its barbecued ribs and as the barroom not only functions as a "house away from home" but also is usually suffused with cigarette smoke.

2. I borrow the idea of "expressive practices" from Douglas Foley, who uses it both to refer to the agentive/inventive site of social production and the object of the ethnographic study of class culture (1989, 1990).

3. In a richly textured ethnography of Appalachian life, *A Space by the Side of the Road,* Kathleen Stewart (1996) worries obsessively about the problem of reducing the complex poetics of human lifeworlds to tautological systems of representation when cultures are tense, dynamic, conflicted processes. The problematic of representation is further complicated by the effects of anthropology as cultural critique: Stewart describes her own work as "an ethnographic/theoretical discourse that shifts nervously back and forth between story and exegesis. At times it performs a sharp disjuncture between discourses—mine and theirs—and enacts the politics of the dialogic, or the diacritical, contest between them" (1996:40). My own ethnography is similarly "nervous" and demonstrates a similar shifting between culture rendered and culture interpreted, a shifting that is both cause and effect of making the struggle between rhetorical agendas (mine and others at the Smokehouse) the object of analysis.

4. To *what* extent local forms and practices are determined by political economies has been an issue much in debate. For an excellent discussion of how this debate has been configured in cultural studies, see Foley (1990:161–187).

5. There continues to be a surprising dearth of information about actual communicative practices in working-class social networks in the United States, and especially about practices explicitly linked to political identity. However, ethnographers interested

179

in issues of social class have, in the tradition of Paul Willis's study of cultural reproduction in a British youth cohort (1977), produced a handful of critical studies of working-class identity formation in the United States (Eckert 1989; Foley 1990; Fox 1993, 1995, 1996; Weis 1989, 1990).

6. Much has been said about the relationship between culture and class in cultural studies and critical theory. Critics of the Frankfurt School have tended to regard the non-elite classes as a homogeneous "mass," as uncritical consumers of the products of culture. Herbert Marcuse and Theodor Adorno, for example, have treated cultural products as if dominant market forces wholly determine them. Though such approaches offer useful heuristics for thinking about the problematics of the class- culture relation, they offer nothing that assesses the situation from the point of view of the "mass man" (much less the mass woman!) himself; these theories have little to say about how meanings are locally produced.

7. Willis's ethnography of British "lads," *Learning to Labour* (1977), though generally regarded as the seminal ethnography of class culture, has been critiqued on several grounds: Willis subordinates his rendering of cultural practices to the voice of Theory; he unproblematically assumes the lads' expressive practices to perform functions of "resistance" (thus failing to account for apparent residues of hegemonic processes in the lads' speech); Willis is too much of what Van Maanen (1983, 1988) would call a "realist," that is, his tale too easily assumes correspondences between signifiers and their referents, such that his ethnography is rhetorically ill-equipped to account for moments of tension, contradiction, and flux (see Foley 1989, 1990; Limon, 1994; Marcus 1986). Foley himself does not hold Willis to be beyond critique, pointing out that Willis works from an underdeveloped notion of "ideology," and fails to fully prove that the "lads" are in fact engaging in acts of resistance. Foley's own work on Chicanos in Texas describes practices of the everyday as "what people invent to find dignity in an oppressive class society" (1990:139).

8. Foley (1989) arrives at his argument for treating the expressive practices of class cultures as "alienated communicative labor" and objects of ethnographic study by looking to Habermas to enrich Marx's theory of commodity fetishism with "new concepts of speech and communication" (146); in turn, Foley sees Goffman, with his emphasis on strategic miscommunication, as a corrective to Habermas's idea of consensus-via-dialogue in the public sphere. Foley explains: "Each class performs its speech style during ritualized class interactions in various institutional settings" (146). Thus, class inequalities are reproduced dramaturgically from moment to moment.

9. This project comes, finally, in response to the calls of those seeking to approach problems in cultural studies with anthropological methods—as, for example, Jose Limon (1994), who complains of "the neglect of folklore in general within the cultural studies enterprise, a neglect in favor of written literature and media cultural production" (11). Rhetoric, with its emphasis on the oral and strategic uses of language, can return the folkloristic dimension of everyday life to the general study of cultural forms and processes.

10. To illustrate this irony, Fox (1994) recounts his encounter with Tyler Foote, a "working-class Vietnam veteran, on parole after spending time in prison on major felony charges" (3). Foote is clearly no cultural dupe; rather, he is a remarkably skilled performer of working-class discursive forms: he is, as Fox would have it, "a literary ethnographer of his own culture." In speaking with Foote, Fox notices that his subject's own professed political philosophy, alert as it seemed to be to issues of power and subjectivity, echoed postmodern and Marxist theorists' ideas articulated within Foote's own distinctive discursive paradigm. Fox concludes that Foote's philosophical savvy un-

settles—"ironizes"—the "disciplinary project of 'theorizing' his discourse using any of these classic accounts of false or limited consciousness" (3). Fox holds that his conversation with Tyler Foote "demonstrates some of the ways in which ethnography and class culture are tropologically saturated with pervasive irony. The 'object' of ethnographic writing is a speaking subject; the cultural experience of class is a subjective, individuated refraction of objective, collective social relations. These ironies are compounded when the hybrid practice of ethnography frames the hybrid domain of class culture as its speaking, subjective object" (3).

11. Ralph Cintron (1997) applauds the "rhetoricizing" of cultural anthropology and its resultant attention to the textual politics and problematics of knowledge produced through ethnography. Yet, he maintains, a full penetration of rhetoric into anthropology would attend to rhetorics at work beyond the text, for example in the field and in cultural scenes. This wider view of rhetoric is especially patent in making sense of performativities in the field (whether "in" cultural practice, or "in" ethnographic encounters themselves). Cintron asks us to consider that rhetoric throughout history has given heed to processes of display (a focus which, in classical treatises, came to be known as epideictic); in this way, we might be equipped to discuss rhetorics of a variety of cultural phenomena from artifacts to rituals, including public processes. "Sociocultural anthropology," writes Cintron, "is rhetorical long before its texts, its ethnographies and theoretical treatises, come into being because the cultural stuff that becomes a fieldnote is rhetorical, as is the fieldnote itself" (3).

12. Kathleen Stewart (1996) describes her own ethnography of Appalachian life as a story that "fashions itself in a tension between interpretation and evocation, mimicking the tension in culture between the disciplinary and the imaginary" (7). As a rhetoric always implies a poetics in that forms and representations inevitably have suasive (hortatory) force in the context of everyday life, to preserve "rhetoric" as the object of study acknowledges disciplined and imaginative cultural processes.

13. To say that rhetoric is well-equipped to attend to the "performative and conflictual" dimensions of everyday speech is not to suggest that sociolinguistics proper offers no analytical resources with which to account for communicative conflict as well as consensus (see Briggs 1996, for example). Recent developments in sociolinguistics challenge, or at least complicate, the traditional sociolinguistic idea of "speech community" in which speakers share assumptions about the "rules" for linguistic behavior (Eckert and McConnell-Ginet, 1992; Lave and Wenger 1991; Wenger 1998). These scholars have suggested replacing the notion of "speech community" with that of "community of practice" as a site of linguistic activity to better show how social organisms are maintained, despite varied social roles and conflictual attitudes among members (see Holmes and Meyerhoff 1999). Eckert and McConnell-Ginet identify a community of practice (CofP) as

> An aggregate of people who come together around mutual engagement in an endeavor. Ways of doing things, ways of talking, beliefs, values, power relations—in short, practices— emerge in the course of this mutual endeavor. As a social construct, a CofP is different from the traditional community, primarily because it is defined simultaneously by its membership and by the practice in which that membership engages. (1992: 464)

Inasmuch as the Smokehouse is a site of negotiated public and personal identities, and insofar as it establishes these identities and enforces group boundaries through the practice of speech genres (and in particular, argument), it operates as a community of practice.

14. Ralph Cintron (1997) sees rhetoric as a way to apprehend the *agon* of cultural processes, asking his readers to consider his own ethnography of Latino gang life to be

"a project in the rhetorics of public culture or the rhetorics of everyday life. . . . [B]oth try to name an approach that, consistent with the discipline of rhetoric, is interested in the structured contentiousness that organizes, albeit fleetingly, a community or culture" (x). He goes on to say that, unlike sociocultural anthropologists, he aims to treat cultures as "systems of contention in which a contentious position does not exist without its structured opposite and the two together have much to do with the specificities of everyday life" (xi). The other thing that differentiates his work from the anthropological, writes Cintron, is his "reliance on a certain amount of rhetorical vocabulary," namely, classical concepts of *tekhne* and *ethos*. Cintron, in other words, treats cultures as communities of practice while foregrounding concepts in classical rhetorical theory. Cintron sees a project in "the rhetorics of public culture" as a novel synthesis of traditional ethnographic field methods, critiques and theories of cultural studies, and questions raised in the history of rhetorical theory. This synthesis describes the parameters of my own project as well, even if the disciplinary intersections slightly differ from Cintron's.

15. Cintron (1997) invokes the classical notion of ethos not only (as I do) to locate authority in discursive acts but also to delineate the problematics of ethnographic authority: creating a convincing ethnographic tale, argues Cintron, is a function of the ethnographer-author's appeals to ethos.

16. I take seriously Kathleen Stewart's warnings about the dangers of representative overconfidence in telling ethnographic tales. She is right, I think, in suggesting that the most profound cultural truths are visible in the most fleeting moments, as her ethnography (1996) of Appalachian culture so skillfully demonstrates. But whereas Stewart is after a cultural poetics, I am after a cultural rhetoric—not entirely different projects, as I've suggested already, but cultural rhetoric focuses on tensions between what is stable and what is emergent, what is aesthetic and what is hortatory, between what is said in doing and what is done in saying. To attempt an ethnography of rhetoric *is* to offer an account of how a culture explains itself to itself and how this challenge is taken up as praxis.

17. Older people who frequent the Smokehouse have come from, and still strongly identify with, urban working-class neighborhoods on the South Side. These ex-Roselanders or ex-Fernwooders speak as if they were forcibly uprooted and displaced from neighborhoods in which they once enjoyed a utopian society of camaraderie and mutual support. When these men and women speak of "change" in a neighborhood, they inevitably mean change in racial composition (though conceivably neighborhoods could "change" in countless other ways). This, to them, is the most significant social change.

18. Cintron (1997) argues that uses of memory as a heuristic in the process of retrieving and interpreting data from the field are part of the "unacknowledged history of ethnography" and that the intervention of memory into cultural interpretations means that ethnographic knowledge is always autobiographical whether or not it is recognized or presented as such. "For it would seem," writes Cintron, "that the ethnographic process of observing the world and making sense of it requires making tenuous negotiations between knowledge claims and memory, particularly the memory of very old experiences whose details have been forgotten" (8). The autobiographical narrative I include here, offered in the spirit of this claim, attempts to recognize and focus on the heuristic pressures of my own history of class conflicts.

19. In a bibliography of ethnographic research in American culture published in 1992, Michael Moffett counts four studies situated in bars or including accounts of barroom culture: Read (1980), Bell (1983), Halle (1984), and Weston (1991). Other studies that take life in bars as a focus of investigation include Cavan (1966), LeMasters (1975), and Spradley and Mann (1979). More recently, ethnomusicologist Aaron Fox has pub-

lished work on the production and consumption of musical forms and working-class communicative practices, in bars in Texas and the Midwest (1993, 1995, 1996).

20. See Hoggart (1957) and Thompson (1966) for studies of British working-class social life that include the pub as a site of social practice.

21. The analogy to drama is not accidental: newcomers to the bar have remarked on its similarity to the famous TV sitcom tavern, *Cheers,* and more established regulars have compared my own role at the Smokehouse to Diane Chambers (veteran waitress Roberta, on the other hand, has been said to be 'just like' Carla).

22. Ethnographers of working-class cultures (Eckert 1989; Fox 1995; Willis 1979) have often noted the ideological cross-linking of class and gender significations. Ortner (1991) sums up these observations in arguing that "in working-class culture women are symbolically aligned, from both the male point of view and, apparently, their own, with the 'respectable, middle-class' side of those oppositions and choices" such that "every sexual choice is also a class choice, for better or worse" (173).

23. Admittedly, there have been times when it has been difficult not to give in to the temptation to give issues of gender more analytical space; however, I have tried to remain aware that elaborating the (considerable) complexities of class and gender ideology would ultimately have the effect of occluding, or at least endlessly complicating, the focus on communicative practices as class productions. But it is interesting to note that in *The Second Sex* (1989), Simone de Beauvoir points to a parallel between the plight of women as "other" and the particular kind of otherness attributable to the working classes. She suggests that women and the "proletariat" are analogous in the sense that "neither ever formed a minority or a separate collective unit of mankind. And instead of a single historical event it is in both cases a historical development that explains their status as a class and accounts for the membership of *particular individuals* [emphasis hers] in that class" (xxiv).

3. A Place to Be

1. I have long struggled with the problem of what to call the network of people who are the subjects of this research. Though I'm not entirely comfortable with "Smokehousers," which implies that association with the bar is *the* salient social feature of the lives of those it names, "Smokehouse group" seems to connote a much more corporate, more explicitly identified organization than is actually the case. Even though people at the Smokehouse express fierce loyalties to each other, they would not identify themselves as a "group," which would, I suspect, suggest to them a purposeful set of common interests beyond the implicit concerns of proximity, support, and reciprocity that normally characterize local cohorts.

2. Greendale (a pseudonym) is a town of approximately 10,000 residents located about 20 miles south of Chicago's downtown Loop. It is not a poor community: the average annual income of is residents is around $64,000. Houses range from $50,000 to $109,403. Yet not all Smokehousers live in Greendale; many come to the bar from nearby, lower-income communities. Those most likely to have houses in Greendale are skilled laborers and craftsmen or retirees.

3. Many observers of working-class life have noted the damage done to marriages and families by men spending too much leisure time drinking with their "buddies" at bars (e.g., LeMasters 1975, Rubin, 1976). What I have seen at the Smokehouse bears out the observation that the matter of male defections from home to bar is the source of real conflict between many couples. As a bartender, I was expected, as when a woman called looking for her missing husband at the bar, to *ask* the deserter whether he was "here" or

not before calling him to the phone. But bartenders, who tended to identify with women left at home, often (in small gestures of resistance) "forgot" to ask permission before disclosing the presence of men at the bar.

4. See Eckert (1989) for a well-developed discussion, grounded in long-term ethnographic research among Detroit adolescents, of the constitution, organization, and function of working-class social networks.

5. Spending time with Smokehousers *outside* the bar has helped me to understand the power of the barroom to constitute social roles and relationships. This is not to suggest, however, that the bar overdetermines relationships such that its social practices are wholly a function of the barroom setting itself. Sherri Cavan (1966) concludes, following from her observations of barroom behavior in a hundred San Francisco-area bars, that bars enforce an entirely distinctive set of roles for social practice and that these predictable codes of conduct cut across class lines. I would argue, however, that such a conclusion doesn't take into consideration that these codes may in fact emerge from the historical status of bars as working-class institutions and that behavior in bars is by no means, as Cavan believes, empty of significance for patterns of social organization that prevail outside.

6. Or, in the terms of Spradley and Mann's (1975) helpful taxonomy of the population of Brady's Bar, these are the "real regulars."

7. Regulars who are not also employees are usually men over 30 employed in skilled and unskilled labor jobs. They are truck drivers, construction workers, telephone linemen, heavy equipment operators, and the like. Women work in service jobs as waitresses, bartenders, clerks, child-care providers, and hairdressers.

8. At the time of this research, Perry (the owner of the Smokehouse) decided to abandon his old way of scheduling bartenders (in 12–hour shifts, from 4–2) in favor of a new split-shift schedule; this decision was made in response to bartenders' complaints about not being scheduled for enough hours in some weeks. But this plan, too, was eventually abandoned in favor of the old system after bartenders complained that it became too difficult to arrange child care for the extra days they'd have to work under the split-shift arrangement.

9. In their study of gender roles at in a college-town tavern, Spradley and Mann (1975) found that the social hierarchy of "Brady's Bar" was held in place by tacitly shared understandings about gender roles, social territory, and division of labor; this hierarchy was rigidly maintained despite frequent transgressions against the authority of those in high-status positions. This nicely describes the situation at the Smokehouse, as well.

10. It is not the case that nonwhites are actively excluded from the social world of the bar—occasionally black customers do visit the Smokehouse and participate in talk at the bar. Yet, significantly, they don't have roles as *personae*. The racial composition at the bar clearly doesn't tell the whole story, for the significance of race concerns dynamic processes of identity formation in everyday interactions. As John Hartigan concludes from his research among working-class whites in Detroit, "While racial meanings are often quickly rendered and asserted . . . there are also many situations in which they are superseded, held in abeyance, or simply do not come to mind." He suggests further that "any analysis of racial categories and meanings must be able to take into account the play between and active and passive articulations of racial identity," an analytical posture that "does not imply alternate modes of presence or absence such that, at times, a person's racialness might be simply not present" but instead "points to an interpretive continuum according to which the racial aspect of an event or situation is either significant or not to the participants" (1997b:188).

11. To what extent the communicative situations from which data have emerged have been affected by alcohol consumption is a valid question, but a difficult one to an-

swer. Though some of the regulars whose voices appear in the chapters to follow are heavy drinkers, none habitually indulges in the public, out-of-control drunkenness that Smokehousers find disruptive to the social life of the bar. I gave up as impossible the problem of trying to decide when a person who'd been drinking was most authentically "himself" (or herself), which struck me as an insoluble problem of both chemistry and representation. Yet I intuitively did not take as "data" conversations among people who were obviously drunk and whose behavior seemed a departure from what I'd come to expect from them. I myself did not drink alcohol as I worked behind the bar (my usual data-collecting position) but would sometimes take a drink with others after finishing an early shift at the service bar or when I visited the bar on my day off.

12. The extent to which assumptions about gender roles are tied to the *practice* of Smokehouse society has become increasingly apparent to me in the process of researching and writing this study. Over time, I have found it ever more difficult to abide by the unspoken rules governing gender and have been more and more inclined to speak the unspeakable. That I am now willing to challenge tacit assumptions about gender means that I can no longer claim the same solidarity with the group's practice and therefore can much less comfortably issue challenges at the level of *theory* (i.e., in argument).

13. The idea that under certain social conditions women can sometimes take on roles as "honorary males" must be credited to Marcia Farr (personal communication), whom I first heard use the term to describe her own provisional status among the men in a community of Mexicanos in which she had just begun to conduct ethnographic research. Farr explains that as a teacher, or *maestra,* she was originally assigned a role in the group reserved for members of higher status (i.e., the role of a man).

14. For an extensive and very well-articulated overview of postmodern and cultural-studies critiques of ethnography, see Stewart (1996:25–26). At the heart of these critiques, writes Stewart, are calls for "a renewed sense of context and history, the recognition of transnational cultural production and precise cultural proclivities, and theories of culture that might highlight internal contestation and intercultural hybridity, cultural invention and imagined community, and an ironic self-consciousness" (25).

15. How completely one needs to abandon one's prior cultural frames of reference to wholly inhabit the phenomenological world of one's ethnographic subjects is a subject of vigorous debate among ethnographers working in this tradition. Some "radical" ethnographers, who worry about the ethical implications of representing ethnographic data (however "accurate" they may be) in a language that is incompatible with the emic meaning of that data, argue that one must abandon prior cultural commitments altogether. Dan Rose (1990), for example, argues that the ethnographer must "go native" as a way to subvert established assumptions about the practice of ethnography, thus encouraging an ongoing critique of the means and ends of ethnography itself.

16. It may seem ironic—given the usual construction of me as a supercilious intellectual—that in order to present my research to others, I went about convincing people of my good intentions by presenting myself as defender of the interests of working people against (my construction of) the arrogance and naïveté of "those academic types." Yet this indicates, I think, only that the "oppositions" I describe here are not fixed roles, but rather relational positions. However polarized such positions appear to be in argument, they really represent provisional locations along shifting axes of identification.

17. Golde (1986) sees places like bars as so fraught with gender taboos as to be prohibitive sites for female fieldworkers: Warren (1988) paraphrases Golde's observation that "while women anthropologists have a somewhat varied response to norms for dress and appearance, they seem almost uniformly to keep away from male-drinking locations." Warren goes on to speculate that female ethnographers avoid such sites "probably

because of the common and cross-cultural association between male drinking and sexual license. A woman who goes drinking with men, in their settings, opens herself up to overtures" (29). As one would expect, a bartender at the Smokehouse is subject to "overtures" from males as a matter of course. And in fact, Perry exploits his male customers' hopes that their overtures will be successful: he has made it a matter of policy that bartenders' husbands or boyfriends not be permitted to drink at the bar while their wives or girlfriends are at work. In this way, the illusion of a bartender's sexual availability is maintained. Yet a bartender is free to reject any sexual intimations, advances, or invitations to which she is subjected. Over the years, there have been many Smokehouse bartenders who have been in monogamous relationships with someone outside the group and who have never "gone out with" anyone at the bar. Perry's strategy, however, is to seduce male patrons with the hope that, at the Smokehouse, they might in fact "get lucky."

4. Across the Table

1. This is not to presume, however, that this knowledge somehow exists prior to its activation in argument. My point is precisely to show public knowledge, or ideology, to be a process under construction. What is said here is as much a *product* as it is the *material* of rhetorical processes. But cultural practices and forms can never be pinned down, only rendered in different narratives, reflected under different lights.

2. Whether to use Smokehousers' real names has been a vexing ethical problem. People at the Smokehouse agreed to speak to me in interviews because they assumed that I was interested, at least in part, in what they had to say as individuals. Some would not, I suspect, want their individual identities to be erased by pseudonyms. Just recently, "Arlen" asked me what I was going to call him in my "story." When I asked him what he wanted me to call him, he responded, "Why not use my real name?" But I decided to preserve anonymity across the board, finally, because I knew that identifying some Smokehousers (even if they agreed to such identifications) would implicate others who may not wish to be identified; I could not be entirely sure that all Smokehousers could have completely anticipated how their voices would be presented here. (For a helpful discussion of the implications of preserving anonymity, see Lofty and Blot 1997).

3. In other words, interviews are not transparently referential of "cultural meaning"—as Briggs (1986) demonstrates, interviews are discursively complex, motivated, political events. Briggs cautions against the naïve assumption that "different responses to the same question are comparable," as if interviewers and interviewees (and even all interviewees!) are similarly motivated. Briggs argues that interviews are always a (more or less) hegemonic genre but are most ethically questionable and least rhetorically valid when they comport with the "usual practice," which is to solicit "statements that pertain to a given theme, event, symbol or what have you from fixed notes or transcriptions . . . [which are] then juxtaposed, yielding a composite picture of things that seem to go together in the eyes of the researcher on the basis of referential, decontextualized content" (102). Although I am in fact "juxtaposing" field and interview data, I am treating the interview—as event—as a meaningful source of data in its own right, the terms of various engagements (and resistances to) that are themselves subject to scrutiny as social and ideological phenomena. How Smokehousers play against me in the role of interviewer, and how they present themselves as "subjects" speaking *to* and *through* me, does not disqualify, but rather mediates in significant ways, the "contents" of their narrated responses.

4. The practice of interviewing ethnographic informants to uncover unconscious taxonomies of tacit knowledge is characteristic of ethnosemantic approaches to inter-

viewing, such as the one elaborated in Spradley (1979). Spradley's aim is to design questions that, through dialectic and example, infer cognitive categories evidenced through patterns of language use; his assumption is that cultural meaning is systematic, stable, and submerged. According to Spradley, "informants have already learned a set of categories into which their culture is divided. . . . Our goal is to employ methods of analysis that lead to discovering this organization of cultural knowledge. . . . Most of the time this internal structure as it is known to informants remains tacit, outside their awareness" (93). My own approach departs from Spradley's in that I am less interested in recovering a stable "core" of cultural knowledge than I am in learning how Smokehousers represent, and theorize, this knowledge narratively.

5. Smokehousers are all too aware that the bar is a place for performance. To represent their views outside ritual spaces struck me as an ethically sound, as well as rhetorically appropriate, move: Smokehousers would not want to identified solely by their argumentative personae any more than any actor wishes to be narrowly associated with his or her dramatic role.

6. Briggs (1986) is unequivocal about the hazards invited by introducing the interview into a community whose linguistics repertoire does not include the interview as a naturally occurring event. Explains Briggs: "The hiatus between the communicative norms of interviewers and researcher can greatly hinder research. . . . If the fieldworker does not take this gap into account, he or she will fail to see how native communicative patterns have shaped responses; this will lead the researcher to misconstrue their meaning" (3).

7. Even as interviews are metacommunicative events that function to "report" or "evaluate," they nonetheless (in Briggs's words [1986]) "rely on the referential or descriptive function of language" and thus are "ineffectual" in treating certain issues beyond speakers' conscious frames of reference (98). When juxtaposed with other data, interviews can, perhaps, point out the parameters of these frames.

8. See Stewart (1996) for an exhaustive summary of treatments of narrative in cultural studies, linguistics, anthropology, and folklore (29). After listing several possible functions of narrative, Stewart concludes that "whatever its presumed motives are traceable effects, and whether it takes a relatively authoritative, monologic form or a more open, dialogic form, narrative is first and foremost a mediating form through which 'meaning' must pass." To put it another way, she says, "stories are productive. They catch up cultural conventions, relations of authority, and fundamental spatio-temporal orientations in the dense sociality of words and images in use and produce a constant mediation of the 'real' in a proliferation of signs" (30).

9. In approaches to the study of verbal art as developed by Bauman (1977), Briggs (1988), and others, the conventional research approach would be to focus on the most prominent and skillful performers in the community. Although such "lead" performers are often the source of my own data on performed argument in the chapter to follow, I attempt here to draw no direct comparison between what people claim to do in argument and what they "really" do. Rather, I wish to invoke data from interviews to illustrate tensions between individual players and the collective ethos that shapes contexts in which arguments happen.

10. That Walter recommends Joe as a subject for interviews speaks, I think, to the general perception among Smokehousers that those who have highly stylized and visible rhetorical personae—who show themselves to be good performers—can't, when all is said and done, be counted on to speak honestly. Walt recommends Joe as someone who, in his mind, would be least likely to offer ritual, publicly sanctioned responses, to enact the stylized persona of the Smokehouse "workin' man" that Smokehousers stage pub-

licly for my benefit. It also speaks to Walter's awareness of my purpose in holding one-on-one conversations with Smokehousers: he understands that I wanted to interview people as a way to get them to speak outside the constraints of their public personae.

5. A Place to Tell It

1. The idea that Smokehouse ideology is organized into "themes" derives from James Spradley's treatment of "cultural themes," which Spradley defines as "any cognitive principle, tacit or explicit, recurrent in a number of domains and serving as a relationship among subsystems of cultural meaning" (1979:186). Here the language of "rhetorical theme" aims to account for what is *unstable* in Smokehouse theories of practice, to account for the activation of ideologies in strategic discourse.

2. Cooper (1932), writing about the place of topics of Aristotlian rhetoric, describes a topic as "a pigeonhole in the mind of a speaker" (xxiv). I find this conception helpful inasmuch as it suggests internalized structures of ideology. Yet this use (or any such application) of the concept of topoi is necessarily a simplification of its theoretical complexities. As scholars of classical rhetoric (e.g., Covino and Jolliffe 1995; Crowley and Hawhee 1999) are quick to point out, treatments of the nature of topoi—how they are mobilized in discourse, what forms they can take–have varied throughout the corpus of classical rhetorical theory and criticism. What I find especially relevant to the study of local rhetorical practices is the geographical metaphor implied in the concept of topoi: in classical Greek, *topos* meant, simply, "place." Crowley and Hawhee understand the rhetorical topos as "an intellectual source or region that could be inserted into any discourse where appropriate" (75).

3. The question of the precise extent to which class identity is linked to the material circumstances of work itself, and to what extent to "lifestyle," (i.e., leisure activities outside of a work) gets to the heart of the debate about the structural determinants of ideology. See Willis (1977), Halle (1984), and Fox (1994) for theoretical and empirical treatments of the issue.

4. In asking people about their class affiliations, I am asking them to theorize what would otherwise be narrated in conjunction with everyday practices. As Halle notes, "In the United States the term 'working class' is hopelessly ambiguous. There are no questions that allow a researcher to investigate perceptions of the class structure in America without suggesting to respondents a particular image of that structure" (1984:203). Still, it is instructive to note what narratives rush in to fill the representational void created by a construct that has no emic analogue.

5. LeMasters (1975), Halle (1984) and Foley (1990) find strong connections in their own ethnographic work between working-class identity and patterns of residence. For Halle's chemical workers, for instance, home ownership ad sites of residence had enormous import as a means to establish economic stability (or to announce mobility). Halle writes that for these workers, "residential property is the most important way of saving, accumulating and inheriting wealth. Few workers deal in stocks, shares, or securities. . . . A house is a solid asset whose value, in these men's experience, is prone to rise" (11). Likewise, for Smokehousers, a house in a "stable" residential area assures economic security and signals social status.

6. Fox, "The Poetics of Irony and the Ethnography of Class Culture" (1994). See chapter 1, note 10, for a summary of Fox's interaction with Foote.

7. The distinction I make here between "social" and "cultural" categories is an attempt to differentiate between how Smokehousers see themselves as positioned in the socioeconomic hierarchy and how they identify as a cohort defined by values, practices,

language, taste, artifacts, and so on. In other words, whereas Smokehousers see their so-cioeconomic situation as a consequence of their status as whites, the cultural milieu in which they participate is, at least in part, seen as a result of specific ethnic alliances.

8. See Hartigan (1997a, 1997b) for a richly theorized treatment of how "white-ness" operates as a class signifier (for poor whites in Detroit).

9. This means that I am either naïve (can't distinguish between worthy produc-tions and useless ones) or overprivileged (have the luxury of thinking what I do really matters). There is a sense in which Smokehousers regard naïveté as a class luxury, one that in my case—because I'm not really different in class—becomes a character trait to be (usually half-affectionately) chastised, deplored, or ridiculed.

10. In a discussion of British "shop floor culture," Paul Willis (1979) emphasizes the importance of the semiotics of physical labor to the ideologies of work. He writes, "A whole range of jobs . . . still involve a primitive confrontation with exacting physical tasks . . . [and] the basic attitudes and values developed in such jobs are still very im-portant in general working-class culture, and particularly the culture of the shop-floor." Willis goes on to observe that " this importance is vastly out of proportion to the num-ber of people actually involved in such heavy work" (190). This out-of-proportion sig-nificance of the ethos of "primitive confrontation with exacting physical tasks" is much in evidence at the Smokehouse, where it prevails despite individual Smokehousers' vari-able proximities to such work in time and space.

11. Halle (1984) writes that workers at the Imperium chemical plant found valu-able and relevant to their own status as "working men" only jobs that have certain "pro-ductive" features. "Blue-collar work is generally seen as productive. But . . . big business and in general the upper- and lower-white-collar sectors are not. When it comes to ex-amples of nonproductivity, the professions workers mention most often are lawyer, doctor, and teacher. The dominant attitude toward all these groups is mistrust and often hostility, rooted in a belief that part or all of their activity is some way unproductive." (208). Implicit in this ideology is an assumption that women, whose jobs tend not to in-volve heavy physical labor, can't be considered truly productive. (See Willis 1977 as well for an illuminating discussion of how the "principle of abstract labour" is rhetorically cross-linked with the "symbolic sexual realm").

12. Working-class alienation from, and forms of identification against, middle-class institutions of formal education has been well-documented ethnographically both in sociolinguistics (see, for example, Heath 1983 and Eckert 1989) and in cultural stud-ies (see Willis 1977; Foley 1990; Weis 1990).

13. In an ethnographic study of social categories in a suburban Detroit high school, Eckert (1989) found that working-class students assumed adult roles much ear-lier than their middle-class counterparts, for whom the high school years are a time of preparation for an adult life marked by stages of upward mobility. "Continuity between high school and early adulthood," explains Eckert, "resides in different spheres [for middle- and working-class adolescents]" (139).

14. Fox (1995) shows vernacular working-class speech forms to display "covert prestige," or power that arises from values attributed to speech in local marketplaces. Al-ternative sources of power notwithstanding, Smokehousers know that I represent the dominant linguistic marketplace, one where vernacular forms are devalued.

15. The tendency of Smokehousers to express loyalties to the very institutions and social structures from which they are excluded points to a paradox that seems to be cen-tral to working-class conventional wisdom. In the chapter to follow, I explore how this and other tensions inherent in the common logic play out in speech events.

16. At one time in recent Smokehouse history, the group at the bar did, however,

develop a written—perhaps even a literary—tradition of its own. Once, for a period of several months, Smokehousers amused themselves by writing limericks about each other and reading them aloud to others at the bar. These inevitably bawdy verses were always about central characters in the group. Most often, these limericks took as their subjects the physical features or idiosyncratic personality traits of particular Smokehousers and functioned as rather benign written caricatures. The tradition of writing limericks was begun by Maggie, who one day wrote a limerick about Roberta and posted it on the bulletin board in the kitchen. Soon after this first "publication," several people at the bar were madly scribbling verses on cocktail napkins and performing public "readings" of this literature. For as long as the trend continued, I enjoyed acclaim at the bar for my ability to dash off rhymes. Here is an example of a limerick about a fellow bartender Maggie and I composed collaboratively:

> Mimi, a chesty old lass,
> Had a bosom of great weight and mass.
> She said, "Perfect balance
> Ain't one of my talents,"
> But she never once fell on her ass.

17. Of course, the practice of argument—and in particular, performed argument—is a coherent oral tradition tied to group identity. But because this practice is marked by generic rather than linguistic (phonological and syntactic) features, Smokehousers do not count it as a linguistic tradition directly linked to their historical and political identity as a social group, though it does in fact work to define social boundaries.

Sometimes, however, Smokehousers consciously use nonstandard linguistic features to communicate social affiliations, as when Jack affects a Southern dialect to advance what he knows would strike me as a particularly reactionary point of view. (Perry, by contrast, tries to speak Standard English in argument and therefore to claim alliance with the middle-class society he believes to share his "liberal" views.) Smokehousers' differential attitudes toward social mobility in their linguistic code are actually *allowed* by the act of consenting to a conventional speech genre—argument.

18. Halle (1984) learned that Imperium workers believed in the potential of the democratic system, but they were convinced that the politicians themselves ensured that this potential would never be realized. Halle explains that Imperium workers speak for American workers more generally in that they "fully subscribe to the ideals of a democratic society while firmly believing that current politics falls homelessly short of these ideals." This failure, is in large part the fault of "venal politicians" [who are] to blame for what's wrong" (201). For Imperium workers, as for Smokehousers, the criticism is leveled at the practice of politics, not at the theory itself.

19. Perot's great popularity among Smokehousers can be attributed to his demonstration that material capital can be accumulated without, and ultimately confers more social power than, cultural capital.

6. A Place to Stand

1. The concept of *communicative competence* derives from the idea, central to theoretical linguistics, that native speakers of a language have a natural capacity, or competence, to form grammatically appropriate utterances. In the ethnography of communication as developed by Hymes (1974), the idea of linguistic competence takes on a pragmatic component: that is, speakers show communicative competence when they know what utterances are socially (and not just grammatically) appropriate according

to the rules of their speech communities. Marcia Farr explains that "each speech community has its own repertoire of 'ways of speaking,' and its own standards for evaluating appropriate and inappropriate uses of language in particular contexts" (1994:3).

2. Ethnomethodologists such as Garfinkel (1967, 1974), Sacks (1974, 1979), and Schegloff (1972, 1982) have noted that social interaction shapes discourse recursively and that the cultural rules of speaking are negotiated *in* interactions (Briggs 1996). Argument is a generic construct inasmuch as it functions as a means by which cultural rules about how to structure meaning are legislated as well as enforced.

3. Methodologies developed within the field of the ethnography of communication, as conceived by Hymes (1974) and later explained by Saville-Troike (1982), take the *speech event* as the essential unit of communication for analysis. Saville-Troike defines the speech event as a set of utterances (or speech acts) set off in discursive space by "a unified set of components throughout, beginning with the same general purpose of communication, the same general topic, and involving the same participants, generally using the same language variety, maintaining the same tone or key and the same rules for interaction, in the same setting" (1982:27). (Here, both Walter and Maggie express a faith in the capacity of argument to engender real dialogue and to provide opportunities for persuasion. Although this view as it is articulated here could well have something to do with Walt's and Maggie's efforts to present themselves as "open-minded," it nonetheless supplies evidence that "argument" as such is regarded by Smokehousers as a unit of communication, or speech event. Still, even as Smokehousers seem in one sense to hold a kind of Habermasian faith in the power of dialogue in the public sphere, Maggie and Joe imply elsewhere that the kind of performance that goes on at the Smokehouse impedes dialogue and makes persuasion impossible.)

4. In their investigation of "conflict talk," conversational analysts Marjorie Harness Goodwin and Charles Goodwin report report similar findings, concluding that, however "disruptive" argument may be, it "is in fact accomplished through a process of very intricate coordination between the parties that are opposing each other" (1990:85).

5. Folklorist Ben-Amos explains that genres are given meaning as such by communities in which they operate and are therefore "cultural affirmation of the communication rules that govern the cultural context" (1976:225). According to ethnographers of speaking such as Gumperz and Hymes, speakers who belong to the same speech community "share knowledge of the communicative constraints and options governing a significant number of social situations." (1972:16). One may describe the Smokehouse cohort as a community of speakers in terms of the knowledge its members share about what counts as a genre and about how genres work.

6. An ethnosemanticist would no doubt be quick to observe that the scatalogical metaphor implicit in "bullshitting" and "giving shit" is meaningful and connotes unproductive, "wasteful" speech, whereas "telling it" (like it is) implies communicative economy and referential validity.

7. Joking practices, and the interpersonal relationships they interpret and constitute, have been a subject of enduring interest to scholars of social discourse and have been the focus of an extensive body of literature in sociolinguistics, anthropology, and folklore (see Radcliffe-Brown [1965] for a general discussion of the anthropology of joking). Ritual insults as a prominent communication style have traditionally been associated with urban African Americans culture (Abrahams 1962, 1974; Labov 1972), but research on communicative styles in white working-class communites have noted similar joking practices (Applebaum 1981; Halle 1984; LeMasters 1975).

8. Though women frequently take part in joking, the gender-indexed nature of this expressive style is apparent in both form and function. Most joking rituals involve men

symbolically emasculating each other (as the designation "ball-busting" would suggest) by impugning sexual potency and other signs of virility such the capacity to "hold liquor" and willingness to spend money for rounds. (See Willis 1979 and Fox 1995 for discussions of how male control of working-class discursive space is asserted through joking events).

9. Here I borrow the idea of "storyability" from Amy Shuman (1986), who uses it to distinguish a story's "content" from its "tellability," or terms of public presentation. Others (e.g., Robinson) have noted that storyable events are, in Shuman's apt paraphrase, a "transforming of the commonplace into the remarkable" (74). In the episode to follow, Roberta does just that: she renders a commonplace (i.e., the topic of race relations) as an *event*.

10. See Van Dijk (1993) for a discussion of race narratives as genres.

11. Bauman (1977) holds that one way to understand the meaning and role of a given speech event is to observe how it is related to performance: "The association of performance with particular genres is a significant aspect of the patterning of performance within communities" (25). Is is, as I will argue, the status of argument as a conventional but unstable genre that accounts for its association with performance.

12. Kenneth Burke's (1945) proposition that *all* language functions in some capacity as performance ("dramatistically," according to Burke) was elaborated by language philosopher J. L. Austin in *How To Do Things With Words* (1959). In that work, Austin claimed that because utterances perform social actions, they should be regarded not merely as referents but as *acts*. The idea of looking at language for what it does was later taken up in studies of oral narrative and verbal art and became an established paradigm in empirical investigations of language behavior. Whereas Austin's essential idea that language has a metacommunicative component is the philosophical basis of the ethnography of speaking in general, researchers of verbal art have made the conventions for establishing metameanings through ritually stylized speech the focus of their scholarship (e.g., Babcock 1977, Bauman 1977, 1986; Briggs 1988; Farr 1993, 1994). Babcock (1977) calls metacommunication "any element of communication which calls attention to the speech event as performance and to the relationship which obtains between the narrator and his audience vis-a-vis the narrative message," such that "the subject of discourse is narrative itself and those elements by which it is constituted and communicated" (68).

13. Memorable performances may be especially volatile or may include many people in active roles. The flag argument certainly qualifies as memorable on both counts. The nature of the performance itself, combined with my relative nonparticipation (and construction as antagonist despite my unwillingness to participate), suggests that the event that served as catalyst for the performance presented profound challenges to the common logic.

14. Bauman (1977) attempts to apprehend this complexity, listing several ways cultures mark speech events as performances: "special codes; figurative language; parallelism; special paralinguistic features; special formulae; appeal to tradition; disclaimer of performance"(16). In later work, however, Bauman warns that the student of performance should be careful not to apply such "keys" to observed performances in such a way as to foreclose discovery of culturally and situationally specific features of performance: "while there are a number of devices and patterning principles that have been widely documented as features of verbal art, the discovery of keys to performance cannot rely on a priori formal assumptions about what constitutes artful language" (Hill and Irvine 1992:195). He does, however, offer a generally applicable definition of performance as "a metacommunicative frame, the essence of which resides in the assumption of responsibility to an audience for a display of communicative competence" (1992:182).

15. The choice of metaphor is not accidental. For a helpful discussion of the gender politics of class identities, see Ortner (1991).

16. It is no accident that the most notorious barroom performers are men. Others who have studied working-class discourse have remarked on this phenomenon. In his research on "redneck" discourse in a Texas bar, for example, Aaron Fox found that "full performance is metapragmatically associated with powerful males" (1995:2) (though Fox goes on to show how women subvert this in a speech event he calls the "reverse"). The masculine ethos of performers and performances cannot be overlooked. In entering into performance with me, Jack and Walter are—in addition to asserting a cultural logic against the class interests I am presumed to stand for—realigning this logic with male experiences and interests. (See Willis 1979 for an excellent discussion of the hegemonic articulation of class logics as masculine ethos.) Both Walter and Jack display an ethos of tempered virility, of modulated aggression, one that communicates that their maleness has effectively oriented them to the immediacy of production and the value of productivity itself.

17. To say that there is such a thing as "private" belief would seem to suggest that a level of "theory" is held somehow apart from the social world from which it derives its meaning. But, rather, I mean "private" to signify that layer of belief in which an individual's theory of how the world works not only informs but impels his or her everyday practice (or the kind of belief-in-the-flesh that Bourdieu [1984] would call *habitus*). By "public," on the other hand, I refer to professed views that function as negotiated cultural capital in the social sphere. Thus, *public* belief animates the arena of rhetoric and debate and is therefore subject to definition by the imperatives of social roles, conflicts, and so on.

7. A Place for What If

1. Some scholars of working-class communicative patterns have speculated that performed agonistic discourse is a legacy of honor codes that have traditionally defined male relationships (e.g., Philipsen 1992). I am suggesting, however, that (even though the Smokehouse acts as male ceremonial space and has an institutional ethos that derives from tacit rules governing the conduct of men) the performance of agonistic rhetoric is as much a function of Smokehousers' class identity—that is, of their perceived position in sociopolitical space—as it is of gender expectations.

2. Though this volume focuses on schools as institutional sites of cultural production, the editors offer a comprehensive bibliographic treatment of scholarship that addresses questions of social reproduction and cultural production more generally. See Woolard (1985) for a convincing argument that more studies of cultural reproduction must be located *outside* dominant institutions to see how hegemony works as a process of consent (rather than of coercion).

3. Since I began this study, I have had several one-on-one conversations with Smokehousers that have convinced me that rhetorical positions taken at the bar are not altogether as intractable as they appear. I was surprised to learn, for instance, that Perry believed my arguing at the bar had caused Arlen to change his "politics." Speaking of my "effect" on others at the bar and on Arlen in particular, Perry remarked, "It's interesting to listen to how Arly's views have changed over the years. . . . [O]h, yeah, you have an influence. . . . [Y]ou've had a liberalizing influence on Arlen." It is significant, I think, that Perry regularly sees Arlen when the bar is closed (and not, therefore, functioning as public space).

4. That argument must serve both social and epistemic functions for the group means that at the Smokehouse, there is no such thing as a "personal opinion." Opinions,

as orientations to the common logic and as symbolic resources, inhabit the public sphere. One's statement of opinion is therefore a statement of social self. This means that when persuasion does happen, it entails the successful "sale" of a new opinion. The sale is successful only if the seller/rhetor can convince the customer that the opinion will be of some use to him. In order for a person to be convinced of the value (not necessarily the "truth") of a proposition and to claim it as her own, she must be convinced of the value of that proposition as cultural capital. Accordingly, an arguer's ethos can be defined as the ability to "wear an argument well." A Smokehouse rhetor successfully convinces his audience to adopt an opinion not because it is inherently rational but because he has demonstrated the profitable use of it as a way to earn distinction in the group. An individual is free to be persuaded—to make a public change in position—only to the extent that his persona can accommodate such a change.

References

Abrahams, Roger. 1962. Playing the dozens. *Journal of American Folklore* 75: 209–220.

Adler, Patricia A., and Peter Adler. 1987. *Membership roles in field research.* Newbury Park, CA: Sage.

Agar, Michael H. 1986. *Speaking of ethnography.* Newbury Park, CA: Sage.

Applebaum, Herbert. 1981. *Royal blue: The culture of construction workers.* New York: Holt, Rinehart and Winston.

Aronowitz, Stanley. 1989. Working-class identity and celluloid fantasies in an electronic age. In *Popular culture: Schooling in everyday life,* eds. Henry Giroux and Roger Simon. New York: Bergin.

Austin, J. L. 1962. *How to do things with words.* Eds. J. O. Urmson and Marina Sbisa. Cambridge: Harvard University Press.

Babcock, Barbara A. "The story in the story": metanarration in folk narratives. In *Verbal Art as Performance,* Ed. R. Bauman. New York: Newbury, 1977.

Bakhtin, M. M. 1986. *Speech genres and other late essays.* Ed. Caryl Emerson. Trans. Vern McGee. Austin: University of Texas Press.

Bauman, Richard, and Joel Sherzer, eds. 1974. *Explorations in the ethnography of speaking.* Cambridge: Cambridge University Press.

Bauman, Richard. 1977. *Verbal art as performance.* New York: Newbury.

———. 1986. *Story, performance, event.* Cambridge: Cambridge University Press.

———. 1992. Disclaimers of performance. In *Responsibility and evidence in oral discourse,* eds. Jane Hill and Judith T. Irvine. Cambridge: Cambridge University Press.

Bell, Michael J. 1983. *The world from Brown's lounge: An ethnography of black middle-class play.* Urbana: University of Illinois Press.

Ben-Amos, Dan, ed. 1976. *Folklore genres.* Austin: University of Texas Press.

Bourdieu, Pierre. 1984. *Distinction: A social critique of the judgment of taste.* Trans. R. Nice. Cambridge, MA: Harvard University Press.

———. 1991. *Language and symbolic power.* Cambridge: Harvard University Press.

Briggs, Charles. 1986. *Learning how to ask: A sociolinguistic appraisal of the role of the interview in social science research.* Studies in the Social and Cultural Foundations of Langauge 1. Cambridge: Cambridge University Press.

———. 1988. *Competence in performance: The creativity of tradition in Mexicano verbal art.* Philadelphia: University of Pennsylvania Press.

———, ed. 1996. *Disorderly discourse: Narrative, conflict, and inequality.* Oxford Studies in Anthropological Linguistics 7. New York: Oxford University Press.

Briggs, Charles, and Richard Bauman. 1992. Genre, intertextuality, and social power. *Journal of Linguistic Anthropology* 2: 131–172.

Bruner, Jerome. 1990. *Acts of meaning.* Cambridge, MA: Harvard University Press.

———. 1991. The narrative construction of reality. *Critical Inquiry* 18 (1991): 1–21.

Burke, Kenneth. 1969. *A grammar of motives.* Berkeley: University of California Press.

Campbell, Karlyn Kohrs. 1982. *The rhetorical act.* Belmont, CA: Wadsworth.

Cavan, Sherri. 1966. *Liquor license: An ethnography of bar behavior.* Chicago: Aldine.

Cintron, Ralph. 1997. *Angels' town: Chero ways, gang life, and rhetorics of the everyday.* Boston: Beacon Press.

Clarke, J., C. Critcher, and R. Johnson. 1979. *Working-class culture: Studies in history and theory.* New York: St. Martin's.

Clarke, John. 1979. *Capital and culture: The post-war working class revisited.* In *Working-class culture,* eds. J. Clarke, C. Critcher, and R. Johnson, 238–254. New York: St. Martin's.

Clifford, James. 1988. *The predicament of culture.* Cambridge, MA: Harvard University Press.

Clifford, James, and George Marcus, eds. 1986. *Writing culture: The poetics and politics of ethnography.* Berkeley: University of California Press.

Cooper, Lane. 1932. *The rhetoric of Aristotle.* London: Prentice-Hall.

Covino, William, and David Jolliffe. 1995. *Rhetoric: Concepts, definitions, boundaries.* Boston: Allyn and Bacon.

Crowley, Sharon, and Debra Hawhee. 1999. *Ancient rhetorics for contemporary students,* 2nd ed. Boston: Allyn and Bacon.

de Beauvior, Simone. 1989. *The second sex.* Trans. H. M. Parshley. New York: Vintage Books.

Dius, Perry R. 1983. *The saloon: Public drinking in Chicago and Boston 1880–1920.* Urbana: University of Illinois Press.

Eckert, Penelope. 1989. *Jocks and burnouts: Social categories and identity in the high school.* New York: Teachers College Press.

Eckert, Penelope, and Sally McConnell-Ginet. 1992. *Think practically and look locally: Language and gender as community-based practice. Annual Review of Anthropology* 21: 461–490.

Farr, Marcia. 1993. Essayist literacy and other verbal performances. *Written Communication* 10.1: 4–38.

———. 1994. Echando relajo: Verbal art and gender among Mexicanos in Chicago. *Proceedings of the Berkeley Women and Language Conference.* Berkeley: Department of Linguistics.

Fetterman, David. 1989. *Ethnography step by step.* Newbury Park, CA: Sage.

Foley, Douglas. 1989. Does the working class have a culture in the anthropological sense? *Cultural Anthropology* 4.2: 137–163.

———. 1990. *Learning capitalist culture: Deep in the heart of Tejas.* Philadelphia: University of Pennsylvania Press.

Fox, Aaron A. 1993. Split-subjectivity in country music and honky-tonk discourse. In *All that glitters: Country music in America*, ed. George H. Lewis, 131–140. Bowling Green, OH: Bowling Green State University Popular Press.

———. 1994. The poetics of irony and the ethnography of class culture. *Anthropology and Humanism Quarterly* 19.1: 53–72.

———. 1995. The "redneck reverse": Language and gender in Texas working-class women's verbal art. *SALSA II Conference Proceedings,* 189–1999.

———. 1996. "A blue-blooded woman and a redneck man": performing working-class feminism. Paper presented at the American Anthropological Society meeting, San Francisco.

Fox, Richard G., ed. 1991. *Recapturing anthropology.* Santa Fe: School of American Research Press.

Garfinkel, H. 1967. *Studies in ethnomethodolgy.* Englewood Cliffs, NJ: Prentice-Hall.

———. 1974. On the origins of the term "ethnomethdology." In *Ethnomethodology,* ed. R. Turner. Harmondsworth: Penguin.

Geertz, Clifford. 1988. *Works and lives: The anthropologist as author.* Stanford, CA: Stanford University Press.

Georges, Robert. 1968. *Studies in mythology.* Homewood, IL: Dorsey Press.

Goffman, E. 1981. *Forms of talk.* Philadelphia: University of Pennsylvania Press.

Golde, P., ed. 1986. *Women in the field: Anthropological experiences.* Berkeley: University of California Press.

Goodwin, Charles, and Marjorie Harness Goodwin. 1990. Interstitial argument. In *Conflict talk: Sociolinguistic investigations of arguments in conversation,* ed. Allen D. Grimshaw, 85–117. Cambridge: Cambridge University Press.

Grimes, Michael. 1991. *Class in twentieth-century sociology.* New York: Praeger.

Gumperz, J., and D. Hymes, eds. 1972. *Directions in sociolinguistics.* New York: Holt, Rinehart.

Halle, David. 1984. *America's working man: Work, home, and politics among blue-collar property owners.* Chicago: University of Chicago Press.

Hartigan, John. 1997a. Locating white Detroit. In *Displacing whiteness: Essays in social and cultural criticism,* ed. Ruth Frankenburg, 180–214. Durham, NC: Duke University Press.

———. 1997b. Name calling: Objectifying "poor whites" and "white trash" in Detroit. In *White trash: Race and class in America,* eds. Matt Wray and Annalee Newitz, 41–57. New York: Routledge.

Heath, R. 1986. *Realism and relativism: A perspective on Kenneth Burke.* Macon, GA: Mercer University, 1986.

Heath, Shirley Brice. 1983. *Ways with words: Language, life and work in communities and classrooms.* Cambridge: Cambridge University Press.

Hill, Jane H., and Judith T. Irvine. 1993. *Responsibility and evidence in oral discourse.* Cambridge: Cambridge University Press.

Hoggart, Richard. 1957. *The uses of literacy: Aspects of working-class life, with special references to publications and entertainments.* New York: Oxford.

Holmes, Janet, and Miriam Meyerhoff. 1999. The community of practice. *Language in society* 28: 171–172.

Hymes, Dell. 1974. *Foundations in sociolinguistics.* Philadelphia: University of Pennsylvania.

Johnson, Richard.1979. Three problematics: Elements of a theory of working-class culture. In *Working-class culture,* eds. J. Clarke, C. Critcher, and R. Johnson, 201–237. New York: St. Martin's.

Labov, William. 1972. *Sociolinguistic patterns.* Philadelphia: University of Pennsylvania Press.

———. 1972. Rules for ritual insults. In *Studies in social interaction,* ed. David Sudnow. New York: Free Press.

Lave, Jean, and Etienne Wenger. 1991. *Situated learning: Legitimate peripheral participation.* New York: Cambridge University Press.

LeMasters, E. E. 1975. *Blue-collar aristocrats: Life-styles at a working-class tavern.* Madison: University of Wisconsin Press.

Levinson, Bradley A., Douglas E. Foley, and Dorothy C. Holland. 1996. *The cultural production of the educated person.* Albany: SUNY Press.

Lévi-Strauss, C. (1979). *Myth and meaning.* New York: Schoeken.

Limon, Jose E. 1994. *Dancing with the devil: Society and cultural poetics in Mexican-American South Texas.* Madison: University of Wisconsin Press.

Lofty, John, and Richard Blot. 1997. Covering one's tracks: Respecting and preserving informant anonymity. In *Voices and visions: Refiguring ethnography in composition research.* Portsmouth, NH: Bonyton/Cook.

Marcus, G., and M. Fischer. 1986. *Anthropology as cultural critique.* Chicago: University of Chicago Press.

Milroy, Leslie. 1980. *Language and social networks.* Oxford: Basil Blackwell.

Moffatt, Michael. 1992. Ethnographic writing about American culture. *Annual Review of Anthropology* 21: 205–229.

Ortner, Sherry. 1991. Reading America: Preliminary notes on class and culture. In *Recapturing anthropology,* ed. Richard G. Fox, 163–191. Santa Fe, NM: School of American Research Press.

Paules, Greta Foff. 1991. *Dishing it out: Power and resistance among waitresses in a New Jersey restaurant.* Philadelphia: Temple University Press.

Peacock, James L. 1986. *The anthropological lens: Harsh light, soft focus.* Cambridge: Cambridge University Press.

Philipsen, Gerry. 1992. *Speaking culturally: Explorations in social communication.* New York: SUNY Press.

Radcliffe-Brown, A. 1965. On joking relationships. In *Structure and function in primitive society.* New York: Free Press.

Read, K. E. 1980. *Other voices: The style of a male homosexual tavern.* Novato, CA: Chandler and Sharp.

Robinson, John A. 1981. Personal narratives reconsidered. *Journal of American Folklore* 81: 58–85.

Rosaldo, Renato. 1989. *Culture and truth: The remaking of social analysis.* Boston: Beacon.

Rose, Dan. 1990. *Living the ethnographic life.* Newbury Park, CA: Sage.

Rosenwieg, Ray. 1983. *Eight Hours for What We Will.* New York: Cambridge University Press.

Rubin, Lillian B. 1976. *Worlds of pain: Life in the working-class family.* New York: Basic Books.

Sacks, Harvey. 1974. An analysis of the course of a joke's telling. In *Explorations in the ethnography of speaking,* eds. Richard Bauman and Joel Sherzer, 337–353. Cambridge: Cambridge University Press.

Sacks, Harvey, and Emmanuel Schegloff. 1979. Two preferences in the organization of reference to persons in conversation and their interaction. In *Everyday language: Studies in ethnomethodology,* ed. George Psathas, 15–21. New York: Irvington.

Saville-Troike, Muriel. 1982. *The ethnography of communication.* New York: Basil Blackwell.

Sennett, Richard, and Jonathan Cobb. 1972. *The hidden injuries of class.* New York: Vintage.

Schegloff, Emmanuel. 1972. Sequencing in conversational openings. In *Directions in sociolinguistics*, eds. John Gumperz and Dell Hymes, 346–80. Cambridge, MA: Basil Blackwell.

———. 1982. Discourse as an interactional achievement: Some uses of "uh-huh" and other things that come between sentences. In *Analyzing discourse: Text and talk, Georgetown University Round Table on Languages and Linguistics 1981*, ed. Deborah Tannen. Washington, DC: Georgetown University Press.

Shuman, Amy. 1986. *Storytelling rights: The uses of oral and written texts by urban adolescents.* Cambridge: Cambridge University Press.

Slayton, Robert A. 1986. *Back of the yards: The making of a local democracy.* Chicago: University of Chicago Press.

Spradley, James, and Brenda Mann. 1975. *The cocktail waitress: Women's work in a man's world.* New York: Knopf.

Spradley, James. 1979. *The ethnographic interview.* Fort Worth: Harcourt Brace.

Stewart, Kathleen. 1996. *A space at the side of the road: Cultural poetics in an "other" America.* Princeton, NJ: Princeton University Press.

Tannen, Deborah. 1989. *Talking voices: Repetition, imagery, and dialogue in conversational discourse.* Cambridge: Cambridge University Press.

Tedlock, Dennis. 1983. *The spoken word and the work of interpretation.* Philadelphia: University of Pennsylvania Press.

Thompson, E. P. 1966. *The making of the English working class.* New York: Vintage.

van Dijk, Teun A. 1993. Stories and racism. In *Narrative and social control: Critical perspectives.* Sage Annual Reviews of Communication Research 21. Newbury Park, CA: Sage.

Van Mannen, John. 1983. *Representation in ethnography.* Thousand Oaks, CA: Sage.

———. 1988. *Tales of the field: On writing ethnography.* Chicago: University of Chicago Press.

Warren, C. A. B. 1988. *Gender issues in field research.* Newbury Park, CA: Sage.

Weber, Max. 1978. *Max Weber: Selections in translation,* ed. W. G. Runcinan. Cambridge: Cambridge University Press.

Weis, Lois. 1989. The 1980s: De-industrialization and change in white working-class and female cultural youth forms. In *Politics and the processes of schooling*, eds. S. Walker and Len Barton. Milton Keynes: Open University Press.

———. 1990. *Working class without work: High school students in a de-industrializing economy.* New York: Routledge.

Wenger, Etienne. 1998. *Communities of practice.* Cambridge: Cambridge University Press.

Weston, K. 1991. *Families we chose: Lesbians, gays, kinship.* New York: Columbia University Press.

Williams, Raymond. 1981. *The sociology of culture.* New York: Schocken.

Willis, Paul. 1977. *Learning to labour: How working-class kids get working-class jobs.* New York: Columbia University Press.

———. 1979. *Shop-floor culture, masculinity, and the wage form.* In *Working-class culture*, eds. J. Clarke, C. Critcher, and R. Johnson, 185–201. New York: St. Martin's.

Woolard, Kathryn. 1985. Language variation and cultural hegemony: Toward an integration of sociolinguistic and social theory. *American Ethnologist* 12.4: 738–747.

Index